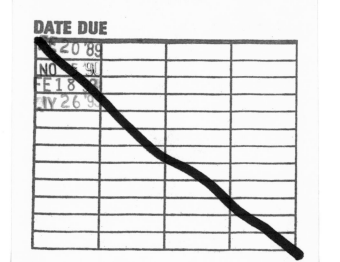

# PSYCHOLOGICAL DYNAMICS OF SPORT

Diane L. Gill, PhD
The University of Iowa

**Human Kinetics Publishers, Inc.**
**Champaign, Illinois**

**Library of Congress Cataloging-in-Publication Data**

Gill, Diane L., 1948-
  Sport psychology.

  Bibliography: p.
  Includes index.
  1. Sports—Psychological aspects. 2. Motivation
(Psychology) I. Title.
GV706.4G55 1986        796'.01        86-10440
ISBN 0-87322-070-6


Developmental Editor: Linda Anne Bump
Copy Editor: Kevin Neely
Production Director: Ernie Noa
Text Design: Julie Szamocki
Typesetter: Brad Colson
Text Layout: Denise Mueller
Cover Design: Jack W. Davis
Cover Photography: Cheryl A. Traendly
Printed by: Braun-Brumfield, Inc.

Printed in the United States of America.

10  9  8  7  6  5  4  3  2

Human Kinetics Books
A Division of Human Kinetics Publishers, Inc.
Box 5076, Champaign, IL 61820
1-800-DIAL-HKP
1-800-334-3665 (in Illinois)

To my parents and grandparents,
who always knew I could do it.

# Contents

## Chapter 9    Behavior Modification in Sport     133

## Chapter 10    Cognitive Approaches: Intrinsic     147
## Motivation in Sport

# Preface

This book provides a comprehensive review of *sport psychology*, the branch of sport and exercise science that focuses on the psychological aspects of human behavior in sport and exercise. As a relatively young discipline, sport psychology has grown and changed dramatically over the past decade. Ten years ago sport psychology was just emerging as an identifiable field. Most of that early work took place in traditional physical education programs and focused on the application of experimental social psychology concepts and methods to motor performance. Today, individuals with varied backgrounds in psychology, health sciences, and related fields, as well as those from physical education and exercise science programs, investigate sport psychology issues ranging from competitive anxiety to group cohesiveness. The application of sport psychology to physical education and competitive athletics remains prominent, but sport psychology, along with the other sport sciences, is extending increasingly into nontraditional settings such as corporate fitness, exercise rehabilitation, and health behavior programs.

During the past 10 years, I have taught sport psychology courses to undergraduate and graduate students of varying backgrounds without the aid of a comprehensive text. I have attempted to fill that void in the sport psychology literature by writing a text that presents basic sport psychology theory and research in a comprehensive and readable manner. Because sport psychology students have diverse backgrounds, I have not assumed that readers of this text have any particular expertise in either psychology or exercise science. The book should be appropriate for undergraduate sport psychology classes, introductory sport psychology classes at the graduate level, and as a supplementary text for related interdisciplinary courses.

I have organized the text into five parts representing the major topics within sport psychology. Part I provides a general orientation to the field, including an introduction and description of sport psychology in chapter 1 and a discussion of the history and current status of the field in chapter 2. The four remaining parts present sport psychology theory and research in the general areas of personality, motivation, social influence, and group dynamics. Those four parts not only reflect the primary divisions of sport psychology knowledge but also progress gradually from a focus on the individual to an emphasis on group interaction processes.

Part II reviews the individual or personality characteristics that influence human behavior in sport and exercise. Chapter 3 presents an overview of sport personality theory and research, whereas the remaining chapters focus on specific individual characteristics. Chapter 4 covers cognitive styles and abilities, especially attentional styles and imagery in sport. The prominent sport psychology work on achievement behavior, competitiveness, and competitive anxiety is discussed in chapter 5. Chapter 6 examines gender roles in sport, including work on masculinity and femininity as personality characteristics and gender differences in achievement behavior. Chapter 7, the last chapter of part II, focuses on attitudes and sport behavior.

Part III reviews motivation, a prominent concern of sport participants. Arousal, the intensity or activation of behavior, is discussed in chapter 8. Specifically, chapter 8 reviews theories and research on the arousal/performance relationship and information on the rapidly expanding area of anxiety management in sport. Chapter 9 considers the use of reinforcement and behavior modification in sport, and chapter 10 reviews the diverse topics within the general area of cognitive motivation, including the relationship between extrinsic rewards and intrinsic motivation, the role of expectations and self-confidence in sport, and the influence of attributions on sport achievement behavior.

In part IV the focus shifts from individual characteristics to social situational factors. Chapter 11 reviews the influence of other people as spectators, competitors, teachers, and coaches on sport performance and behavior, and chapter 12 focuses on social interaction, specifically aggression and prosocial behavior in sport.

In part V, we turn to the dynamics of sport groups. Chapter 13 focuses on group performance, particularly the relationship of individual abilities to group performance. Finally, chapter 14 covers the interpersonal relationships of leadership and cohesiveness in sport groups.

Although specific individual characteristics and situational factors are discussed in separate parts and chapters, these factors do not operate independently. Throughout this text I have tried to emphasize that individual and situational factors interact in complex ways to influence sport and exercise behavior. For example, personality characteristics such as competitive anxiety exert considerable influence in some sport situations but not in others. Similarly, the motivational influence of rewards and coaching strategies depends on how individuals interpret those tactics, and group performance is the product of the interaction of individual members who have diverse motives and characteristics. Because human behavior in sport and exercise is complex, we must consider complex relationships and interactions to understand that behavior.

Several people made important contributions to this text. First, I must acknowledge the many contributions of Rainer Martens. As my former advisor, current publisher, and most helpful critic and colleague, Rainer has contributed to my sport psychology work in many direct and indirect ways. All of the people at Human Kinetics Publishers, including Rainer and Marilyn Martens,

Gwen Steigelman, and Linda Bump, devoted considerable time and effort and provided many helpful suggestions through several drafts of this text. Thelma Horn reviewed the first draft of the text and provided numerous insightful comments and suggestions that were incorporated in the final version. As anyone who has written a text knows, and as anyone contemplating writing a text should know, such a task requires a concentrated period of time. I began working on this text several years ago but completed the most substantial writing only with the aid of a developmental leave from the University of Iowa. I am especially grateful for the support services and collegial atmosphere provided by University House at the University of Iowa.

# *Orientation to Sport Psychology*

Part I provides an orientation to sport psychology, the scientific study of human behavior in sport and exercise. General topics and specific issues related to human behavior in sport are introduced in chapter 1, and sport psychology is discussed as a component of sport and exercise science. Chapter 2 presents an historical overview of sport psychology from the pioneering sport psychology efforts during the 1920s and 1930s, through the emergence of sport psychology as an organized discipline in the 1960s, and finally to current research and applied activities. The information in these introductory chapters provides a general framework to guide the reader through the more specific material in the following chapters.

# CHAPTER 1

# *Introduction to Sport Psychology*

Sport psychology is the branch of sport and exercise science that seeks to provide answers to questions about human behavior in sport. Teachers, coaches, athletes, and recreational sport participants must answer questions similar to those below on a daily basis. Because they must base their activities on the answers to such questions, sport participants need accurate, reliable information about the psychology of sport behavior, just as they need information about the physiological aspects of exercise and the biomechanical principles of movement to guide their decisions and actions.

In order to become acquainted with some of the practical questions raised about topics in sport psychology, answer the following questions by circling *yes* or *no*. The answers to these questions will be discussed at the end of the chapter.

1. **Are distance runners more introverted than basketball players?**

   Yes or No

2. **Should tennis players "psych up" to get the adrenalin flowing and prepare for a championship match?**

   Yes or No

3. **Will more children participate in a community soccer program if T-shirts and awards are offered?**

   Yes or No

4. **Will the employees in the Good Time Company's noon jogging program run longer if they run in a group than if they run alone?**

   Yes or No

5. **Should we encourage aggressive play and fighting in ice hockey as a way to "let off steam?"**

   Yes or No

6. **Is there an "I" in team? (Consider the idea, not the spelling.)**

   Yes or No

# Sport and Exercise Science

As one branch of sport and exercise science, sport psychology is part of the overall scientific study of human movement. Sport and exercise science is a multidisciplinary field that draws upon knowledge from broader, "parent" disciplines and applies that knowledge to sport. As used here, the term *sport* is not restricted to highly organized competition or to highly skilled athletes. Indeed, sport activities range from aerobic dance classes to the Olympic games, and sport participants include 8-year-old gymnasts and 72-year-old joggers as well as professional athletes. Sport and exercise science also extends to skilled movements and physical activities that we seldom consider "sports," such as movement efficiency with an artificial limb or exercise in the weightless environment of space. Of course, most sport and exercise science work involves more traditional settings, such as physical education classes and intercollegiate athletics. Nevertheless, sport science is not limited to those settings, and sport psychology and the other sport sciences will continue to expand into areas such as corporate fitness, exercise rehabilitation, wellness programs, and exercise within health behavior and preventive medicine programs.

Sport psychology has close ties to the other subareas of sport and exercise science. The most prominent subareas of sport and exercise science are (a) *exercise physiology*, which draws upon the disciplines of anatomy and physiology, (b) *biomechanics*, which applies principles and knowledge from physics to the mechanics of human movement, (c) *sport sociology*, which explores the sociological dimensions of sport, and (d) *sport psychology*, which incorporates theory and research from the larger field of psychology. All of the subareas of sport and exercise science draw upon the broader, associated disciplines for information, but they draw from these fields *selectively*. Not all information in physiology and anatomy is equally applicable to exercise. Similarly, not all issues and branches of psychology are equally applicable to sport and physical activity. Thus sport scientists apply selected theories and concepts from the parent disciplines to sport and exercise.

The various sport sciences do more than "borrow" theories and information from other disciplines, however. In addition to selecting relevant information from other sciences, sport scientists often must develop their own theories and concepts to explain sport behavior. Indeed, much recent writing in sport psychology emphasizes the need to develop sport-specific theoretical models, concepts, and measurement techniques that address the unique aspects of sport and exercise.

One good illustration of the value of sport-specific constructs and measures is Rainer Martens' work on competitive anxiety, which is discussed in more detail in chapter 5. Anxiety is a common research topic in psychology; theoretical models have been proposed, and several methods to measure anxiety already exist. Martens (1977) proposed that anxiety in sport competition has unique characteristics and that a sport-specific anxiety measure would provide greater insight and understanding of anxiety within sport. The research of Martens and others confirmed that individuals who tend to become anxious in sport competition can be identified more effectively through a sport-specific measure of anxiety than by more general anxiety measures and provided a sport-specific measure that now can be used to probe other aspects of competitive anxiety.

Other sport psychologists have developed sport-specific constructs and measures related to attentional style (see chapter 4) and cohesiveness (see chapter 14). These efforts show promise for providing insights and information about sport behavior that cannot be gleaned from more general psychological research. Sport psychology, like the other sport sciences, thus borrows selected, relevant information from its associated parent discipline and also develops theoretical models and constructs that are unique to sport.

Because sport psychology is part of the multidisciplinary field of sport and exercise science, it draws upon theories, constructs, and measures from the other sport sciences as well as from psychology. A thorough understanding of sport behavior requires the integration of information from all the subareas that constitute sport and exercise science. For example, if we want to study the psychological effects of aerobic activities such as distance running, cycling, or swimming, we will understand their *psychological* effects more fully and perhaps with greater insight if we also consider the *physiological* effects of such training. Indeed, some of the emerging research on exercise as an approach to improving mental health and the often discussed but seldom documented "runner's high" phenomenon suggests that psychological effects and mood changes may be associated with physiological factors such as beta-endorphin levels. Psychophysiological research is still in its infancy, and its findings are inconclusive. However, as sport psychologists and exercise physiologists continue their endeavors, we will expand our knowledge of the psychological effects of exercise training.

Dishman (1982, 1984) is a particularly vocal advocate of the psychobiological approach in sport psychology. He proposes a psychobiological model to predict an individual's adherence to an exercise program. Dishman's model of exercise adherence incorporates biological factors, such as body composition, along with psychological factors, particularly self-motivation. Dishman's model is discussed more thoroughly in chapter 3. Similar psychobiological approaches may further advance our understanding of many sport behaviors.

Knowledge and techniques from biomechanics, sport sociology, and other areas of sport and exercise science may provide further insights into the psychological aspects of sport and exercise behavior. Biomechanical measures and procedures may help us probe the psychological aspects of skilled movement with unique insights, and sport sociology constructs and measures are already prominent features of sport psychology research on social influence and group dynamics. Indeed, several of the studies on leadership and cohesiveness cited in chapter 14 were conducted by sport sociologists.

# Psychology of Sport and Exercise

Now that we have considered the role of sport psychology within the overall field of sport and exercise science, we will consider sport psychology as a distinct discipline in more detail. We have described sport psychology as the branch of sport and exercise science that focuses on the psychological aspects of sport and exercise. Sport psychology thus clearly incorporates the theoretical models and approaches of psychology. Psychology texts typically define psychology as the scientific study of human behavior. Sport psychology, then, may be defined as *the scientific study of human behavior in sport.* As noted earlier, sport should be construed broadly to include various recreational activities, competitive sports, and health-oriented exercise programs.

In contrast to this wide-ranging interpretation of sport, most sport psychologists take a more limited approach to psychology. The term *sport psychology* could imply the application of all aspects of psychology to sport. However, psychology itself is a far-reaching field with many subareas. The American Psychological Association (APA), the primary professional organization in psychology, lists 42 different divisions, including the larger divisions such as clinical psychology, experimental psychology, and personality and social psychology as well as divergent specialties such as military psychology, consumer psychology, psychopharmacology, and rehabilitation psychology. At this time the APA does not have a separate division for sport psychology, but an exercise and sport psychology interest group has formed and has begun to pursue divisional status.

Given the wide scope of psychology, it is not surprising that sport psychology does not incorporate all aspects of psychology. In fact, sport psychology itself is divided into specialized areas. The North American Society for the Psychology of Sport and Physical Activity (NASPSPA), the main professional organization for sport psychology in North America, is composed of three interest areas, including (a) *motor learning/control*, (b) *motor development*, and (c) *sport psychology*. These three areas reflect the general division of psychological study within sport and exercise science.

The motor learning/control area is aligned most closely with the psychology areas of cognition, perception, and the experimental psychology of learning and performance. Within sport science, motor learning/control specialists tend to focus on cognitive and perceptual processes involved in the learning and performance of skilled movements and the cognitive and neuropsychological processes underlying controlled movement. Magill (1980), Marteniuk (1976), and Schmidt (1982) offer an overview of the motor learning/control area.

Motor development, as its name implies, focuses on developmental psychology issues related to sport and motor performance. Although motor development is the newest and least established subarea within sport and exercise psychology, several motor development specialists are investigating issues related to the development of motor patterns and skilled performance. Texts by Espenschade and Eckert (1980), Haywood (1986), and Wickstrom (1983) may be consulted for an overview of the changing nature of the motor development area.

Sport psychology, the third subarea within sport and exercise psychology, is the focus of this book. Although the term *sport psychology* implies that the field includes all aspects of psychology within the context of sport, this is not the case. Sport psychology, as commonly interpreted and as used in this text, emphasizes certain subareas of psychology, namely *personality* and *social psychology*. Like social psychology, sport psychology focuses on meaningful social behavior rather than portions of behavior. Subareas of psychology that focus on portions of behavior, such as perception, cognition, and physiological psychology are not generally considered within the realm of sport psychology. Of course, perception, cognition, and other psychological processes related to learning and performance are important for a complete understanding of sport behavior, but these issues are typically taught and investigated under the rubric of motor learning/control or the growing field of motor development. Thus the term *sport psychology*, as used in this text, should be interpreted as referring to the influence of personality and social factors on meaningful social behavior in a variety of sport and exercise settings.

Sport psychology is not, however, restricted to personality and social psychology, and many other aspects of psychology are addressed. Within the last few years, many sport psychologists have developed an interest in applying their knowledge to actual sport situations, specifically by educating and training sport participants in psychological skills. Interest in applied sport psychology has introduced a number of counseling and clinical psychology theories and techniques to sport psychology. Sport psychology also incorporates some work from developmental psychology, cognitive psychology, and physiological psychology. As noted earlier, those topics typically fall into the separate subareas of motor learning/control and motor development. However, sport psychology overlaps a great deal with those areas of study.

Just as a thorough understanding of sport psychology issues often requires incorporating information from the other sport sciences, the subareas within the psychology of sport and exercise have much to offer each other, and the dividing lines between the subareas are quite permeable. As we will discuss in chapter 4, attentional style and the relationship between attention and sport performance is a prominent topic in both sport psychology research and applied work with sport participants. Attention is also a very prominent topic within motor learning/control. Thus sport psychologists and motor learning/control specialists interested in attention share many theoretical models and methods, and the work within each subarea provides insights that enrich the overall work on attention in sport.

Many other examples of topics that cross the boundaries between sport psychology and motor learning/control could be cited. Motor development also addresses many of the same issues. For example, Frank Smoll, a motor development specialist, and psychologist Ron Smith have conducted some of the most systematic and widely cited sport psychology research on coaching behaviors in youth sports (see chapter 11). Thus the subareas of motor learning/control, motor development, and sport psychology share many concerns, even though they emphasize different issues and approaches.

The emphasis of sport psychology is on meaningful social behavior in sport and exercise. In focusing on such behavior, a central theme of this text is that both individual differences and situational factors affect sport behavior. This premise reflects a basic tenet of social psychology set forth in a formal but simple way by Kurt Lewin (1935) as $B = f(P, E)$; that is, behavior is a function of the person and the environment. Parts II and III of this text focus on the individual difference factors, including personality characteristics, attitudes, and motivational orientations. Part IV shifts our attention to environmental factors, particularly the influence of other people. Finally, part V explores the social interaction processes in sport groups.

This shift in focus sounds straightforward but is actually quite complex. Personal and situational factors do not operate independently; they interact. Personal characteristics influence some situations and not others; situational factors affect different people in different ways; and the person affects the situation just as the situation affects the person. For example, individual ice hockey players might differ in aggressiveness; some players are more likely to fight and display aggressive behavior than others. However, the more aggressive individual does not *always* display more aggressive behavior. For example, in one game a player who is usually quite nonaggressive could have a frustrating shooting night, be harrassed excessively by the coach, sustain a painful shoulder injury, and eat too many candy bars before the game. Those situational factors might provoke aggressive behavior from the normally restrained individual. Furthermore, those same situational factors might not provoke the same reactions in other players. One player might react to an overly critical coach by bearing down and improving play; another might become frustrated and play even worse. Yet another player might retaliate by challenging the coach's comments and changing the coach's behavior and the situation. Thus any particular behavior takes place within the context of many interacting personal and situational factors. In short, human behavior in sport, like human behavior in general, is complex and dynamic.

With that caveat in mind, let's return to the questions posed at the beginning of the chapter.

### 1. Are distance runners more introverted than basketball players?

*No.* Although we hold many stereotypes about the personalities of athletes, sport personality research has not uncovered any consistent differences among sport participants. Athletes appear to represent the entire range of personality characteristics and, as a group, do not differ consistently from nonathletes. Varying subgroups of sport participants (e.g., distance runners and basketball players) do not differ consistently in personality characteristics. A discussion of research on personality profiles of athletes is included in chapter 3.

2 . **Should tennis players "psych-up" to get the adrenaline flowing and prepare for a championship match?**

*No, or at least not usually.* Again, many of us hold stereotyped beliefs about preparing for competition. We often believe that the best athletes are those who can increase arousal ("psych-up"); thus many precompetition coaching techniques aim to increase athletes' arousal levels. In contrast to popular belief, however, most athletes need to calm down or *control* arousal prior to competition. Exceptions exist; some top athletes, especially those involved in strength or endurance tasks such as weight lifting, may use psych-up or arousal-increasing techniques effectively to improve performance. These are exceptions, however. Arousal control methods should be used much more frequently than they currently are, especially with younger, less experienced, or less skilled sport participants. For a discussion of arousal and sport performance, see chapter 8.

3 . **Will more children participate in a community soccer program if T-shirts and awards are offered?**

*Yes, but awards create problems.* The chance to receive T-shirts and awards may act as an incentive to some children who would otherwise not participate. However, most children participate in sport for intrinsic reasons such as fun and challenge. If nearly all children would participate anyway, nothing is gained by using rewards and many problems are introduced. Research indicates that the extensive use of rewards may undermine intrinsic interest in an activity. When rewards are introduced, the children may see themselves as participating to get the rewards, thus lowering their intrinsic interest. The more we emphasize extrinsic rewards, the more likely we are to undermine intrinsic motivation. This may result in many children (or adults) who will participate only when extrinsic rewards are offered. Intrinsic and extrinsic rewards are discussed in chapter 10.

4 . **Will the employees in the Good Time Company's noon jogging program run longer if they run in a group than if they run alone?**

*Yes.* Research on social influence and performance indicates that people usually run longer and work harder when other people are watching or doing the same thing. Many people find that they can run farther more easily if they jog with others. However, the presence of other people does not improve performance for all sport and exercise activities. In general, the performance of relatively simple or well-learned skills, especially speed and endurance tasks, is enhanced by the presence of others, whereas the presence of others usually interferes with the learning and performance of more complex skills that require coordination and timing. Additional discussion of social influence is presented in chapter 11.

5. **Should we encourage aggressive play and fighting in ice hockey as a way to "let off steam"?**

   *No.* Many different theoretical explanations or reasons for aggression exist. Some theories propose that aggressive behavior is a natural, instinctive response and that we should channel those inevitable behaviors into nondestructive outlets such as sport. The most accepted theories and most research evidence, however, suggest that aggression is a learned social behavior. Encouraging aggressive play in hockey does *not* "let off steam" and reduce the likelihood of other aggressive behaviors. Instead, encouraging aggression in sport probably teaches and reinforces aggressive behavior and increases the likelihood of aggression in other settings. Issues surrounding aggression in sport are reviewed in chapter 12.

6. **Is there an "I" in team?**

   *Yes.* The standard locker room slogan, "There is no I in team," provides a spelling lesson but unwise psychological advice. Often we use such slogans to imply that team members should forget about individual goals and performances and focus only on team goals and outcomes. However, research findings indicate that we elicit the best performances from both individuals and groups when we explicitly recognize and reinforce individual contributions. When individual efforts are not recognized, individuals tend to slack off, which lowers the performance of the overall group. Most successful coaches realize the importance of individual recognition and often take elaborate steps to ensure that individual goals are set and that individual achievements are reinforced. More detailed explanations of group performance are found in chapter 13.

How do your answers compare? How many questions did you answer correctly without guessing? Perhaps some of the answers surprised you. Based on the most recent sport psychology research and theory, many of the answers run counter to popular beliefs and practices in sport and exercise.

Additionally, as you probably noted, many of the answers are not simple or absolute. Sport psychology is a relatively new field of study, and new findings often change our answers to questions. Only 10 years ago, for example, few people thought that rewards could have any negative effects; most people thought that at worst they had no effect. Now, recent research findings demand that we reconsider our practices in light of the possible detrimental effects of rewards. Future research may again change our approaches.

The remainder of this text will elaborate on these and other psychological issues in sport and exercise. Do not expect to find simple *yes* or *no* answers. Instead, you will find information on how *some* personality factors affect *some* sport behaviors in *some* situations. Such information is never complete, but as sport psychology advances our understanding of human behavior in sport will gradually increase.

## *Summary*

Sport psychology is the branch of sport and exercise science defined as the scientific study of human behavior in sport. Like the other disciplines within sport and exercise science, sport psychology can be applied to varied skilled movements, physical activities, and exercise programs such as corporate fitness, exercise rehabilitation, and health-oriented exercise programs as well as traditional physical education and competitive athletics.

Within the psychology of sport and exercise, *sport psychology* is differentiated from *motor learning/control*, which encompasses cognitive and perceptual processes in motor learning and performance, and from *motor development*, which addresses developmental issues in sport and motor performance. Sport psychology focuses on both individual differences and social situational factors that interact in complex ways to influence human behavior in sport and exercise. Sport psychology is a relatively young discipline, and sport psychologists are only beginning to provide answers to some of our many questions about sport and exercise behavior. As you read through the text, you may find ideas and research findings to help you answer not only the questions posed in this chapter but also questions that arise in the future about human behavior in sport and exercise.

# CHAPTER 2

# History and Current Status of Sport Psychology

A precise date for the beginning of sport psychology cannot be easily pinpointed. Different aspects of the field emerged at different times. Some isolated early work was never continued, and one could claim with some justification that the field is just emerging today. Some commonly cited bench marks do exist, however, and those bench marks are described in this chapter.

## The First Social Psychology Experiment: 1898

Triplett's (1898) experiment on the motor performance of individuals acting alone and in pairs has been widely cited as the first laboratory experiment in social psychology and represents an important bench mark for sport psychology. The experiment was prompted by Triplett's observations of competitive cyclists. Triplett, a cycling enthusiast, noted that cyclists performed faster with a pacing machine (with other cyclists on a tandem bicycle) than when alone and that they performed even faster when competing against other cyclists. Triplett reasoned that the presence of others aroused a competitive drive in the cyclists that elicited better performance. Like any good scientist, Triplett tested his ideas in a controlled setting and confirmed his predictions when he observed that children wound fishing reels faster when in pairs than when alone.

Because of his reference to sport and use of an experimental motor task, Triplett's work is widely recognized in sport psychology, particularly with respect to social influence variables (see chapter 11). Of course, Triplett did not identify himself as a sport psychologist nor even as a psychologist interested in sport. During the early twentieth century, several other psychologists also conducted research involving sport or motor tasks. Although many of those findings are cited in the sport psychology literature, the intent of these researchers was to examine general psychology constructs and relationships rather than to study sport or exercise behavior per se.

# The Genesis of Sport Psychology: 1925

During the early twentieth century, a few farsighted individuals recognized the importance of psychological factors in sport and initiated sport psychology research. Although sport psychology had not yet emerged as a distinct discipline, the pioneering work of these early sport psychologists raised numerous issues and paved the way for much of our current work and research.

## Sport Psychology in the United States

Coleman Griffith, pictured in Figure 2.1, was a highly respected psychologist at the University of Illinois in the early 1900s and the first person to pursue sport psychology issues in the United States. In 1923 Griffith taught a course entitled, "Psychology and Athletics," and in 1925 he established the Athletic Research Laboratory at the University of Illinois.

Although Griffith's primary training and responsibility were in general psychology, he conducted an amazing amount of sport psychology work in the 1920s and 1930s. As well as teaching classes and directing the Athletic Research Laboratory, Griffith wrote two major texts, *Psychology of Coaching* (1926) and *Psychology of Athletics* (1928), published numerous articles based on both laboratory and field research on the psychological aspects of sport, and consulted with professional and intercollegiate sport teams.

For his sustained, high-quality contributions, Griffith has been described as the "father of sport psychology" in the United States (Kroll & Lewis, 1970).

**Figure 2.1** Coleman Griffith, the father of sport psychology in the United States. *Note.* From the Coleman Griffith Collection, University Archives, University of Illinois at Urbana-Champaign.

However, this designation is somewhat of a misnomer. "Father" implies that Griffith began a line of work that was carried on by his followers. To sport psychology's misfortune, Griffith had no followers, despite the fact that his publications, research activities, and thoughtful insights now rank him among the most respected and significant figures in the history of sport psychology.

## International Sport Psychology

While Griffith was initiating sport psychology research in the United States, sport psychology was also emerging in other countries. In discussing the emergence of sport psychology after World War I, Cratty (1983) specifically cited the ground-breaking work of Schulte in Germany and Roudik in Russia. Dr. Yuri Hanin, a senior researcher in sport psychology at the Research Institute of Physical Culture in Leningrad, reports in a postal interview that sport psychology emerged as a discipline of study in the Soviet Union during the years 1945-1957. He suggests that Soviet sport psychology had two "fathers," Peter Roudik and A.C. Puni, who is shown in Figure 2.2 (Hanin & Martens, 1978).

# Formal Organization in Sport Psychology: 1965

Despite the innovative, farsighted work of the pioneers in sport psychology during the first half of the twentieth century, sport psychology did not become an organized discipline in either North America or Europe until the 1960s. Coleman Griffith's systematic sport psychology work was an anomaly in the 1920s. Although a few psychologists and physical educators conducted occasional studies on sport psychology issues, especially on motor learning topics, sport psychology did not emerge as an identifiable subdiscipline until the mid

**Figure 2.2**   A.C. Puni, one of the fathers of Soviet sport psychology.

1960s. In the 1960s, some individuals such as William Morgan at Wisconsin and Daniel Landers and Rainer Martens at Illinois began to identify sport psychology or the social psychology of physical activity as their primary interest. A complete listing of others who pioneered sport psychology as a distinct discipline is not attempted because some notable contributors would likely be omitted. Simultaneously, many individuals became active sport psychologists in other countries, particularly in Europe, and sport psychology became an established area of sport and exercise science and practice.

As individuals developed interests in sport psychology, they began to organize. In 1965, the International Society of Sport Psychology (ISSP) formed and held the first International Congress of Sport Psychology in Rome. The ISSP continues to hold meetings every four years, normally after the Olympic year, and has become a forum for the international exchange of sport psychology information. At the same time that the ISSP was forming, initial steps were being taken to form a sport psychology organization in North America. Organizational meetings were held in 1965 and 1966, and in 1967 the North American Society for the Psychology of Sport and Physical Activity (NASPSPA) was officially incorporated. Today, NASPSPA is the primary sport psychology organization in the United States. NASPSPA now holds an annual conference, publishes a newsletter, and maintains close ties with the ISSP and the more recently formed Canadian Society for Psychomotor Learning and Sport Psychology (CSPLSP) to facilitate the exchange of ideas and research findings within the sport psychology community.

Dr. Miroslav Vanek, a prominent sport psychologist from Czechoslovakia, summarized the emergence of sport psychology in his 1985 presidential message to ISSP members:

> The psychology of sport has become an institutionalized discipline within the sport sciences in the later half of this century. . . . It is now possible to say that sport psychology has emerged as a distinctive subdiscipline and as a recognized member of the sport sciences. Our membership has grown, we have journals devoted to sport psychology, national and international societies, coursework and textbooks, specific courses for training in sport psychology, increasing research efforts, and so on. In fact, sport psychology has become a profession in many countries. (Vanek, 1985, p. 1)

## Today: Research Plus Application

Sport psychology expanded tremendously from 1965 to the present both in North America and at the international level. Sport psychology research proliferated during the 1960s and 1970s, and much of that research adopted experimental social psychology approaches. Concern for theoretical development and attention to experimental control advanced sport psychology knowledge and encouraged the recognition of sport psychology as a viable academic discipline. More recently, however, the emphasis on experimental social psychology models has waned, and sport psychology is now devoting increased attention to sport-specific issues and approaches.

As sport psychology knowledge has expanded, the dissemination and communication of that information has also expanded. Communication takes many forms, including classes and seminars, publications in both scientific and more popular sources, presentations at conferences and workshops, and direct application of sport psychology information through work with sport participants. Many physical education and exercise science programs include sport psychology courses, and several universities offer specialized graduate training in sport psychology. The *International Journal of Sport Psychology*, an official publication of the ISSP, disseminates sport psychology information at the international level, and the *Journal of Sport Psychology*, which began publication in 1979, is the dominant sport psychology research publication in North America. Considerable sport psychology information also appears in various sport and exercise science publications as well as in the general psychology literature.

At least in North America, the most recent expansion of sport psychology is the growth of applied sport psychology through work with sport participants. Several sport psychologists and some psychologists with clinical orientations are devoting considerable time and effort to working directly with sport participants, typically by providing psychological skills training or consultation to athletes. A new organization, the Association for the Advancement of Applied Sport Psychology (AAASP), has recently formed that promises to become a major force in the field. AAASP has established three distinct sections that focus on health psychology, social psychology, and intervention/performance enhancement. AAASP has begun publishing a newsletter, selected officers, and organized an initial conference to be held in the fall of 1986. In chapter 8 we will discuss anxiety management, a major component of most applied sport psychology programs, and some specific techniques that have been used with athletes.

To date, most applied sport psychology programs have been limited to elite athletes. The same techniques and approaches may be neither effective nor desirable for young athletes, physical education classes, health-oriented exercise programs, or sport participants with no interest in moving to more intense, demanding performance levels. As sport psychology research and knowledge continue to expand, the application of sport psychology will probably expand into such alternative sport and exercise settings. Applied work may well become more sophisticated as our knowledge increases with alternative techniques and approaches for varied activities.

## Sport Psychology as Science

Regardless of how sport psychology information is applied, applied techniques and programs are only as sound as the research and theories on which they are based. Carefully designed and conducted research is necessary if sport participants are to receive accurate, reliable information about human behavior in sport. Sound research and theory development are especially critical in sport psychology because it is a relatively young scientific discipline with a limited knowledge base.

As part of sport and exercise science, sport psychology is a scientific discipline that builds its body of knowledge about human behavior and sport by following the scientific method. The scientific method is not one rigid set of procedures but rather a general approach encompassing a variety of investigative strategies. Sound, relevant research could be conducted in a field setting with a volleyball team or in a controlled laboratory setting using a rotary pursuit task. Similarly, it might involve self-report questionnaire measures or physiological indicators. Different approaches have different advantages and limitations, and the researcher must consider the options to best answer each particular question. For example, field studies conducted in real-life settings typically allow greater generalization and immediate application of results, whereas laboratory settings provide greater control of critical variables and extraneous factors to allow more precise testing of theoretical predictions. Regardless of the question, the researcher must always attempt to ensure the greatest control possible with the greatest generalizability, balancing the two to best suit each particular question. The important consideration is to match the research design and method to the question.

Regardless of the specific question or approach of a particular study, the scientific method involves the systematic acquisition and evaluation of information with the goal of understanding the behavior or phenomenon under investigation. Neale and Liebert (1973) described the scientific method as follows:

> Most generally, science refers to the pursuit of objective knowledge gleaned from observation. Thus, the term refers to a *method* (systematic acquisition and evaluation of information) and a *goal* (identifying the nature or governing principles of what is being studied) rather than to any particular phenomena. (p. 2)

Science thus relies on observed evidence rather than biased judgments or vague impressions and seeks to go beyond those observations to *explain* and *predict* events and behavior. Simple descriptions of behavior or events at one time may have some value in that specific situation. If we can develop general principles or theories on the basis of our observations, however, we can better understand the causes and consequences of behaviors and apply those theories and principles to predict behavior and guide us as we encounter new situations. The aim of science, and the aim of sport psychology research, then, is to develop *theory*.

Theory is not merely an opinion, as we often imply with statements such as, "That's only a theory, not fact." A theory is actually a systematically derived explanation of a phenomenon based on empirical evidence gathered from carefully designed and conducted research. Soundly developed theories allow us to go beyond our observations to *explain* and *predict* behavior.

For example, in answering the question about aggressive behavior in ice hockey posed in chapter 1, I invoked a social learning *theory* of aggression. Social learning theory is not an idea casually tossed out but rather a carefully developed set of principles based on considerable research that help *explain* why aggressive behavior occurs. According to social learning theory, the hockey player has learned aggressive behavior in that situation by observing others and by being reinforced for aggressive behavior in similar situations. The social learning theory further *predicts* that a young hockey player who is reinforced for aggressive behavior is likely to exhibit aggressive behavior later, whereas another youngster who is reinforced for nonaggressive responses is likely to exhibit nonaggressive behaviors in similar situations.

In the scientific method, theories are never accepted as complete or absolute but are constantly tested and modified or replaced. The social learning theory of aggression, for example, suggests many additional questions such as the following: Are some athletes more likely to be imitated than others? Does reinforcement from coaches or parents have more or less influence than reinforcement from teammates? What factors in a sport situation (e.g., score, time in game, opponent's actions) provoke aggressive responses? Theories guide researchers in asking significant questions, and new findings help to create, revise, and develop theories.

Many sport psychologists are conducting sound research and attempting to develop theories that explain human behavior in sport. Because sport psychology is an emerging discipline, however, few established theories and general principles exist at this time. Research continues to increase our understanding and to affect our practices in sport, but many questions that sport participants raise about psychological issues have not yet been addressed through the scientific method. Thus sport participants, who must operate in the here and now, often rely on their own experiences and common sense. Sport participants depend on sport psychologists and other sport scientists to provide accurate, reliable scientific information to supplement their nonscientific insights and experiences.

New research findings may call into question some of our current practices. One sport practice questioned by recent research is the practice of giving rewards such as trophies, uniforms, and certificates. Several years ago most people believed that rewards could only help sport performance and behavior; at worst rewards might have no effect, but certainly rewards would pose no problems. As we discussed in chapter 1, however, recent research indicates that emphasis on *extrinsic* rewards can undermine *intrinsic* motivation and reduce later sport participation. Thus teachers, coaches, and program directors who previously used rewards as much as possible must now use rewards more cautiously in ways that do not undermine intrinsic motivation but do enhance feelings of success and satisfaction and the desire to participate in sport activities. A more complete discussion of this issue is presented in chapter 10.

Of course, not all research is equally helpful to sport participants. Furthermore, not all research is equally reliable and valid, regardless of how the findings might be applied. Some researchers do a better job than others of matching their research design and methods to the question, and some studies are more carefully conducted, which allows us to place more confidence in their findings. Sport psychologists who communicate information to sport participants often try to filter out poorly conducted research and irrelevant material. In selecting material for this text, I attempted to include reliable, well-designed studies that address significant issues in sport psychology. Of course, this selection involves subjective judgment and may be influenced by some biases. Readers who wish to delve more deeply into various topics should consult additional sources and make their own judgments. In addition, forthcoming research may well bring new insights and challenge some of the interpretations and conclusions presented here.

Science is not a final answer but a continuing process. Furthermore, the communication of sport psychology information is not a one-way street. Researchers must communicate their findings to sport participants, but participants also have much information to offer sport scientists. Participants can make scientists aware of issues that need attention and, because of their direct experience in sport activities, may provide special insights that an "objective" scientist might overlook.

## Summary

Sport psychology began with the isolated but farsighted work of pioneering psychologists in the 1920s and 1930s. In the 1960s and 1970s, sport psychology expanded at a phenomenal rate as formal organizations and various publications and communication forums emerged. Sport psychology continues to expand today, with many sport psychologists building the knowledge base of the discipline by following the scientific approach. An increasing number of sport psychologists are devoting their primary efforts to the direct application of sport psychology by helping participants to develop psychological skills. At present, most applied sport psychology work involves elite athletes. As our knowledge increases, however, direct application of sport psychology may extend to recreational activities, health-oriented exercise programs, and other nontraditional settings. Sport psychology is a relatively new and emerging discipline within sport and exercise science. We know far more about human behavior in sport than we did 20 years ago, but we have much more to learn. The continued application of the scientific method and the exchange of information among sport scientists and sport participants should advance sport psychology in exciting directions over the next 20 years and beyond.

# PART II

# *Individual Differences and Sport Behavior*

In part II we will begin to examine theories and research findings that help to explain human behavior in sport and exercise. Specifically, part II reviews the literature on personality and individual differences that influence sport behaviors. Chapter 3 considers general personality theories and the research on personality profiles of sport participants. Although much sport personality research has been conducted, existing studies on the personality profiles of sport participants tell us very little about sport behavior. As you will discover, the most useful sport personality research considers specific individual differences together with relevant situational factors that influence sport and exercise behavior.

The sport psychology research on specific personality characteristics is reviewed in chapters 4, 5, and 6. Recently, sport psychologists recognized the important role of individual differences in cognitive skills and attentional style, and that emerging literature is covered in chapter 4. The substantial sport psychology work on competitiveness and competitive anxiety is presented in chapter 5. Sport psychologists have drawn upon the extensive psychological research on achievement motivation and anxiety to help explain individual differences in competitive behavior. Furthermore, we have advanced our understanding greatly by addressing issues specific to sport with sport-specific measurement techniques and approaches. Because the role of females in sport has changed dramatically in recent years, the investigation of gender roles is prominent in sport psychology. Individual differences in gender role characteristics, particularly the literature on masculinity/femininity, are examined in chapter 6. Chapter 6 also presents information on the "fear of success" construct, as well as more current explanations of gender differences in achievement behavior. Finally, chapter 7 examines the literature on attitudes and sport behavior. The material on personality and attitudes in part II should help you to better understand the role of individual differences in sport and exercise behavior.

# CHAPTER 3

# *Personality*

Individual differences among sport participants are obvious. One youth soccer player relishes the center stage while a teammate shuns the limelight; one coach nervously paces the sideline while a rival calmly plots strategy. One gymnast consistently rises to the challenge of competition, but another chokes and performs far below expectations. Such individual differences reflect *personality*. Not only do we recognize that individual differences exist in sport, but we often assess personality informally when we "size up" opponents or evaluate our own strengths and weaknesses. Those personality assessments then affect our sport behaviors. A diver waiting on deck before the first dive of a meet might ask, "Can I maintain my poise and concentration through this competition?" The diver who answers, "Yes, I am confident and ready to hit that first dive," likely will perform differently and feel differently about the performance than one who answers with hesitation or worries about making mistakes. We also use personality judgments when interacting with others. Coaches and instructors do not make the same comments to players they consider to be fragile or sensitive that they do to players judged to be mentally tough.

The goal of sport personality research is to provide accurate and reliable information about individual differences in sport and the implications of such personality differences for sport performance and behaviors. In this chapter we will discuss general personality theories and measures and then focus on the sport psychology research on personality characteristics and sport behavior.

## *Personality Defined*

Personality is the individual's unique psychological makeup or, more formally, "the underlying, relatively stable, psychological structures and processes that organize human experience and shape a person's actions and reactions to the environment" (Lazarus & Monat, 1979, p. 1). Thus defined, personality denotes characteristic or *consistent* individual differences in behavior. An individual who consistently displays aggressive behavior (e.g., often argues, easily angers, initiates fights) is attributed the personality characteristic of aggressiveness. Personality can be described as the sum total or overall *pattern* of such characteristics and tendencies. We commonly think of personality as including characteristics related to social behaviors, such as introversion, independence, or aggressiveness. Those characteristics are part of personality, but personality also includes perceptual and cognitive characteristics, such as the ability to concentrate or focus attention.

# Theories of Personality

Several theories have been proposed to explain and predict personality. Ranging from primitive biological explanations, through more complex biological theories, and continuing with the more predominant theoretical representations such as psychodynamic and organismic theories, trait theories, social learning theories, and interactionist theories, personality has been the subject of a large percentage of both psychological and sport psychological literature.

## Early Theories

As far back as ancient Greek civilization people have attempted to understand and explain individual differences in personality and behavior. The early Greeks believed that all persons had four basic body fluids or "humors" in varying proportions. Varying individual temperaments or personalities were due to different relative proportions of the four humors. Blood was associated with a "sanguine" or cheerful temperament; a preponderance of yellow bile led to "choleric" or irritable behavior; black bile was associated with a "melancholic" or sad temperament; and the "phlegmatic" temperament, associated with phlegm, was characterized by indifferent, apathetic behavior.

## Biological Theories

Today's theorists, of course, do not offer the four body humors as explanations of personality. However, other biological explanations of individual differences in personality and behavior have considerable credibility in the modern scientific community. Biological explanations for aggressive behavior, for example, are quite prevalent. It is important to note, however, that proponents of biological explanations do not claim a biological basis for all behavior tendencies, or even for all aggressive behaviors. Moyer (1973), in discussing the physiological basis of aggression, clearly points out that no physiological characteristic or process explains all aggressive behavior and further acknowledges the crucial role of learning and situational factors. For example, as we will discuss in chapter 12, some evidence indicates that heightened physiological arousal (a biological factor) increases aggressive behavior. However, research also indicates that situational factors and information greatly influence aggressive responses to increased arousal.

Certainly biological factors influence behavior, including sport behavior. A 6-foot, 4-inch high school student may be encouraged to play basketball or volleyball and may find considerable success, whereas a 5-foot, 4-inch classmate may find more encouragement and challenge in wrestling or gymnastics. No one in sport psychology, however, claims that such biological characteristics are the basis of personality. Instead, some sport psychologists advocate consideration of biological characteristics along with personality characteristics to explain sport behavior.

One biological explanation of personality with some credibility in personality psychology, and one that has attracted several sport and physical education researchers, is Sheldon's constitutional theory (Sheldon & Stevens, 1942). Sheldon developed a widely recognized system of assessing body build or *somatotype*. Somatotyping involves rating a person's physique along the three dimensions of endomorphy (roundness), ectomorphy (linearity), and mesomorphy (muscularity). Sheldon proposed that each dimension is associated with a distinct set of personality characteristics. Endomorphy is characterized by affection, sociability, and relaxation; jolly Santa Claus is the prototypical endomorph in both body type and personality. Ectomorphy is characterized by tenseness, introversion, and a preponderance of artistic and intellectual types. The mesomorph, with the typical athletic build, has the stereotypical personality characteristics of aggressiveness, dominance, and risk-taking.

Sheldon reported correlational evidence to support the proposed relationship between body type and personality, but subsequent studies failed to confirm his findings. Furthermore, the popular images we have of different body types may lead us to see more stereotyped personality characteristics and assume stronger correlations between body type and personality than actually exist. Although some sport literature still cites Sheldon's work, constitutional theory receives little attention in contemporary personality psychology, and even Sheldon noted that body type is not a complete explanation for personality.

Dishman (1982, 1984) explicitly advocates consideration of both biological and psychological factors in his psychobiological model of exercise adherence. Dishman proposes that both biological factors, such as body composition, and psychological factors, particularly self-motivation, influence individuals' adherence to an exercise program. Persons who are relatively lean and recover rapidly from exercise will find the activity more enjoyable and feel greater accomplishment than individuals who are overweight or who have knee problems that limit activity. Different goals and approaches may well have different effects on those two types of individuals. Similarly, personality factors affect exercise adherence. Individuals who are highly self-motivated may set personal goals and strive for them with little guidance, but less self-motivated individuals may need more conducive exercise settings or social support to maintain their exercise programs.

Thus biological factors are important considerations, along with psychological factors, but they do not fully explain personality. Within the sport personality literature, biological factors are most prominent as possible explanations for the effects of exercise on moods and psychological well-being. Even in these areas, however, as we will discuss later in this chapter, biological explanations are not clearly established and many factors play important roles.

## Psychodynamic and Organismic Theories

One of the three most prominent current approaches to personality is the class of clinically oriented theories that includes *psychodynamic* and *organismic* theories. These two approaches are distinct classes of theories, but they are similar in that both are primarily clinical approaches that involve the in-depth analysis of a single individual. The most notable psychodynamic approach is the psychoanalytic theory of Freud and the neo-Freudians. Psychoanalytic theory proposes that the resolution of conflicts in early life lays the foundation for the adult personality. As the individual progresses through developmental stages, the ego arbitrates between the basic unconscious drives of the id and the values, attitudes, and conscience of the superego.

Freud certainly made a tremendous impact on psychology, and on life in general, as evidenced by the familiarity of Freudian terms and concepts. We will not delve into the complexities of Freudian personality theory here, however, because psychoanalytic approaches have had little impact on sport psychology. Psychodynamic theory is mainly an after-the-fact explanation based on informal observations and clinical intuition; psychoanalytic approaches focus on psychopathology and offer few testable predictions, especially about healthy personalities. By and large, sport participants do not have pathological personalities, and the main issue for sport psychology is the relationship between personality characteristics and behaviors in typical, "normal" sport settings.

Organismic theories of personality, such as Maslow's self-actualization theory, are more optimistic and humanistic than the Freudian or neo-Freudian approaches. Rather than focusing on instincts and early conflicts, organismic theories see personality as being shaped by the overall field of forces and posit self-change or growth as central features. Like psychoanalytic theories, however, organismic theories offer few testable predictions about the relationship of personality characteristics to specific sport behaviors. Thus, although a few sport psychologists doing applied work with individual athletes have adopted some psychodynamic or organismic ideas, these clinically oriented approaches have not played a significant role in sport psychology or even in general personality research.

## Trait Theories

In contrast to psychodynamic and organismic approaches, *trait* theories have generated a tremendous amount of personality research, including most sport personality studies. Most of our familiar personality measures (e.g., *Cattell 16PF, Minnesota Multiphasic Personality Inventory* or MMPI) are based on trait theories, which conceptualize personality as a collection of traits or factors. Traits are relatively stable, highly consistent attributes that exert widely *generalized* causal effects on behavior (Mischel, 1973). Trait theories thus imply consistency and generalizability of behavior. According to trait theory, a person with a high level of the trait shyness should consistently display shy behavior, such as remaining quiet and restrained, across a wide range of settings, including the classroom, team meetings, and social gatherings. An extreme trait approach assumes that once we assess an individual's personality, we can predict that individual's behavior in all situations. If a basketball player is identified as assertive, we can expect that player to behave assertively (e.g., going after the ball, taking the open shot without hesitation) regardless of the situation.

In reality, however, traits are notoriously poor predictors of behavior. Critics of trait theories (e.g., Mischel, 1968) point out that even the most psychometrically sound trait measures at best predict only a small proportion of actual behavior. The assertive basketball player does not display assertive behavior in every contest and every situation. Furthermore, even the player who is consistently assertive on the basketball court may display nonassertive or even reserved behavior in the classroom or on the job.

## Social Learning Theories

The inability of trait measures to predict behavior has led many personality researchers to renounce trait theories, and those critics often adopt a *social learning* approach. Social learning theory focuses on situational factors and learned behaviors and downplays the role of personality traits or innate dispositions. In expressing a social learning view, Bandura (1977a, pp. 11-12) stated, "Psychological functioning is explained in terms of a continuous reciprocal interaction of personal and environmental determinants." An extreme social learning view, such as B.F. Skinner's behaviorism, discounts the role of personality altogether. In Skinner's view, the basketball player exhibits assertive behavior because the situation calls for assertive behavior, and because assertive behavior has been reinforced in the past; any person in the same situation would display assertive behavior.

## The Interactionist Approach

In recent years, sport psychology and general personality psychology have moved away from trait theories and closer to social learning theories. Most personality psychologists do not accept traits as primary determinants of behavior, but most do acknowledge the existence of some consistent individual differences. The preferred approach today is an *interactionist* approach that considers the interrelated roles of both personality factors and situational factors as determinants of behavior. Particular personality characteristics are considered relevant predictors of behavior in certain but not all situations. A tennis player may consistently become anxious when faced with competitive matches, but that player may not become anxious when facing other challenges, such as academic tests or verbal presentations.

$B = f (P, E)$, the general formula presented in chapter 1, represents the interactionist approach in simple terms. The interactionist approach, however, is far from simple. Any behavior, such as aggressive behavior in an ice hockey game, is the function of a seemingly limitless number of personality and environmental factors. Selected personality characteristics may have considerable influence on behavior at one time but little effect in a later situation. A certain factor, such as an insult from an opponent, may provoke an aggressive response from one player but not from another in the same situation, and perhaps not even from the same player again in a slightly different situation (e.g., perhaps the aggressive response was facilitated by lack of sleep or problems outside of sport).

An interactionist approach, then, does not make simple, absolute predictions about the relationship between personality and behavior. Instead, considerable research is needed to identify personality characteristics that influence specific behaviors in varying situations and to determine how those personality characteristics interact with varying situational factors. The interactionist approach thus implies a complex explanation of behavior but offers a more realistic explanation than the simpler predictions of either the extreme trait or situational approaches. To reiterate a statement from chapter 1, human behavior in sport, like human behavior in general, is complex, and we should not expect simple answers.

## *Personality Assessment*

Whether a psychologist is conducting research or providing therapy, personality assessment is necessary if the psychologist hopes to examine the relationships between personality characteristics and behaviors. The general classes of personality assessment techniques include life histories, interviews, objective psychological inventories, projective psychological inventories, and behavioral observations. The use of these personality measures varies with the theoretical approach and purpose of the assessment.

Interviews and life histories are used primarily by clinical psychologists who want to examine the whole person in depth. Projective or unstructured inventories present ambiguous stimuli, such as pictures or inkblots, and allow the person to project his or her personality by telling or writing a story. Presumably the person's true personality is reflected in the responses. Projective measures, such as the *Rorschach Inkblot Test*, are more popular in clinical settings than in research, but one projective measure, the *Thematic Apperception Test* or TAT, has been used extensively in research on achievement motivation, which is discussed more fully in chapter 5.

Objective psychological inventories also are used in clinical work and are by far the most common measures in personality research. Objective inventories, which involve structured responses (e.g., multiple choice or true-false items), are easily administered and scored, and their wide use allows researchers to compare results with other samples and studies. Many of the most widely recognized objective inventories (e.g., the *Cattell 16PF*, MMPI, and *California Personality Inventory* or CPI) assess overall personality. Some objective inventories, such as Spielberger's (1966) *Trait Anxiety Inventory* (TAI) and Rotter's (1966) *Internal-External Locus of Control Scale*, assess only selected personality characteristics. Objective inventories are popular in sport psychology, and several objective measures such as the *Sport Competition Anxiety Test* (SCAT), *Test of Attentional and Interpersonal Style* (TAIS), and *Personal Attributes Questionnaire* (PAQ) will be discussed in later chapters. Sample objective items from the SCAT are presented in Figure 3.1; the entire test is included in Appendix A.

Behavior samples or ratings, which involve the direct observation of behavior, are not very popular in either clinical or research settings. Behavioral observations are not very feasible in clinical settings and do not provide the in-depth analysis that many therapists require. It is probable that behavioral measures are seldom used in research because such measures are time-consuming and more difficult to standardize and quantify than objective

|  | Hardly Ever | Sometimes | Often |
|---|---|---|---|
| When I compete I worry about making mistakes. | ☐ A | ☐ B | ☐ C |
| Before I compete I am calm. | ☐ A | ☐ B | ☐ C |

**Figure 3.1** Sample items from the Sport Competition Anxiety Test (SCAT; Martens, 1977).

inventories. One behavioral observation measure that has been used effectively in sport psychology is the *Coaching Behavior Assessment System* (CBAS) developed by Ron Smith, Frank Smoll, and Earl Hunt. Smith, Smoll, and Hunt (1977) developed the CBAS for their work with youth sport coaches. When using the CBAS, an observer notes each communication and response by a coach and classifies the behavior into one of 12 categories, such as reinforcement or general communication. The CBAS is a carefully developed, reliable measure that has provided valuable information about coaches' behaviors and the effect of those behaviors on young performers. Like most behavioral measures, however, the CBAS is time-consuming and requires that observers be trained in order to achieve reliable results. The use of the CBAS is discussed more fully in chapter 11.

Objective inventories have been the choice in most sport personality research. Clinically oriented measures, such as life histories, interviews, and projective inventories are seldom used because sport psychology rarely involves therapy, even in applied work. Despite the use of the CBAS and TAT, neither projective measures nor behavioral ratings are widely used in sport psychology. Sport psychologists usually select objective inventories that assess overall personality, such as the 16PF or MMPI, or inventories that measure selected characteristics, such as the SCAT, which has the added advantage of being a sport-specific measure.

## Sport Personality Research

The study of personality characteristics and profiles of sport participants is one of the most popular areas in sport psychology research. Perhaps the apparent, unique physical characteristics and talents of athletes prompt sport psychologists to look for analogous psychological profiles. The bulk of the sport personality research involves assessing personality profiles of sport participants to answer questions such as the following: Is there an "athletic personality"? Do personality profiles differ by sport? Are team sport participants more sociable than individual sport participants? Are runners more introverted than volleyball players? Do certain personality characteristics lead to success in athletics, and, if so, can we identify those characteristics to predict success? Each question addresses the influence of personality on sport behavior.

A few sport psychologists have posed the reverse question: How does sport behavior affect personality? We often claim that sport participation affects personality when attempting to justify our programs. For example, we may claim that sport builds character, develops leadership skills and sporting behaviors, or fosters a spirit of teamwork and cooperation. More recently, exercise and fitness programs have been promoted as avenues to improve mental health. At this time the research supporting such claims is sparse at best. We will consider some of this work later in the chapter after discussing the work on personality profiles of sport participants.

## Personality Profiles of Sport Participants

Research on the personality characteristics of sport participants is prolific. Countless theses and research articles attest to the continuing popularity of sport personality research. As part of his pioneering sport psychology work in the 1920s and 1930s, Coleman Griffith (1926, 1928) examined the personality profiles of successful athletes. Based on observations and interviews with college and professional athletes, including his participation-observation work with the Chicago Cubs, Griffith identified the following "characteristics of great athletes": ruggedness, courage, intelligence, exuberance, buoyance, emotional adjustment, optimism, conscientiousness, alertness, loyalty, and respect for authority. Griffith's list was more of a global observation than a scientifically derived conclusion, and you may notice that his list reflects the "All-American boy" image that characterized athletes of Griffith's day.

Many athletes have filled out many personality inventories between Griffith's time and the present, and some reviewers do see some consistency in the sport personality literature. Ogilvie (1968), for example, after reviewing the literature, concluded that certain personality characteristics are associated with successful athletes. With his colleagues, Ogilvie developed the *Athletic Motivation Inventory* (AMI) to measure those characteristics, including drive, determination, leadership, aggressiveness, guilt proneness, emotional control, self-confidence, conscientiousness, mental toughness, trust, and coachability (Tutko, Lyon, & Ogilvie, 1969). You may notice the similarity of this list to Griffith's list, which was derived from global methods without the benefit of considerable research.

Morgan (1978, 1980) offers the most systematic and strongly supported work on the relationship of personality to success in sport. On the basis of a series of studies, Morgan proposed that a "mental health model" effectively predicts success in athletics. In essence, the mental health model suggests that positive mental health and athletic success are directly related, whereas psychopathology and success are inversely related. In separate studies with college and Olympic wrestlers, national team rowers, and elite distance runners, Morgan demonstrated that successful athletes did indeed possess more positive mental health characteristics and fewer negative mental health characteristics than the general population. The pattern of characteristics emerging from Morgan's research is depicted in Figure 3.2 and has been appropriately termed the "iceberg profile." On *Profile of Mood States* (POMS) scores, successful athletes were above the waterline (population norm) on vigor, but below the surface on the more negative moods of tension, depression, anger, fatigue, and confusion.

Although Morgan's model is based on sound research, some cautions are in order. The model is quite general; not every successful athlete has the iceberg profile, and many less-than-successful athletes do have the profile. It is not surprising that psychopathology is negatively related to success in athletics; quite likely, psychopathology is negatively related to success in most

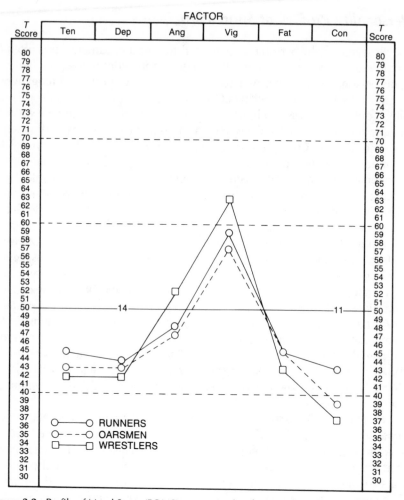

**Figure 3.2** Profile of Mood States (POMS) summaries for elite wrestlers, distance runners, and rowers. *Note.* From "Psychological Characterization of the Elite Runner" by W.P. Morgan and M.C. Pollock, 1977, *Annals of the New York Academy of Sciences,* **301**, p. 387. Copyright 1977 by the New York Academy of Sciences. Reprinted with permission.

endeavors. Furthermore, the iceberg profiles of athletes do not necessarily imply that positive mental health (personality) leads to success; success in sport may enhance positive mental health and create more positive mood profiles. It is notable that Morgan's clearest findings are with the POMS, a measure of moods, rather than with traditional inventories of more global and stable personality traits.

## *Problems with Sport Personality Research*

Despite Morgan's work, most sport psychologists take a more skeptical view of the sport personality literature. In 1974, a group of prominent sport psychologists (Fisher, Ryan, & Martens, 1976) discussed personality and sport and concluded that global personality traits have little if any relationship to sport participation or performance. Even a quick review of the sport personality research reveals that the findings are as varied as the studies; different studies find different traits that characterize athletes, with some findings in direct contradiction. For every study that finds runners to be more introverted than volleyball players, another finds no difference. There are no general findings across all studies. Little evidence exists to support the existence of a given athletic personality type, a personality profile that separates elite athletes from the rest of us, or specific personality types associated with specific activities. With such diverse and unreliable findings, sport personality information cannot predict meaningful sport behavior or be of much help to sport participants.

With such vast quantities of sport personality research yielding such meager and conflicting information, we might easily ask if personality relates to sport behavior at all. Although the sport personality literature to date tells us little about human behavior in sport, individual differences probably play a crucial role in sport behavior. Unfortunately, many sport personality studies were undertaken because they were easy to conduct rather than because they sought to answer meaningful questions. Such studies have yielded a vast amount of literature but have seldom addressed the more provocative sport personality issues.

If sport psychologists address relevant issues about personality and sport behavior and improve the quality of their research, sport personality information can be valuable to both sport psychologists and participants. First, we need to consider some of the problems with the existing research and how those problems might be remedied. Martens (1975) has classified the problems with sport personality research into the three general categories of *conceptual, methodological,* and *interpretive* problems.

**Conceptual Problems.** Conceptual problems are problems in the basic theory or reasoning underlying a study. The major conceptual problem in sport personality research is that many studies were done without a good reason. Research should be designed to answer meaningful questions, and that research should be initiated from a theoretical framework. In other words, the researcher should first consider the sport behavior of interest and then, on the basis of existing theory and empirical evidence, determine which personality variables are relevant and devise a study to test logical relationships between these personality variables and sport behavior. Unfortunately, sport personality studies have seldom been so carefully thought out and designed. Instead, as described by Ryan (1968),

> The research in this area has largely been of the "shot gun" variety. By this I mean the investigators grabbed the nearest and most convenient personality test, and the closest sport group, and with little or no theoretical basis for their selection fired into the air to see what they could bring down. It isn't surprising that firing into the air at different times and at different places, and using different ammunition, should result in different findings. In fact, it would be surprising if the results weren't contradictory and somewhat contrary. (p. 71)

A sound conceptual basis is critical to sport personality research. If researchers do not ask meaningful questions, their efforts cannot produce meaningful answers.

**Methodological Problems.**  Once the researcher has identified a relevant, testable question, the soundness of the study's methodology must be ensured; that is, the sample and measures must be appropriate, and the design and procedures must ensure that the research question is addressed without introducing confounding or extraneous variables. All too often, sport personality researchers have tested inappropriate samples, such as testing a single basketball team as representative of all basketball players, or used inappropriate measures. The *Minnesota Multiphasic Personality Inventory* (MMPI), for example, is composed of ten clinical scales (e.g., depression, paranoia) that were designed and validated for diagnosing clinical populations rather than assessing personality differences that might relate to sport behaviors. However, the MMPI often has been used to assess personality differences among athletes within a "normal" range.

**Interpretive Problems.**  Even if a study is conceptually and methodologically sound, the researcher must exercise caution in interpreting its findings. The most common interpretive error is overgeneralization. Many researchers try to make too much of their research findings. Relationships found with one sample of athletes may not generalize to sport participants in other activities or programs. Similarly, laboratory results may not generalize to sport settings.

When interpreting data, it is also important to remember that even if certain groups of sport participants possess a particular characteristic, we cannot infer that this characteristic *led to* or *caused* sport participation or success or that the characteristic relates to any specific behaviors. As discussed earlier, personality traits are notoriously poor predictors of behavior. Furthermore, sport has many powerful situational factors, such as training, set plays, coaching instructions, and team norms, that likely have a much stronger influence than personality has on specific behaviors. For example, suppose someone designed and conducted a sound study and found that intercollegiate volleyball players are more independent than the norm. Should we assume that players who score high on independence will be better volleyball players? Should we use such independence scores when selecting players? No! First of all, we cannot assume that independence helps make a person a better volleyball player. Even if we have data from several studies showing that volleyball players are independent, the data are *correlational*. Correlations indicate a relationship, but not necessarily a cause-effect relationship. Perhaps the experience of playing volleyball somehow leads to higher independence scores, or perhaps some other factor or factors that we do not know about influence both independence scores and volleyball participation. From a practical perspective, why would a coach want volleyball players with high independence scores? What does high independence mean in terms of actual performance and behavior in volleyball? Are high scores on independence (or any other personality factor) really likely to override or alter the influence of coaching instructions, strategies, training, or team norms?

## Use of Personality Tests to Select or Screen Participants

Of course, some personality characteristics may relate to important behaviors in sport. Some athletes become extremely anxious when faced with competition, and a reliable, valid measure of competitive anxiety might help to identify athletes who need training or instruction in anxiety management. Even the best personality measures, however, are not even close to absolute predictors of behavior, and certainly the state of sport personality knowledge does not justify the use of personality measures to screen and select sport participants.

Unfortunately, some personality tests have been used to screen athletes, and some sport participants and potential participants may have suffered as a result. One of the most widely known sport personality tests, and one that is especially likely to be misinterpreted and misused, is the *Athletic Motivation Inventory* (AMI; Tutko, Lyon, & Ogilvie, 1969). The AMI presumably assesses personality traits relevant to success in athletics. Data to support that claim are meager at best, but the marketing of the AMI, primarily to coaches, allows for considerable misinterpretation. Following the typical procedures, a coach might readily administer the AMI to a team, send the exams (along with a hefty fee) to the Institute for the Study of Athletic Motivation, receive the results (including scores and advice on handling each player), and find that a particular player scored low on one or more traits that the coach considers important (e.g., drive, coachability). Even with the best of intentions, the coach might expect certain behaviors, key on particular actions, and alter the coach-athlete and intrateam relationships. At worst, the athlete might be slotted into certain roles or dropped from the team. Such actions would be unjustified and unfair to the athlete, the coach, and other team members.

No evidence has been published to show that any of the traits assessed on the AMI relate to any specific behaviors in sport. Furthermore, even if the traits predicted certain behaviors, that would not justify dropping athletes. Height is related to success in volleyball; a stronger, more reliable relationship between height and volleyball success can be established than between volleyball success and any personality trait on the AMI. Also, that relationship has a logical basis: Taller players can get better angles for shots. Even with such a strong, logical relationship, most coaches would not automatically eliminate short players or select one starter over another simply because the first player was 1 inch taller. Certainly such selection on the basis of personality traits would be even more unfounded when strong, logical relationships between personality traits and specific sport behaviors have *not* been established.

The AMI's lack of validity and its reliance on the trait approach, as we have just discussed, are major flaws, but the most disturbing part of the AMI results is the advice to coaches on dealing with players. Competent clinical psychologists seldom give advice without extensive face-to-face contact. The standard advice given in the AMI results for a player scoring low on a desired trait is to work on increasing that trait (e.g., speak to the player and help the player to develop a stronger sense of trust). This approach may not be workable. Would we tell a volleyball coach, "Player A is far below the norm on height. You should work on that."? We do not know that we can change personality any more than we can change height, and, even if we could, we do not know that changing personality would change sport behavior or success.

In general, personality tests, even reliable, valid ones, have limited practical use in sport at this time. Global personality measures do not relate very well to specific sport behaviors, and even when specific personality factors relate to selected behaviors, strong situational factors may override that relationship. Coaches and others working with sport participants can probably learn more about individual differences through observations and talking with participants than through existing personality inventories.

## Effects of Sport and Exercise on Personality

Although most sport personality work explores the influence of personality characteristics on sport participation and behavior, the other side of sport personality research—the influence of the sport experience on the individual—is becoming more popular. Persons organizing and administering sport programs often claim that sport builds character or that participants develop values and a sense of teamwork. Such claims are seldom supported by research. In fact, some of the few studies that have been done suggest that sport participation may actually decrease individuals' emphasis on ethical behaviors and values such as fair play.

In general, no evidence suggests that sport and exercise programs affect the overall personality profiles of participants. However, some work in the rapidly emerging health psychology approach to exercise implies that physical exercise may lead to improved psychological well-being and mental health. Notably, these studies focus on psychological states, such as anxiety or depression, rather than more global and stable personality traits. Currently, the testimony about the psychological benefits of programs such as jogging for anxiety reduction, aerobic dance to increase confidence, survival training to improve self-esteem, and fitness training for postcardiac recovery is stronger than the empirical evidence, but some emerging work suggests that the proponents of such programs may have some basis for their claims.

An excellent review by Folkins and Sime (1981) provides a good discussion of the research on exercise and psychological well-being. Folkins and Sime and others who have reviewed this line of research (e.g., Buffone, 1984; Hughes, 1984; Mihevic, 1981; Morgan, 1981, 1985; Sachs, 1984) agree that participation in general sport activities does not seem to affect personality, but vigorous exercise and programs that increase fitness levels may have positive effects on mood, self-concept, and general mental health. Except for self-concept, general personality traits do not seem to be affected by improvements in physical fitness. Some evidence suggests that improved fitness and the accompanying changes in body image may positively affect self-esteem, especially for participants who had low self-esteem prior to the fitness program. Recently, Varca, Shaffer, and Saunders (1984) conducted a long-term study of sport participation and life satisfaction. Their findings indicated that sport participation during adolescence led to increased life satisfaction for men at the start of college and five years after graduation, but no relationships were found for women. Other work implies that improved cardiovascular fitness is linked with an increased sense of well-being and more effective management of emotional stress. Persons who were more psychologically distressed or more physically unfit at the start of the programs were the most likely to report improvements, and several studies with clinical patients suggest that exercise may aid in relieving depression or anxiety.

To date, few controlled studies have been conducted, and even those researchers who agree that exercise and fitness may improve mental health do not agree on an explanation. Some propose that exercise increases the individual's sense of control and mastery and leads to improved psychological health, and others refer to an altered state of consciousness or distraction from anxiety-provoking thoughts. Some assert that exercise induces the release of morphine-like chemicals called *endorphins* that may account for at least some psychological effects, and others consider the psychological improvement associated with exercise to be a function of attention given to participants or a placebo effect. At this time, then, research on the psychological effects of sport and exercise is far from conclusive. Considerable research is needed to clarify the relationships between exercise and mental health, but the suggestive findings give cause for optimism.

## *Improving Sport Personality Research*

Despite the problems, not all sport personality research is futile. Many important questions should be and are being addressed. Administering general personality tests and assessing overall profiles that predict few sport behaviors, however, is not very productive. Research with general personality measures has revealed little about sport participants or sport behaviors. Personality characteristics have little relationship to sport participation or behaviors, and sport participation has little effect on general personality. A more promising approach involves identifying and investigating relevant personality characteristics and situational factors that affect sport and exercise behaviors in theoretically based interactive models. That is not an easy task, but some sport psychologists are taking that approach.

Dishman's (1982, 1984) psychobiological model of exercise adherence illustrates the interactive approach to personality and exercise behavior. Within the model, Dishman incorporates both individual characteristics and situational factors to predict adherence to an exercise program. The key personality variable with a logical and empirically demonstrated relationship to exercise adherence is self-motivation, which is the tendency to persevere independently without situational reinforcements. Dishman and his colleagues (Dishman & Ickes, 1981; Dishman, Ickes, & Morgan, 1980) developed a self-motivation questionnaire and demonstrated its reliability and validity for predicting exercise adherence. However, self-motivation alone is an inadequate predictor of exercise adherence. As mentioned earlier in this chapter, other individual characteristics, including biological factors and situational factors such as the exercise setting and program strategies, also affect exercise adherence. Furthermore, those individual and situational factors interact; situational factors do not affect all individuals the same way. A highly self-motivated individual may persist longer when allowed to set personal goals, whereas an individual with low self-motivation may persist longer in a more structured exercise setting.

# *Summary*

Personality is the overall pattern of psychological characteristics that makes each person a unique individual. Individual differences are obvious in sport, and understanding such personality factors can help to explain sport and exercise behavior. Although much sport personality research has been conducted, that research tells us little about sport behavior because surveys of sport participants' personality profiles do not relate very well to specific behaviors.

We can learn more about sport behaviors by investigating the interactive effects of specific personality characteristics and situational factors on sport and exercise behaviors. Dishman's psychobiological model of exercise adherence incorporates both individual and situational factors in an interactionist framework, and several other sport psychologists are also adopting an inter-actionist approach to investigate specific personality characteristics and sport behavior.

Some of the relevant work on specific sport personality characteristics is discussed in the next three chapters, specifically the work on cognitive strate-gies and attentional styles in sport (chapter 4), competitiveness and competitive anxiety (chapter 5), and gender roles and sport (chapter 6). Although the sport personality research conducted to date has produced little useful information, the current work on self-motivation, attentional style, competitive anxiety, and other relevant personality characteristics is beginning to help us explain the complex, interactive relationships among individual and situational factors in sport.

# CHAPTER 4

# *Individual Differences in Cognitive Styles and Abilities*

Although sport psychology work on general personality profiles and social psychological personality characteristics has provided little useful information and few insights, the investigation of individual differences in cognitive styles and abilities appears to be much more promising. Within the last few years both sport participants and sport psychologists have become increasingly concerned with cognitive skills. Sport psychologists who work with athletes often devote considerable time and effort to promoting concentration exercises and imagery or mental rehearsal. Mahoney (1979) specifically cites imagery and attentional focus, along with arousal regulation and self-confidence, as major cognitive-behavioral concepts with important implications for sport psychology.

We do not need to consider elaborate psychological skills programs or research to recognize the central role of cognitive skills in sport. We could go to the local youth baseball game and listen to a coach tell a 10-year-old batter to "Keep your eye on the ball" or watch high jumper Dwight Stones and notice that we can almost see him go up and over the bar as he stands on the approach mentally rehearsing the jump. Furthermore, individual differences in cognitive skills and strategies are quite evident. Anyone who has worked with a group of 10-year-old baseball players knows that some youngsters are better at keeping their eye on the ball than others. Similarly, some gymnasts clearly maintain their concentration through a complex routine, whereas others are easily distracted and slip off balance. Dwight Stones and tennis player Chris Evert Lloyd report that imagery helps them perform, but other athletes find imagery more troublesome than beneficial. Some people effectively use imagery to practice sport skills; some batters are good at concentrating on the ball, and some soccer players quickly perceive the overall view of the field and readily find the open player for the pass. On the other hand, some individuals are equally poor at each of those cognitive skills.

The investigation of such individual differences in cognitive skills and their relationship to sport behavior is a sport personality issue. Certain cognitive skills such as the ability to focus and maintain attention have clear, demonstrable implications for performance and behavior. Thus the investigation of cognitive personality characteristics may be much more relevant to sport behavior than the traditional sport personality research discussed in chapter 3. Even one of the strongest critics of traditional personality trait research (Mischel, 1973) advocated consideration of cognitive characteristics and processes in personality psychology. It is clear that cognitive characteristics and processes also play a role in sport psychology.

Systematic research and concern for the effective use and practice of cognitive techniques is a recent development, but some initial findings suggest that cognitive styles and characteristics have important implications for sport performance and behavior. A number of investigators have begun to look at individual differences among sport participants in terms of specific cognitive/ perceptual characteristics and styles. At this time, such research is largely descriptive and suggestive, but its findings are promising.

Mahoney and Avener (1977) examined psychological factors and cognitive strategies of qualifiers and nonqualifiers for the U.S. Olympic men's gymnastics team. Qualifiers were found to be more self-confident, more likely to think and dream about gymnastics, and more likely to use self-talk and internal mental imagery (imagining doing the activity), and they appeared to be more able to control worry and concentrate on the task at the time of performance. Other studies have replicated many of these findings, especially the higher self-confidence of more successful athletes (Gould, Weiss, & Weinberg, 1981; Highlen & Bennett, 1979; Meyers, Cooke, Cullen, & Liles, 1979), and, as will be discussed in chapter 8, the ability to control anxiety seems to be characteristic of successful performers. To date, these studies have involved small, limited samples, the measures have not established reliability and validity, and causality has not been established. We do not yet know whether the cognitive psychological differences indicate pre-existing individual differences or the consequences of training or experience or whether those characteristics can be changed. Nevertheless, the initial findings are encouraging, and the investigation of cognitive psychological factors appears to be a promising direction for sport personality research.

## *Attentional Style*

Attention is a long-standing subject of discussion and investigation within psychology. In his classic text, *The Principles of Psychology*, William James (1890) described attention as follows:

> Everyone knows what attention is. It is taking possession by the mind, in clear and vivid form, of one out of what seems several simultaneously possible objects or trains of thought. Focalization, concentration of consciousness are its essence. It implies withdrawal from some things in order to deal effectively

with others, and is a condition which has a real opposite in the confused, dazed, scatterbrained state which in French is called *distraction*, and *Zerstreutheit* in German. (pp. 403-404)

We still understand attention in much the same way that James described it, but modern cognitive psychologists have much more to say about attentional processes and their role in learning and memory. In relation to attention and sport, we are generally concerned with *selectivity* and *alertness*. Selectivity relates to how a person limits attention to selected objects or ideas:

- Can you pick out the open player for a pass?
- Can you pick up on cues to your opponent's movements, or do you get faked out?

Alertness relates to the keenness of cognitive attention:

- Are you alert and paying attention for the starting signal?
- Can you maintain your concentration at the end of a long and tiring endurance event?

Readers who wish to probe further into theories and research on attentional processes and their relationship to motor performance should consult sources on cognitive psychology and motor behavior (e.g., Keele, 1973; Marteniuk, 1976; Norman, 1976; Schmidt, 1982). Certainly cognitive psychologists and motor behavior researchers will continue to investigate attentional processes and increase our understanding of the cognitive factors within sport and motor behavior. At the same time, sport psychologists are beginning to examine attentional styles and the relationship of individual differences in attentional style to sport performance and behavior. The combined efforts of researchers in these areas should improve our understanding of attention in sport and exercise.

## Nideffer's Attentional Model

Largely due to the initial work of Nideffer, attentional style is the subject of considerable sport psychology research. Nideffer (1976a) proposes that attentional style exists along two dimensions, *width* and *direction* (see Figure 4.1). Width ranges from narrow to broad; narrow attention is focusing on a limited range of cues, whereas a broad focus takes in a wide range of cues. Direction shifts on a continuum from an internal focus on one's own thoughts and feelings to an external focus on objects and events outside the body.

Nideffer posited that varying combinations of attentional width and direction are appropriate for varying sport activities and that the use of the appropriate

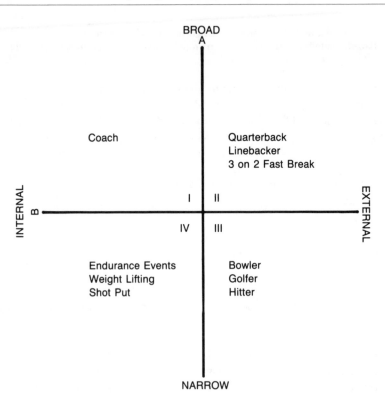

**Figure 4.1** Nideffer's model of attentional focus. *Note.* From *The Inner Athlete* (p. 49) by R. Nideffer, 1976, New York: Crowell. Copyright 1976 by Robert Nideffer. Reprinted with permission.

attentional focus can enhance performance. A broad-internal focus is an analytical style that is useful for planning strategy and analyzing previous performances; coaches often need a broad-internal style. A broad-external focus involves taking in a good deal of information. Many sport situations call for a broad-external focus, such as a basketball player leading a fast break and a football quarterback trying to pick out primary and secondary receivers. A narrow-external focus is useful for activities that require concentration on a ball or object, such as bowling, batting in baseball/softball, putting in golf, and kicking in football. A narrow-internal focus is appropriate for mentally rehearsing a task or performing strength and endurance activities such as distance running and weight lifting.

Although all the attentional focuses are useful, problems arise when an individual relies too heavily on one style or uses an attentional style inappropriately. In using a broad-internal style, a performer might become preoccupied with analysis and miss the action. Although a broad-external style allows a person to take in important information, a person could take in too much irrelevant information and become confused or overreact. On the other hand, an inappropriate narrow-external focus could lead a performer to miss relevant external information, as in the case of an outfielder who makes a good catch but misses the throw to the base. Finally, an extreme narrow-internal focus could imply focusing on negative thoughts such as past failures or anxiety, causing a lack of attention to important external cues.

## Measures of Attentional Style

In addition to describing attentional styles, Nideffer proposes that individuals differ in attentional skills and in the ability to use the varying styles effectively. Thus attentional style is an individual difference variable—a personality characteristic. Nideffer (1976b) developed the *Test of Attentional and Interpersonal Style* (TAIS) to assess individuals' tendencies to use broad-internal and broad-external information and to narrow attention effectively. The TAIS also assesses tendencies to become overloaded with internal or external information or to become too narrow in attention. The specific attentional subscales measured by the TAIS, along with sample items for each subscale, are shown in Figure 4.2.

Nideffer provided preliminary information on the reliability and validity of the TAIS, but sport psychologists are just now beginning to examine the validity of the test and its implications for sport behavior. Some of the initial work indicates that attention and attentional styles influence sport performance and behavior. However, that work also suggests that the validity of the TAIS for sport and its ability to predict sport behavior are limited. Nideffer (1976b) reported that swimmers who were categorized as inconsistent in performance by their coach were overloaded with internal (OIT) and external (OET) stimuli, and Landers and Courtet (1979) found that rifle and pistol shooters who had an effective broad-internal focus (BIT) had more accurate performance. Otherwise, support for the predictive validity of the TAIS attentional scales is weak.

Van Schoyck and Grasha (1981) reasoned that a sport-specific measure of attentional style might be more reliable and valid than the general TAIS for specific sport activities and developed a tennis version of the TAIS (T-TAIS). The T-TAIS did indeed produce higher test-retest reliability and internal consistency than the TAIS. More importantly, the T-TAIS showed a more consistent relationship to tennis ability and match scores than the TAIS showed. Albrecht and Feltz (1985) recently followed similar procedures and developed a sport-specific attentional measure for baseball/softball (B-TAIS). Like Van Schoyck and Grasha, Albrecht and Feltz found that B-TAIS scores, but not TAIS scores, were related to batting performance.

The studies by Van Schoyck and Grasha and Albrecht and Feltz not only demonstrated the superiority of sport-specific measures of attentional style but also raised questions about Nideffer's two-dimensional model of attention. Van Schoyck and Grasha's factor analysis supported the width (narrow-broad) dimension proposed by Nideffer, but not the direction (internal-external)

BET (Broad-External)

The higher the score, the more the individual's answers indicate that he or she deals effectively with a large number of external stimuli. The individual has a broad-external focus that is effective.

1. I am good at quickly analyzing a complex situation such as how a play is developing in football or which of four or five kids started a fight.

2. In a room filled with children or on a playing field, I know what everyone is doing.

OET (External Overload)

The higher the score, the more the individual's answers indicate that he or she makes mistakes because he or she is overloaded and distracted by external stimuli. He or she has difficulty narrowing attention when he or she needs to.

1. When people talk to me, I find myself distracted by the sights and sounds around me.

2. I get confused trying to watch activities such as a football game or circus where many things are happening at the same time.

BIT (Broad-Internal)

The higher the score, the more the individual indicates that he or she is able to think about several things at once when it is appropriate to do so. He or she has a broad-internal focus.

1. All I need is a little information and I can come up with a large number of ideas.

2. It is easy for me to bring together ideas from a number of different areas.

OIT (Internal Overload)

The higher the score, the more the individual indicates that he or she makes mistakes because he or she thinks about too many things at once. He or she is interfered with by his or her own thoughts and feelings.

1. When people talk to me, I find myself distracted by my own thoughts and ideas.

2. I have so many things on my mind that I become confused and forgetful.

NAR (Narrow Effective Focus)

High scorers indicate that they are able to narrow attention effectively when the situation calls for it.

1. It is easy for me to keep thoughts from interfering with something I am watching or listening to.

2. It is easy for me to keep sights and sounds from interfering with my thoughts.

RED (Errors of Underinclusion)

High scorers have chronically narrowed attention. They make mistakes because they cannot broaden attention when they need to.

1. I have difficulty clearing my mind of a single thought or idea.

2. In games I make mistakes because I am watching what one person does and I forget about the others.

Responses are on a Likert scale with the following anchors: Never, Rarely, Sometimes, Frequently, All the time.

**Figure 4.2** TAIS attentional subscale definitions and sample items. *Note.* Modified from *The Inner Athlete* (pp. 116, 118) by R. Nideffer, 1976, New York: Crowell. Copyright 1976 by Robert Nideffer. Reprinted with permission.

dimension. Instead, they described a bandwidth dimension with two components, scanning and focusing. Albrecht and Feltz's findings also failed to confirm Nideffer's model. Their analysis revealed two factors, an effective attentional style (NAR, BET, BIT) and an ineffective style (RED, OET, OIT), which mix Nideffer's dimensions.

After reviewing the literature on attentional styles and measurement techniques in sport, Landers (1981, 1985) concluded that the TAIS does not differentiate attentional direction, is a poor predictor of sport and motor performance, and has limited value in sport. The TAIS may be useful for examining the breadth or bandwidth of attention, but Landers advocates less reliance on questionnaires and greater use of behavioral measures and physiological indicators in studies of attention and sport behavior. Some sport psychology research is already following the direction proposed by Landers. In an innovative series of experiments discussed in the next section, Allard, Graham, and Paarsalu (1980) and Allard and Starkes (1980) used behavioral measures to examine individual differences in perception in sport. Also, several investigators have incorporated physiological measures in studies of attention and of arousal and performance.

## Perception in Sport

In a series of experiments conducted within a cognitive-perceptual psychology framework, Allard and her colleagues (Allard et al., 1980; Allard & Starkes, 1980) examined individual differences in perception in basketball and volleyball. Allard et al. tested the ability of basketball players and non-players to recall basketball slides after a 4-second view. The slides included scenes from structured situations, specifically an offensive play in progress, and scenes from unstructured situations, such as the action immediately following a turnover. Basketball players were better than nonplayers at remembering the slides, but only for the structured situations, confirming earlier findings with chess players that indicated that increased recall accuracy is specific to game situations (Chase & Simon, 1973).

In a series of five experiments, Allard and Starkes compared volleyball players and nonplayers for speed and accuracy in detecting a volleyball in rapidly presented slides. No differences were found for *accuracy* of detection, but players were much *faster* than nonplayers. The faster speed of players did not seem to be a simple athlete-nonathlete difference because volleyball players were faster than comparably skilled athletes from other sports. Additionally, volleyball players were faster than nonplayers at detecting a volleyball but were not faster at detecting an unrelated object (barns), leading

Allard and Starkes to conclude that the perceptual skill of players is best described as a rapid visual search *specific* to the ball as target. This finding reinforces the interactionist approach discussed in chapter 3. Individual differences in perception exist. Volleyball players were faster at detection, and basketball players were more accurate at recall. However, those differences are relevant only for specific sport situations.

Although the Allard and Starkes findings suggest that perceptual skill is related to playing experience, we do not know whether such skills develop with experience, whether we can train individuals to improve those skills, or whether the better skilled individuals stay with the sport as those with poorer skills are selectively eliminated. We also do not know much about how situational factors, such as competition or specific instructions, interact with individual differences in perception or attentional style in sport.

## Association/Dissociation and Performance

The most widely cited sport psychology work on attentional style and performance is Morgan and Pollock's (1977) study of marathon runners. Many of us who run or jog use a dissociative approach or an attentional style highlighted by distraction; that is, we focus externally on objects or ideas such as replaying the day's events or playing songs in our minds while jogging. One innovative runner interviewed by Morgan and Pollock imagined stepping on the faces of disliked coworkers as she was running. Surprisingly, Morgan and Pollock found that elite marathon runners did not use a dissociation strategy. Instead, elite runners typically reported using an associative strategy; they focused on their breathing, paid attention to the feelings in their leg muscles, or otherwise adopted an internal attentional focus and monitored their bodily sensations. Morgan and Pollock's observations are widely cited to support the claim that an associative or narrow-internal focus is desirable for endurance events such as marathon running. However, Morgan and Pollock did not claim that an associative strategy is advantageous to all marathoners at all times. Other evidence argues against a blanket endorsement of associative strategies for all endurance activities.

A recent study in our laboratory (Gill & Strom, 1985) illustrates that a narrow-internal focus is not necessarily appropriate for all endurance activities. In our study, female athletes performed an endurance task (on the quadriceps machine of the Universal gym) for as many repetitions as possible using two attentional styles, a narrow-internal focus on the feelings in their legs and a narrow-external focus on a picture. Significantly more repetitions were performed when using the external or dissociative focus. Furthermore, nearly all participants preferred that style.

Our study is not unique. Pennebaker and Lightner (1980) demonstrated that distraction led to superior performance in two experiments. In the first experiment, individuals exercising on a treadmill reported less fatigue when distracted than when listening to their own breathing. In their second experiment, Pennebaker and Lightner found that individuals ran faster on a cross-country course, where they were more likely to focus on external cues, than when running laps on a circular track.

Weinberg, Smith, Jackson, and Gould (1984) compared association, dissociation, and positive self-talk strategies on performance of an aerobic task (30-minute run) and an anaerobic task (leg lift). Although no differences were observed with the run, individuals using either dissociation or positive self-talk performed longer on the leg lift task than individuals using association.

Morgan's own research (Morgan, 1981b; Morgan, Horstman, Cymerman, & Stokes, 1983) revealed that a dissociative strategy resulted in superior performance on a treadmill task and that even the elite marathoners sometimes used dissociation as well as associative strategies when running. Dissociation appears to reduce the perception of pain and fatigue and thus improves performance when the primary goal is to keep going or maintain performance in the face of pain or fatigue. On tasks such as the quadriceps machine and jogging for nonelite runners in which maintaining performance may be the primary goal, dissociation may facilitate performance. On the other hand, elite runners usually have specific time or place goals and are concerned with more than simply maintaining performance. The elite runners in Morgan and Pollock's study apparently monitored body sensations to pace themselves and achieve their performance goals.

Thus dissociation may be a useful attentional strategy for some tasks, but for other tasks or other situations association may be more effective. Furthermore, individual differences in attentional styles may determine the efficacy of differing cognitive strategies. Weinberg et al. suggested that the experienced runners who participated in their study may have developed preferred attentional styles that interfered with the strategy manipulations and led to the absence of strategy effects in their study. Even though most individuals in our study preferred dissociation, a few individuals specifically stated that they needed to focus on the feelings in their legs to concentrate and push themselves. As we continue to investigate attentional styles and strategies in sport and exercise, we may discover how varying individual attentional styles interact with task characteristics and situational factors to influence performance and whether such individual differences are relatively stable or can be readily changed through instructions, training, or experience.

## *Imagery*

At the beginning of this chapter we noted that the two topics within the general area of cognitive abilities that have captured the most interest in sport psychology are attentional style and imagery. As we have just discussed, individual differences are prominent in the work on attentional styles and strategies. Individual differences have received less attention in relation to imagery. Instead, most sport psychology work focuses on using imagery techniques to prepare for performance and competition. Imagery can be useful as a general relaxation or anxiety management technique, but more frequently we use imagery to mentally rehearse a skill and improve subsequent performance.

## Individual Differences in Imagery Ability

Although the enthusiasm of sport psychologists for imagery skills and techniques is a recent phenomenon, psychologists have been discussing and investigating imagery for some time. As early as 1883, Sir Francis Galton wrote a book in which he devoted considerable discussion to imagery and reported that he had given a questionnaire on the ability to image to a diverse sample. Thus Galton was probably the first person to examine individual differences in imagery ability. Many books on imagery have been written, and the *Journal of Mental Imagery*, devoted to theory and research on this topic, has been published for several years. Individual differences in imagery abilities and the significance of such differences in imagery processes are important aspects of the imagery literature. For example, Marks (1977), in a review paper, emphasized the role of individual differences in perceptual, encoding, and retrieval mechanisms related to imagery.

Many psychologists have investigated individual differences in imagery abilities, and, as a review of imagery assessment by Sheehan, Ashton, and White (1983) indicates, many different measures have been developed and used. Some investigators have used objective or performance-based assessments in which imagery ability is inferred from performance on sample items or selected tasks. The spatial relations subtest of Thurstone's (1938) test of *Primary Mental Abilities* is a performance measure that has been used in imagery research. As Sheehan and his colleagues note, however, most measures of imagery ability are self-report questionnaires. Some of the most widely known and widely used imagery tests include the following:

1. *Betts' Questionnaire Upon Mental Imagery (QMI)*. The shortened version (Sheehan, 1967) of Betts' (1909) original QMI measures imagery vividness in seven sensory modalities.

2. *Gordon's Test of Imagery Control (TIC)*. Gordon's (1949) test assesses how well individuals can control or transform images.

3. *Vividness of Visual Imagery Questionnaire (VVIQ)*. Marks' (1973) VVIQ is an extended version of the QMI visual imagery subscale.

4. *Individual Differences Questionnaire (IDQ)*. The IDQ (Paivio, 1971) and its abbreviated form, the Verbalizer-Visualizer Questionnaire

(VVQ) developed by Richardson (1977), assess the degree to which an individual uses imaginal and verbal thinking modes.

Although imagery vividness as measured by the Betts QMI was positively related to improvement in a physical skill with the use of mental practice (White, Ashton, & Lewis, 1979), few of the imagery ability measures have been used to investigate imagery with sport and motor tasks. In fact, even in the general psychology literature, none of the self-report scales consistently predicts very much about imagery or performance.

Sheehan et al. suggest that the use of experience-based measures, such as thought sampling, might offer new insights, especially into motivational and emotional processes associated with imagery. The researchers also advocate the use of varied assessment procedures, including psychophysiological measures such as electroencephalogram (EEG) recordings to help probe individual differences.

Kosslyn (1983) proposes a computer metaphor theory of imagery and emphasizes the shortcomings of single self-report scales to assess individual differences. Kosslyn purports that individuals have not one but several imagery abilities. For example, a person might be very adept at picking out specific aspects of an image (e.g., seeing the position of the bat during a swing) but may develop "grainy" images with obscure details rather than sharp, detailed images. Thus multidimensional measurement techniques are needed to assess and investigate individual differences in imagery abilities.

## Imagery and Sport Performance

Although the information just discussed indicates that psychologists are actively examining the role of individual differences in imagery processes, sport psychologists are just now beginning to consider imagery in a systematic way. Obviously many sport participants use imagery and have been doing so for some time. More recently, several sport psychologists involved in applied work with athletes have tried to introduce more structured imagery techniques to help athletes use imagery to enhance performance. Unfortunately, theoretical work and research findings to guide sport participants in the effective and appropriate use of imagery is sparse.

The research most closely related to the current use of imagery techniques in sport is the mental practice research conducted during the early twentieth century and continuing into the 1960s and 1970s. Most of that literature compared mental practice with physical practice and seldom considered individual differences or the various aspects of the imagery process. In reviewing that literature, Richardson (1967a, 1967b) concluded that mental practice improved motor performance, and Corbin (1972) more cautiously suggested that the findings were inconclusive and that varying tasks and characteristics of the studies yielded varying results. In any case, the findings certainly were not entirely consistent and provided little insight into the mental rehearsal process and its effects.

The recent surge of interest and activity in applied sport psychology has brought renewed interest in mental rehearsal or, as it is more popularly termed, imagery in sport. Mahoney (1979) advocated a cognitive-behavioral approach to sport psychology and specifically cited imagery as a key cognitive process with implications for sport performance. Based on his reading of the literature, Mahoney reached the following conclusions:

1. Mental practice may be more effective when the athlete is familiar with the task and when mental practice is interspersed with actual motor practice.

2. Mental practice may be more effective if the athlete uses an internal perspective and imagines the kinesthetic feelings of doing the skill rather than an external observer's perspective or exclusively visual imagery.

3. A coping model who makes mistakes but recovers may help others to develop such recovery skills, but a coping model may also increase the likelihood of errors.

Although some of Mahoney's recommendations are questionable in light of recent research, most sport psychologists actively working with athletes follow Mahoney's advice and give imagery a prominent role in their psychological skills programs.

Imagery or, more specifically, visuomotor behavioral rehearsal (VMBR), is the cornerstone of the applied sport psychology program developed by Richard Suinn (1976, 1983), a psychologist who has done considerable work with Olympic athletes. Suinn (1983) defines VMBR as, "a covert activity whereby a person experiences sensory-motor sensations that reintegrate reality experiences" (p.512). Suinn emphasizes imagery as a total sensory recreation of a skill and not simply a visual picture. In fact, Suinn presents electromyographic (EMG) recordings from a ski racer using imagery that matched the expected activity on the actual course. Suinn reports considerable success with the VMBR technique, and several other researchers confirm that VMBR can be effective for sport participants (Lane, 1980; Titley, 1976).

Many athletes, such as high jumper Dwight Stones and tennis player Chris Evert Lloyd, reportedly make extensive use of imagery, and some case studies indicate that imagery is an effective technique for practicing sport skills. However, as Suinn (1983) concludes in his review of the literature on imagery in sports, controlled studies are rare, and at this point findings tentatively support the *apparent* value of imagery rehearsal in skill enhancement among proficient athletes.

We still know little about how imagery works, if it does, or how we might improve imagery's effectiveness for various individuals. Furthermore, the existing research yields inconsistent conclusions. Mahoney advocates an internal perspective, but others (Epstein, 1980; Meyers, Cooke, Cullen, & Liles, 1979) report no difference between internal and external perspectives. Suinn found clarity of image important in some of his work, but Mahoney and Avener (1977) were unable to confirm these results. Meyers and his colleagues and Start and Richardson (1964) observed that controllability of imagery is related to better performance, but Mahoney and Avener failed to find any relationship. Thus the existing literature provides few clear guidelines. Perhaps our existing knowledge of the role of imagery and mental rehearsal in sport is best summarized in Feltz and Landers' (1983) thorough review of the mental practice literature. Feltz and Landers applied meta-analysis to the existing research and concluded by offering the following four theoretical propositions:

1. *"Mental practice effects are primarily associated with cognitive-symbolic rather than motor elements of the task"* (p. 45). Mental rehearsal seems especially useful for tasks involving movement sequences, timing, or cognitive problem solving.

2. *"Mental practice effects are not just limited to early learning—they are found in early and later stages of learning and may be task specific"* (p. 46). Some authors believe that mental rehearsal is most useful in early learning stages when cognitive elements are most prevalent, and others believe that imagery is more effective after the performer has practiced and become familiar with the task. Feltz and Landers found evidence for both views and asserted that mental rehearsal may operate in different ways at different stages of learning.

3. *"It is doubtful that mental practice effects are produced by low-gain innervation of muscles that will be used during actual performance"* (p. 48). Although Suinn and others report that EMG patterns during imagery mirror those during actual performance, implying that such low-gain neuromuscular activity may account for mental rehearsal effects, Feltz and Landers found no direct evidence to support that claim. Instead, they assert that imagery appears to elicit general muscle innervation rather than the specific muscle activity patterns associated with the imagined skill.

4. *"Mental practice functions to assist the performer in psychologically preparing for the skill to be performed"* (p. 50). Feltz and Landers

propose that the general muscle innervation associated with imagery may act to set appropriate tension levels and attentional focus.

## *Summary*

The existing sport psychology literature on cognitive styles and characteristics offers some practical suggestions but few conclusive findings. Cognitive skills and strategies have important implications for sport performance. Some cognitive characteristics do seem to differentiate between better and less skilled performers. However, Allard's research with basketball and volleyball perception and the work on association and dissociation imply that individual differences may be quite specific to particular activities and may not be applicable across varied tasks or situations. Perhaps more than any other sport psychology topic, cognitive skills and strategies demand investigation and pose exciting questions for sport psychologists.

# CHAPTER 5

# Competitiveness and Competitive Anxiety

Individuals' approaches and reactions to competition provide one of the clearest illustrations of personality differences within sport. Specifically, individuals differ in competitiveness, or the desire to enter and do well in competition, and competitive anxiety, or the tendency to become anxious or upset in competitive situations. Some sport participants eagerly look forward to competition and thrive on the challenge, whereas others become tense and tentative when faced with intense competition. Individual differences in competitiveness and competitive anxiety are important in sport because most of our common sport activities involve competition and because competition is the sport form that elicits the most intense psychological reactions.

## The Competition Process

Before proceeding with a discussion of competitiveness and competitive anxiety, we need to define the competition process. Of course, anyone involved in sport knows intuitively what competition is; the Super Bowl is competition; the Boston marathon is competition; the Wimbledon tennis tournament is competition; and a high school volleyball match is competition. On the other hand, not everyone agrees on whether to classify the following events as competition: a beginning runner trying to finish a 10K race in less than 1 hour, a basketball team dividing into two teams for a scrimmage game, or an individual trying to make 8 of 10 putts from a given spot on the living room rug.

To develop a conceptual framework for understanding the role of personality factors in the competition process, we need a definition of competition that will differentiate competitive and noncompetitive activities. The following definition proposed by Martens (1976b) serves that purpose:

> Competition is a process in which the comparison of an individual's performance is made with some standard in the presence of at least one other person

who is aware of the criterion for comparison and can evaluate the comparison process. (p. 14)

All definitions are arbitrary to some extent, and persons could argue for alternative definitions. Martens' definition, however, sets specific criteria that differentiate competitive and noncompetitive activities and encompasses most of the activities that we commonly call competition.

As defined by Martens, competition is a social achievement situation. Achievement situations, according to most psychologists, involve the evaluation of performance in comparison to a standard. Thus competition, which involves the comparison of performance to a standard, is an achievement situation. However, not all achievement situations can be labeled as competition; competition has the added restriction that at least one other person must be involved, making competition a *social* achievement situation.

In a typical competitive contest an opponent serves as both the performance standard and the other person who creates a social situation. However, Martens' definition also includes a high jumper who continues after all others have dropped out as long as spectators or judges are in an evaluative position. Thus a 10K runner who tries to finish under 1 hour would be competing if other runners or friends knew the goal and could evaluate the runner's performance. If no one else knew what the runner was trying to do, however, the runner would not be competing even though many runners and spectators were present. The runner and the golfer who set personal goals are cases of achievement situations if the individuals evaluate performance against personal standards, but they are not in competition unless others are aware of their goals and can evaluate their performances. The term *competi-*

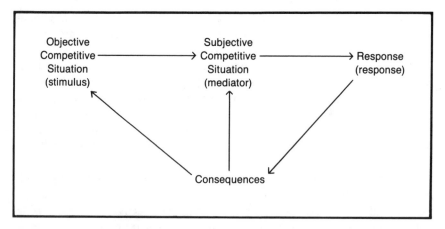

**Figure 5.1** Martens' model of the competitive process. *Note.* From *Sport Competition Anxiety Test* (p. 32) by R. Martens, 1977, Human Kinetics. Copyright 1977 by Rainer Martens. Reprinted by permission.

*tion* is reserved for that subset of achievement situations that involves social evaluation. For the purposes of this text, we can also assume that competition refers to sport and physical activity settings.

Competition, as defined by Martens, is not simply a set of conditions but a *process*. The competition process, depicted in Figure 5.1, includes the following stages:

1. *Objective Competitive Situation.* The objective competitive situation is the set of minimal conditions that must exist to start the competition process. As stated in the definition, the objective competitive situation must include the comparison of performance to a standard and at least one other person who can evaluate the comparison. The objective competitive situation, then, requires a social achievement situation. Once those conditions are met, the competition process can begin.

2. *Subjective Competitive Situation.* The subjective competitive situation involves the individual's perceptions, interpretations, and appraisals of the competitive situation. At this stage personality and individual differences enter the process. One tennis player might look forward to a match with the club champion as a challenge and a chance to gain experience, whereas another player faced with the same objective situation might dread the match. Competitiveness and competitive anxiety are two key personality factors that exert considerable influence on the individual's perception and appraisal of the competition process. That appraisal, or the subjective competitive situation, determines the individual's response to competition.

3. *Response.* The response stage includes physiological responses, such as increased heart rate or sweating, psychological responses, such as feeling anxious or worried, and behavioral responses, most notably performance but also including nonperformance behaviors such as aggression.

4. *Consequences.* The final stage of the competition process is consequences, including the most obvious consequence in competitive sport, winning or losing. Winning and losing are associated with feelings of success and failure, but the relationship is not automatic. A competitor might feel successful after playing well but losing to a highly skilled opponent and might not feel at all successful after winning despite a subpar performance. Feelings of success and failure and other consequences of the competition process do not simply occur in isolation but "feedback" into the process and affect subsequent competitive events. A child who makes an error in a baseball game but who is encouraged and instructed in the correct technique by a coach may improve in baseball skill, thus changing the objective

situation in future games, or the child may develop a positive outlook on the baseball experience, affecting the subjective situation in the future. On the other hand, a youngster whose error is met with criticism may develop a more apprehensive and anxious approach to future situations. Thus the competition process is dynamic; consequences at one point in time may affect skills, conditions, or perceptions for subsequent competitive situations.

Martens' definition of competition as a process contrasts with earlier definitions that typically defined competition as the opposite of cooperation. In competition rewards are distributed unequally—the winner takes all. But in cooperation, all participants share equally in the rewards. Such *reward definitions* guided early psychology research on competition but do little to help us understand sport competition. In sport, competition involves much more than the unequal distribution of rewards. In fact, competition is *not* the opposite of cooperation. Instead, nearly all sport competition also involves cooperation. Cooperation is obvious in team sports when teammates work together on plays and strategies, but less obvious cooperation also occurs between opponents. Both formal and informal cooperation occur as opponents abide by mutual rules, attitudes, and understood conventions. The essence of competition demands that competitors cooperate by challenging each other to achieve optimal performances. Former football player George Sauer, Jr., put it this way:

> Opponents in sport are not enemies. . . . Opponents mutually enrich their challenges by presenting an intelligent unpredictability that is absent in sports without opponents. . . . Opponents reflect ultimately a cooperation in the form of competition. Even the words "compete" and "contest" imply a togetherness rather than separateness. Compete literally means to "seek together," and contest, to "bear witness together!" (Scott, 1971, p. 67)

Just as competition is not simply the opposite of cooperation, competition should be differentiated from rivalry. Competition involves comparing performance to a standard; competition is *goal-directed*, and the goal is superior performance. Rivalry is *person-directed*; the object is to best others, and one's own performance is a secondary concern. Of course, sport competition may well include rivalry, and individual competitors may hold both performance-oriented and person-oriented goals to varying degrees. Nevertheless, competition is, by definition, performance-oriented, and rivalry is not necessarily implied.

## Achievement Motivation in Sport

Using Martens' definition of competition as a goal-directed, social process as a base, we can consider the role of personality characteristics and situational factors as they affect actions and interactions in the competition process. According to Martens (1976a, p. 3), "Competitiveness is defined as a disposition to strive for satisfaction when making comparisons with some standard of excellence in the presence of evaluative others in sport." Thus competitiveness is the tendency to strive for success in sport competition. It is clear that sport participants differ in competitiveness. Some individuals always seem to be at their best in competition, whereas others seem to do everything wrong. One Little Leaguer struts up to bat and dares the pitcher to throw a strike, and a teammate slouches slowly to the plate and prays for a walk.

To date sport psychology has provided little information about how competitiveness develops and how it affects sport participants. However, we do know more about the closely related construct of achievement motivation. Competitiveness is a sport-specific form of achievement motivation, and sport psychologists generally agree that competitiveness develops from achievement motivation. Thus by examining the factors that influence achievement behavior we can begin to understand competitiveness.

Achievement motivation has a rich research tradition that provides insights applicable to sport. Competition is the most common achievement situation in sport, but achievement also occurs in noncompetitive situations when individuals compare their performances to personal standards. For example, a runner might set time goals for training runs, or a tennis player might set the goal of getting in 80% of the first serves. In fact, nearly all sport activities involve some form of achievement behavior. Thus individual differences in achievement behavior and achievement motivation are worthy of attention in their own right and also as a basis for understanding competitiveness.

## Atkinson's Theory of Achievement Motivation

Many explanations for individual differences in achievement behavior exist. Some emphasize the personality characteristic of achievement motivation, whereas others focus on perceptions and interpretations. Despite the diversity of current work on achievement motivation, nearly all approaches are based to some extent on the classic work of Atkinson. Atkinson (1964, 1974) advanced the most widely known and most researched theory of achievement motivation. Atkinson's theory is an interaction model that specifies the role of personality and situational factors as determinants of achievement behavior in precise, formal terms. Because Atkinson's theory is the starting point for most current achievement work, and because the formal theory involves complex but precisely specified relationships, we will now consider Atkinson's theory in detail.

**Personality Factors.** Murray (1938) first discussed achievement motivation as a personality factor and defined the need to achieve as the desire

To accomplish something difficult. To master, manipulate or organize physical objects, human beings, or ideas. To do this as rapidly and as independently as possible. To overcome obstacles and attain a high standard. To excel one's self. To rival and surpass others. To increase self-regard by the successful exercise of talent. (p. 164)

Murray also developed the *Thematic Apperception Test* (TAT) to measure individuals' need to achieve. As discussed in chapter 3, the TAT is probably the most common measure of achievement motivation and is a projective test. We will consider the TAT and other achievement motivation measures later in this chapter after we have discussed Atkinson's theory.

Atkinson extended Murray's work to delineate achievement motivation more clearly as a personality construct. According to Atkinson, achievement motivation actually combines *two* personality constructs: *the motive to approach success ($M_s$)* and *the motive to avoid failure ($M_{af}$)*. The motive to approach success is the capacity to experience pride or satisfaction in accomplishment, and the motive to avoid failure is the capacity to experience shame or humiliation as a consequence of failure. Everyone has both characteristics. We all like to be successful, and we all feel good when we accomplish something. On the other hand, we all feel badly when we make mistakes, perform poorly, or are unsuccessful in our achievement efforts.

Even though we all enjoy and seek success and try to avoid failure, we do not all have the two motives to the same degree. The key personality factor in Atkinson's theory is the difference between the two motives ($M_s - M_{af}$). When discussing individual differences in achievement motivation, we commonly refer to persons as "high" or "low" achievers. Individuals who have a high $M_s$ and low $M_{af}$ are the high achievers; success is very important to them, but they do not worry much about failure. Thus high $M_s$, low $M_{af}$ persons seek out challenging achievement situations and strive hard for success without worrying about possible failures. On the other hand, individuals who have a low $M_s$ and high $M_{af}$ worry about failure a great deal. Even though success would be nice, low achievers prefer to avoid the possibility of failure and the anxiety associated with achievement situations. Individuals who have equal levels of $M_s$ and $M_{af}$, regardless of whether both are high or both are low, fall in between high and low achievers. When neither motive dominates, predictions according to Atkinson's theory are not very clear.

**Situational Factors.** Atkinson's theory does not make predictions solely on the basis of the motives but incorporates *both* personality and situational factors. The main situational factor in Atkinson's theory is task difficulty, or, specifically, the individual's *probability of success ($P_s$)*. $P_s$ ranges from 0 (no chance at all) to 1.00 (certain success). For example, if you are an average tennis player, your $P_s$ in a match with the club champion might be 1 in 10 or .10; your $P_s$ in a match with a beginner might be 9 in 10 or .90; and in a match with someone of equal ability your $P_s$ would be .50.

A second situational factor built into Atkinson's theory is the *incentive value of success* ($I_s$). Like $P_s$, $I_s$ is a characteristic of the task. In fact, as depicted in Figure 5.2, $I_s$ relates directly to $P_s$ as $I_s = 1 - P_s$. This relationship suggests that the lower the chances of success, the greater the incentive value of success. For example, if I were an average tennis player, I would have a very slim chance of winning a game against a top player such as Martina Navratilova (for the sake of the example we will assume I have a $P_s$ of .10). Although I have little chance of success, if I could win a game I would be elated; the incentive value would be high ($I_s = .90$). At the other extreme, I could challenge my 7-year-old niece, who has never held a tennis racquet, to a game. My chance of success would be high ($P_s = .90$) but the incentive value low ($I_s = .10$), and I would not be very inspired by the prospects of success.

When we consider the overall situational component in Atkinson's theory, we consider the product of $P_s$ and $I_s$ ($P_s \times I_s$). With Atkinson's definition of $I_s$ as $1 - P_s$, that product always has its highest value when $P_s = .50$. Readers who are mathematically inclined can work out various products; you will find that when $P_s = .50$, $P_s \times I_s$ (.50 $\times$ .50) $= .25$, and no other products will be that high. The product progressively decreases as you move toward either extreme ($P_s = 0$ or $P_s = 1.00$). For example, at $P_s = .70$ the product decreases as $P_s \times I_s$ (.70 $\times$ .30) $= .21$. The product, $P_s \times I_s$, is the key situational determinant of achievement behavior in Atkinson's theory; the higher the product, the stronger the tendency to engage in achievement behavior. As noted, the

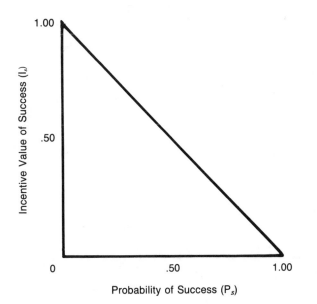

**Figure 5.2** Incentive value of success ($I_s$) as a function of probability of success ($P_s$) as proposed by Atkinson (1964).

product is greatest for everyone at $P_s = .50$. However, not everyone engages in achievement behavior to the same degree. To explain these differences we must also consider the personality factor.

**Achievement Behavioral Tendencies.**  According to Atkinson, the behavioral tendency, or specifically the *tendency to approach success ($T_s$)*, is a product of the individual's motive to approach success ($M_s$) as well as the situational factors. Formally,

$$T_s = M_s \times P_s \times I_s$$

As shown in Figure 5.3, $T_s$ is greatest at $P_s = .50$ and decreases as the chances of success ($P_s$) move away from .50 and closer to either extreme. Although that same curvilinear relationship holds for everyone, the individual's motive ($M_s$) determines the height of the curve, which is the level of achievement behavior. Individuals differ in $M_s$, and thus an individual with a high $M_s$ always

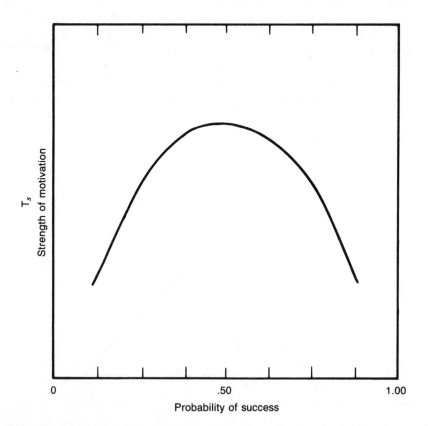

**Figure 5.3**  Behavioral tendency to approach success ($T_s$) as a function of probability of success ($P_s$) as proposed by Atkinson (1964).

has a greater $T_s$ than an individual with a low $M_s$. Table 5.1 illustrates the behavioral tendencies for a high $M_s$ individual ($M_s = 8$) and a low $M_s$ individual ($M_s = 2$). Notice that the high achiever has the greater tendency to approach success for each situation and that the difference between the two individuals is greatest at the challenging ($P_s = .50$) situation.

**Table 5.1** Behavioral tendency to approach success ($T_s$) for a high achiever ($M_s = 8$) and a low achiever ($M_s = 2$) for three different probability of success situations ($P_s = .10, .50, .90$).

| $P_s$ | High $M_s$ (8) $M_s \times P_s \times I_s = T_s$ | Low $M_s$ (2) $M_s \times P_s \times I_s = T_s$ |
|---|---|---|
| .10 | $8 \times .10 \times .90 = .72$ | $2 \times .10 \times .90 = .18$ |
| .50 | $8 \times .50 \times .50 = 2.00$ | $2 \times .50 \times .50 = .50$ |
| .90 | $8 \times .90 \times .10 = .72$ | $2 \times .90 \times .90 = .18$ |

Perhaps you are wondering what happened to $M_{af}$. If we considered only the $T_s$, we would assume that even though individuals differ in the strength of the $T_s$, everyone has at least some $T_s$, and the tendency is greatest in the most challenging situations ($P_s = .50$). When we consider the $M_{af}$ and the associated *tendency to avoid failure ($T_{af}$)*, we find that some individuals are *not* likely to approach achievement situations but in fact have a strong tendency to avoid such challenges.

The $T_{af}$ is determined in much the same way as the $T_s$: as the product of an individual motive or personality factor ($M_{af}$) and situational factors ($P_f \times I_f$). The *probability of failure ($P_f$)*, like $P_s$, is a task characteristic. In fact, $P_f = 1 - P_s$. If you have a .90 chance of success, you have a .10 chance of failure. The *incentive value of failure ($I_f$)* is a negative incentive; essentially, $I_f$ represents how badly you will feel if you fail. The easier the task, the worse you will feel if you fail, and the greater (more negative) the $I_f$. Thus $I_f = 1 - P_f$, with a negative value. As with $P_s \times I_s$, the highest product and most negative value of $P_f \times I_f$ is reached when $P_f = .50$. The behavioral tendency to avoid failure ($T_{af}$) is defined as

$$T_{af} = M_{af} \times P_f \times I_f$$

As with $T_s$, $T_{af}$ varies among individuals, but the greatest negative value is reached when $P_f = .50$. Thus both $T_s$ and $T_{af}$ have their greatest values at $P_s = .50$. Situations in which we are matched with an opponent of equal ability, or in which our chances of success are very uncertain, bring out the strongest achievement behaviors. High achievers especially like challenging situations, and low achievers especially want to avoid those challenges.

Because each individual has conflicting motives and achievement tendencies, an overall achievement tendency must be calculated. According to Atkinson, the overall behavioral tendency, or *resultant achievement oriented tendency ($T_a$)*, is

$$T_a = T_s - T_{af}$$

Considering the component personality and situational factors, the formula can be written as

$$T_a = (M_s \times P_s \times I_s) - (M_{af} \times P_f \times I_f)$$

Because $P_s$, $I_s$, $P_f$, and $I_f$ are all characteristics of the task that can be defined as a function of $P_s$, we can substitute terms and reduce the previous formula to separate the personality and situational factors as

$$T_a = (M_s - M_{af}) \times (P_s \times [1 - P_s])$$

The product, $P_s \times (1 - P_s)$, the situational factor, always has its greatest value at $P_s = .50$, the situation that elicits the strongest behavioral tendencies. Whether the behavioral tendency is positive (to approach) or negative (to avoid) depends on the personality factor ($M_s - M_{af}$). If $M_s$ is greater than $M_{af}$, then the resultant tendency will always be positive and the individual will approach the achievement situation. Conversely, if $M_{af}$ is greater than $M_s$, the resultant tendency will be negative and that individual will always tend to avoid the achievement situation. In either case, the greater the difference between the two motives, the stronger the approach or avoidance tendency.

Thus the high achiever always has a tendency to approach achievement situations, and the low achiever has a tendency to avoid those situations. Furthermore, the difference between the high and low achiever is greatest in the most challenging and uncertain situations ($P_s = .50$) because those situations bring out the strongest behavioral tendencies. (Mathematically inclined readers can work out these relationships for themselves.)

## Achievement Behaviors

The clear and precise formulas in Atkinson's theory, which we have just discussed at length, predict three general categories of achievement behavior: choice, intensity, and persistence. *Choice* refers to the individual's decision to approach or avoid the achievement situation. According to Atkinson, the resultant achievement tendency determines choice. When the resultant achievement tendency ($T_a$) is positive ($T_s$ is greater than $T_{af}$), the individual tends to approach the situation; when $T_a$ is negative ($T_s$ is less than $T_{af}$), the individual tends to avoid the situation. Thus high achievers, who have a greater $M_s$ than $M_{af}$, have a positive $T_a$ and approach achievement situations, whereas low achievers tend to avoid those situations.

In Atkinson's theory, a high achiever always tends to approach competition and other achievement situations and is especially attracted to the most challenging situations, which occur when $P_s = .50$. These situations include competition with opponents of equal ability or personal goals that are challenging but attainable. Low achievers have a tendency to avoid all achievement situations but are especially averse to challenging situations in which $P_s = .50$.

You may note that we sometimes see individuals who seem to be low achievers in competition and other achievement situations. Often those individuals are anxious and hesitate to exert intensive effort. Atkinson acknowledges that low achievers may enter achievement situations because of extrinsic pressures. He suggests that within achievement settings, low achievers still try to avoid the most intense situations ($P_s = .50$). Instead, if they must do something, low achievers choose tasks and situations with more extreme chances of success or failure (e.g., $P_s = .90$ or $P_s = .10$). For example, a 10-year-old girl might be pressured into joining a community tennis program by parents, siblings, friends, or a coach who sees undeveloped talent. If she is a low achiever with a high $M_{af}$, she will become anxious in competition and try to avoid intense matches. Instead, she might choose to play against less skilled players so that she would be assured of success. Or she might play against more highly skilled players so that no one would expect her to win and failure would not seem too bad. Another girl in the same program who was a high achiever and wanted to be successful at tennis would seek out challenging matches with opponents of similar ability.

This forced choice situation in which high achievers prefer challenging ($P_s = .50$) situations and low achievers tend to choose extreme situations ($P_s = .10$ or $.90$) is probably the most widely known of Atkinson's behavioral predictions. Remember, however, that this scenario reflects a *forced* choice situation. Given a *free* choice, high achievers are attracted to achievement situations, whereas low achievers prefer to avoid all challenges. High achievers would rather play the club champion ($P_s = .10$) than no one at all, and low achievers would prefer to avoid all competitive and challenging situations.

To summarize Atkinson's predictions for choice behavior, in free choice situations high achievers choose to enter achievement situations, and low achievers choose to avoid them. In forced choice situations in which the individual must choose something, high achievers are most attracted to the most uncertain, challenging situations ($P_s = .50$), and low achievers find situations that present the most extreme probability of success ($P_s = .10$ or $.90$) the least aversive.

For intensity or effort within achievement situations, the resultant achievement tendency ($T_a$) again determines behavior. The higher the resultant tendency ($T_s - T_{af}$), the greater the intensity and effort, and, consequently, the better the performance. The tendency to avoid failure ($T_{af}$) is a negative or inhibiting tendency that inhibits intense effort and impairs performance. The greater the $T_{af}$, the more anxious the individual becomes. High achievers, then, tend to exert intense effort in achievement situations, whereas low achievers are inhibited. The difference between high and low achievers is most pronounced in the most challenging situations ($P_s = .50$) in which high achievers have the strongest tendency to exert intense effort and low achievers are most anxious and inhibited.

Behavioral predictions for persistence at achievement tasks can be quite complex. In the simplest terms, high achievers tend to persist as long as they have a chance of success. High achievers especially persist in attempts at an easy task (e.g., $P_s = .70$) that they have failed because failure brings their probability of success closer to .50 and makes the task more challenging. Low achievers do not persist if they can avoid achievement tasks, and they especially do not like to keep trying when the task is more challenging ($P_s = .50$).

## Research on Achievement Motivation

Atkinson's theory has inspired considerable research, including some work with sport and motor tasks, much of which supports his predictions. Before reviewing that research, however, we should consider how investigators assess achievement motivation.

**Achievement Motivation Measures.** In discussing personality measures in chapter 3, we noted that objective inventories are the most widely used personality measures. Achievement motivation measures are an exception. The most common achievement motivation measure, the *Thematic Apperception Test* (TAT), is a projective measure. The TAT was developed by Murray (1938) to measure 28 needs, including the need to achieve. It requires the individual to view a sequence of pictures and answer a series of open-ended questions about each picture (e.g., What is happening?). The TAT is scored by looking for achievement "themes" in the person's responses. Like most projective measures, the TAT is time-consuming to administer and to score. Additionally, extensive training is necessary to score the TAT consistently. Because the TAT is difficult to use, especially with large groups, some self-report measures of achievement motivation have been developed, with the Mehrabian scales (Mehrabian, 1968) the most widely known.

Readers who wish to know how they would score on an achievement motivation measure but do not have time to look up one of the published scales may use the following Gill test of achievement motivation:

You are taking a true-false test. This exam has a correction factor. Your score will be the number of correct answers *minus* the number of incorrect answers.

You have done all the questions to which you knew the answer or could make an intelligent guess. You have 10 questions left. If you do all 10 and get them correct, you will have 10 more points. If you do them and get them all wrong, you will lose 10 points from the score you already have. If you get 5 right and 5 wrong, you will neither gain nor lose points and will end up with the same score that you already have for the other questions. Would you answer those last 10 questions or not?

Scoring the Gill test is simple. If you would choose to complete the last 10 questions, you are a high achiever; if you would not attempt them, you are a low achiever. (If you did not come out as you would expect, remember that the Gill test does not have established reliability or validity and misclassification is possible.

The basic premise of the Gill test, like most self-report achievement motivation measures, is that high achievers like challenging, risky situations and low achievers try to avoid those situations. High achievers want to take a chance for success (gaining 10 points), and, because they have a low motive to avoid failure, they do not worry about the possibility of losing 10 points. On the other hand, low achievers do not want to take the chance that they might lose 10 points, and hence they give up the chance of success in order to avoid the possibility of failure. In a similar vein, typical items on the Mehrabian scales ask the respondent to choose between a risky, challenging option and a safer alternative. The more the respondent selects the riskier choices, the higher the achievement motivation score.

Achievement motivation measures are often used along with trait anxiety measures such as the *Taylor Manifest Anxiety Scale* (Taylor, 1953) or the *Test Anxiety Questionnaire* (Mandler & Sarason, 1952). In such cases, the TAT or other achievement scale is considered a measure of the motive to approach success, and the anxiety scale a measure of the motive to avoid failure. Individuals who score high on the achievement measure and low on the anxiety scale are classified as high achievers; those who score low on the achievement measure and high on the anxiety scale are considered low achievers. For research purposes, those who have similar scores on both are not included in subsequent analyses. Whether the various achievement measures are measures of the motive to approach success or the resultant tendency to act is debatable, and some authors have criticized the classification of high and low achievers. Nevertheless, such procedures are standard in achievement motivation research.

**Research with Sport and Motor Tasks.**   Probably the most researched aspect of Atkinson's theory is risk-taking or forced choice behavior. Considerable research indicates that high achievers do indeed prefer risky situations of intermediate difficulty ($P_s = .50$), whereas low achievers are more likely to select very easy or very difficult tasks. Roberts (1974) examined achievement motivation and risk taking with a motor task and found that individuals classified as high achievers preferred tasks of moderate difficulty ($P_s = .50$), whereas the low achievers preferred more difficult tasks with a low probability of success.

Similarly, Ostrow (1976) reported that high achievers set more realistic goals for handball matches than did low achievers.

The relationship between achievement motivation and performance on sport and motor tasks has received less attention, and the findings are not clear. Ryan and Lakie (1965) had high and low achievers perform a ring peg task in competitive and noncompetitive situations. As Atkinson's theory predicts, high achievers showed more improvement over their noncompetitive scores and outperformed the low achievers in the competitive situation. Low achievers performed slightly better than high achievers in noncompetition. Apparently, the avoidance tendency and anxiety associated with the competitive situation interfered with low achievers' performance. Although Ryan and Lakie's findings supported the Atkinson theory, others have reported little or no difference between high and low achievers (Healey & Landers, 1973; Ostrow, 1976; Roberts, 1972). Thus the relationship between achievement motivation and sport performance has not been established and needs more research attention.

**Multidimensional Achievement Motives.**   Several researchers who are working with personality constructs assert that the achievement motives proposed by Atkinson are too global, and they propose a multidimensional achievement motive. Under this approach, an individual may be highly motivated to achieve success on certain achievement tasks, such as academic work, but may not be at all motivated in the area of competitive achievement. Spence and Helmreich addressed the issue of differing achievement motives by developing a multidimensional measure, the *Work and Family Orientation Questionnaire* (WOFO; Helmreich & Spence, 1978; Spence & Helmreich, 1978). The final version of the WOFO includes four factors: *mastery*, the preference for difficult, challenging tasks; *work*, positive attitudes toward work; *competitiveness*, the desire to win in interpersonal situations; and *personal unconcern*, the lack of concern with the negative reactions of others.

Initial work suggests that the WOFO may help probe individual differences in achievement behavior. The competitiveness scale could be especially useful in sport psychology. Initial findings indicate that male and female athletes score higher on competitiveness than their nonathletic peers. Surprisingly, Spence and Helmreich reported that high-achieving male and female scientists scored higher than college students on the mastery, work, and personal unconcern scales but *lower* on competitiveness. This may imply that competitiveness detracts from actual achievement, at least in the area of academics. However, as measured by the WOFO, competitiveness is limited to rivalry and does not include the various types of competition we find in sport. Furthermore, the scale is not specific to sport. Additional work with the WOFO and the development of more sport-specific achievement and competitiveness scales may help us to understand the role of competitiveness in sport achievement behavior.

# Sport-Specific Achievement Motivation: Competitiveness

The work of Spence and Helmreich and others who approach achievement motivation as a multidimensional construct suggests that a specific measure of achievement motivation for sport competition could be useful. Martens (1976a) specifically advocates the development of a sport-specific construct and measure of competitiveness to further our understanding of competitive behavior. Certainly many individuals who are highly motivated to achieve success in sport do not seem equally motivated to achieve success in academics or work situations. Similarly, individuals who seem to have a high motive to avoid failure and who become tense and anxious when faced with sport competition may be much more calm and confident when taking an academic test.

To illustrate, how would you rate yourself on the motive to approach success and the motive to avoid failure in competitive sports and academics? First, do you consider yourself higher or lower than the average student on the motive to approach success in sport? To address this issue, ask yourself the following questions: Is success in sport very important to you? Do you seek challenges? Does intense competition bring out your best performance? Next, do you consider yourself high or low on the motive to avoid failure in sport competition? For example, do you become tense and anxious in close competition? Do you worry about how you will perform? Do you make more errors in highly competitive contests?

After you have rated your $M_s$ and $M_{af}$ for sport competition, do the same for academic achievement. Are you higher or lower than the average student on your motive to approach success in academics? For example, is success in school very important to you? Do academic challenges bring out your best? Finally, do you consider yourself high or low in the motive to avoid failure in academics? Do you choke before important tests or presentations? Do you worry about poor grades? Keeping in mind the Atkinson model, classify yourself as a high achiever in sport competition if your $M_s$ is high and your $M_{af}$ is low; classify yourself as a low achiever if your $M_s$ is low and your $M_{af}$ is high. If both are high or both are low, consider yourself an average achiever. Now, make the same classification for academic achievement. Do you end up with the same high, low, or average classification for both sport and academics?

Usually about half of the students in a typical class find themselves in different classifications for sport and academic achievement. Even if you classify yourself the same for both, you may find that your motives and reactions are more intense or are in some way different from one setting to the other. If we extend the illustration further, perhaps to social achievement or artistic achievement, you might find even greater diversity in your motives.

If individuals are not equally motivated across all achievement settings and tasks, as the illustration and work of Spence and Helmreich suggest, then global achievement motives and measures may not apply equally to all situations. Certainly the Atkinson model and typical measures were not developed for sport, and their value in explaining competitive behavior may be quite limited.

In light of the limitations of general achievement motivation theories and measures, Martens (1976a) advocates the development of sport-specific constructs and measures of achievement motivation, namely, competitiveness and competitive trait anxiety. As defined earlier in this chapter, *competitiveness* is the motive to approach success in sport competition. Similarly, *competitive trait anxiety* is the counterpart of the motive to avoid failure in sport competition. Sport-specific research on competitive anxiety has advanced much further than the work on competitiveness. As we will discuss later in this chapter, Martens and his colleagues have developed a sport-specific measure of competitive trait anxiety and demonstrated the reliability and validity of that measure for predicting anxiety in sport competition.

Although competitiveness is an equally compelling sport personality characteristic, we do not yet have an established, reliable, and valid measure of competitiveness. To remedy that shortcoming, we are developing a sport-specific competitiveness measure here at the University of Iowa (Gill, in press; Gill, Deeter, & Gruber, 1985). We administered the *Competitiveness Inventory* consisting of several sport achievement and competitiveness items to a large sample of college students. Analyses revealed that the inventory contained three factors or subscales. The first and most comprehensive factor, represented by items such as "I look forward to competing" and "I want to be the best every time I compete," reflects *competitiveness* as discussed in this chapter—the tendency to seek and strive for success in sport competition. The other two factors on the inventory reflected a *win* orientation (e.g., "I hate to lose," "I have the most fun when I win") and a *personal goal* orientation (e.g., "I am most competitive when I try to achieve personal goals," "Reaching personal performance goals is very important to me").

Our initial analyses indicate that the three subscales are internally consistent and reliable. More importantly, the competitiveness scale has some validity for predicting competitive behavior; the competitiveness scale differentiated students who enrolled in competitive activity classes from those who enrolled in noncompetitive classes, even when the more general WOFO achievement scores did not differentiate between those students. We are continuing to test the *Competitiveness Inventory* to determine whether the inventory is a reliable and valid predictor of competitive behavior. Our initial findings are promising, but the work is just beginning. As more sport psychologists investigate and measure competitiveness as a sport-specific personality characteristic, we will learn more about individual differences in specific competitive behaviors. At this time, sport psychology research on competitiveness and specific competitive behaviors is noticeably lacking. The most notable work on competitiveness focuses on the development of competitiveness in the individual and its relationship to achievement motivation.

## The Development of Competitiveness

Tara Scanlan (1978) has discussed in detail the development of competitiveness in relation to achievement motivation, and we will consider the main points of that discussion here. Scanlan's discussion is based on two major works and their relationship to sport competition: White's (1959) competence theory and Veroff's (1969) model of the development of achievement motivation. As seen by White, the competence or effectance motive is the basic motive to be competent and effective. We are born with competence motivation. Even infants strive to explore, try tasks, cause outcomes, and otherwise accomplish something. A young child might display competence simply by striking a piano key to cause sound or by pushing a ball to make it roll. Competence motivation develops into achievement motivation when the child begins to set goals and direct effort to reach those goals. A performance goal or standard might be to build a four-block tower or to roll a ball to a parent. As soon as the child is mature enough to set a goal and maintain efforts to reach that goal, achievement motivation may begin to develop.

Veroff (1969) presents one of the most explicit theories of the development of achievement motivation. According to Veroff, an individual develops achievement motivation through three stages: autonomous competence, social comparison, and integrated achievement motivation. The first stage, *autonomous competence*, involves internal standards. A child might decide to set up a row of blocks and try to knock them over with a ball. The child sets the goal, attempts to reach it, and decides if the performance was successful. The child's own autonomous evaluation of achievement is critical at this stage; other people have little to do with setting the goals or evaluating success/failure, and competition is not part of this autonomous stage. This stage could be likened to establishing a personal sense of competence.

A child who has some success in the autonomous stage may advance into the *social comparison* stage. Obviously, social comparison involves social standards of achievement, or competition. Social standards become important when the child begins interacting extensively with peers, usually during the early school years. The individual who succeeds in at least some social comparisons may advance to the final stage of *integrated achievement motivation*. The most advanced, integrated stage involves both autonomous competence and social comparison. An individual at this stage uses either autonomous, internal standards or social standards, depending on which are appropriate for the situation. A golfer, for example, might set personal goals and work toward those goals in practice rounds and informal play, but the same golfer will attend to competitive standards in a match play round.

Not everyone progresses through the three stages of achievement motivation. In fact, some individuals never master the autonomous stage. Those persons are likely to be low achievers who do not attempt any achievement tasks, either competitive or noncompetitive. Individuals who successfully master the autonomous stage but are unsuccessful in social comparison are unlikely to be very competitive. Those individuals might work very hard and be high achievers when personal goals are involved, but they probably would avoid competition. Persons who are successful at social comparison and advance to the integrated stage will be comfortable in competitive situations, but they might also work hard toward personal, noncompetitive goals.

According to Veroff, a person must use social comparison for *informative* purposes to evaluate skills and abilities in order to advance into the integrated stage of achievement motivation. A person who uses social comparison for what Veroff terms *normative* purposes focuses on winning and uses competition as an ego boost. That person cannot be satisfied with autonomous achievement and will not advance to the integrated stage. Such persons often seem to be supercompetitors who will turn any situation into competition. Returning to our earlier discussion of competition and rivalry, the individual at the integrated stage who uses competition to test skills and abilities would be performance- or goal-oriented, whereas the supercompetitive person who must always be the winner would be rivalry-oriented.

## Cultural Differences in Competitiveness

Why do some children develop into avid competitors whereas others dread competitive events? Most experts agree that childhood experiences are the key; achievement motivation and, more specifically, competitiveness, develop when children have the opportunity and encouragement to enter competition and have some success in competitive achievement situations. Unfortunately, the precise situational factors and interactions that encourage the development of achievement motivation are elusive.

Several studies have identified cultural differences in competitive behavior, implying that the social environment plays a role in channeling achievement and competitive behaviors. After observing children in different cultures playing a variety of competitive games, Nelson and Kagan (1972) reported that American children were much more competitive than Mexican children. Similarly, urban children in several countries were found to be more competitive than rural children. According to Nelson and Kagan (1972), American children were "not only irrationally competitive, they were almost sadistically rivalrous" (p. 91). Highly competitive American and urban children gave up the chance to get rewards for themselves in order to keep another child from getting similar rewards. Nelson and Kagan further proposed that cultural differences are related to child-rearing patterns. Specifically, American mothers tend to reward their children contingent upon achievements, whereas Mexican mothers praise and encourage their children noncontingently, regardless of success or accomplishments.

Orlick, a sport psychologist who is quite outspoken about the detrimental effects of intense competition, examined cultural differences in competitive behavior among Canadian children. An advocate of cooperative games or the *new games* approach, Orlick (1978; McNally & Orlick, 1975) introduced a cooperative broomball game to urban children in southern Canada and to Inuit children in the Northwest territories. The cooperative game used no goalies and specified that goals counted for the other team and that scorers changed teams after a goal. Other rules also downplayed the competitive emphasis on winning. Orlick reported that the northern Canadian children were much more positive toward the cooperative game than were children from southern Canada. In addition, girls reacted more positively to the cooperative games than boys reacted. Boys in southern Canada reacted least positively and often tried to circumvent the cooperative rules and somehow turn the game into a competition. Orlick also compared younger and older children within southern Canada and observed that younger children were more positive toward the cooperative game.

Duda (1983) recently examined the achievement and athletic orientations of Anglo and Navajo girls and boys in the southwestern United States. She reported cultural and gender differences similar to those observed by Orlick. Male Anglo children were the most win/loss-oriented and valued athletic ability the most. Duda also investigated both school achievement and sport achievement and noted that gender differences in orientation were greater for sport than for school achievement.

Overall, these observed differences in competitiveness across and within cultures suggest that competitiveness develops through childhood and that social factors and interactions play a major role in determining whether and to what degree competitiveness develops. However, the findings are only suggestive; considerable research is needed to specify the social factors and interactions that enhance or inhibit competitiveness.

We have just spent considerable time discussing achievement motivation and competitiveness in sport. Specifically, we focused on Atkinson's theory with its complex, mathematical formulas and the implications of achievement motivation research for competitiveness. That work is the cornerstone of much current research, including the cognitive approaches, which we will discuss in chapter 10, and the work on gender roles and achievement, which we will consider in chapter 6. Atkinson's precisely defined, mathematical relationships and predictions are very researchable and have been tested, extended, and modified by many researchers. The work on the personality characteristics of achievement motivation and competitiveness helps us to understand achievement behavior in sport. However, sport psychology could advance even further by considering specific sport achievement behaviors. Certainly competitiveness and competitive behavior demand investigation, but we might also consider noncompetitive achievement orientations and behaviors that might be more relevant to exercise rehabilitation or health-oriented fitness programs.

# Competitive Anxiety

As stated earlier in this chapter, achievement motivation is actually composed of two motives: the motive to approach success and the motive to avoid failure. Competitiveness may be defined as the motive to approach success in sport competition. Similarly, *competitive anxiety* is the sport-specific counterpart of the motive to avoid failure, or the tendency to become anxious and worried about failure in sport competition. Individual differences in competitive anxiety are obvious; some individuals, including some highly skilled athletes, become physically ill worrying about an upcoming contest, whereas others remain calm and controlled. Such individual differences have implications for sport participants, whether or not we consider anxiety within the context of achievement motivation. For example, the director of a cardiac rehabilitation program might take special precautions with a highly competitive anxious participant even if the program does not emphasize competition in order to ensure appropriate levels of exertion and goal setting.

Individual differences in competitive anxiety and the ability to control that anxiety are major concerns for participants in competitive programs. Indeed, many sport psychologists doing applied work with athletes focus on anxiety management techniques and spend considerable time helping participants learn to control anxiety levels. Because of such concerns, sport psychology research on the personality construct of competitive anxiety and the implications of individual differences in competitive anxiety for sport performance and behaviors is quite extensive. Much of that research stems from Martens' (1977) theory of competitive anxiety and his development and use of the *Sport Competition Anxiety Test* (SCAT).

## Theoretical Basis of Competitive Anxiety

Competitive anxiety has been recognized as a key sport psychology issue for some time. Sport competition creates some anxiety in nearly all participants, and for some individuals the anxiety is so intense that successful performance and enjoyment of the activity are impossible. Most athletes must deal with intense anxiety at some time, and most coaches must deal with competitors experiencing varying states of anxiety from near normal and under control to utter panic. Martens developed his approach to the pervasive phenomenon of competitive anxiety by building upon the existing knowledge of anxiety and the following four major principles:

1. *Interaction approach.* Competitive anxiety is a topic that illustrates the value of an interaction approach as discussed in chapter 3. We can see individual differences in competitive anxiety; some individuals work themselves into a frenzy at the hint of competition, whereas

others remain relatively calm and under control in close contests. Although individual differences exist, situational factors also play a major role in competitive anxiety. Close, important games create more anxiety than less important contests. Even the calmest athlete can become quite anxious under some conditions; a family problem, a critical exam, or the presence of professional scouts might elicit intense anxiety in a normally calm athlete. Thus to understand competitive anxiety we must consider the interaction of personality, or individual differences in the tendency to become anxious, along with varied situational factors in competitive sports.

2. *State-trait anxiety distinction.* Spielberger (1966) advanced the interaction approach to anxiety by distinguishing the relatively stable personality characteristic of trait anxiety from the immediate, changeable feelings associated with state anxiety. *Trait anxiety* is the tendency or predisposition to become anxious in stressful situations, whereas *state anxiety* is the actual feeling or state of apprehension and tension at any given moment. Persons with high trait anxiety tend to have high state anxiety in stressful situations, but situational factors also affect state anxiety levels.

3. *General versus specific anxiety.* Although highly trait anxious persons tend to become anxious in stressful situations, they do not necessarily become equally anxious in all types of situations. Some individuals become anxious in social situations, whereas others tend to be anxious in competition. Because of this, previous anxiety research demonstrated that a more limited or situation-specific measure of trait anxiety predicts state anxiety more accurately than more general trait anxiety measures. Mandler and Sarason (1952) reported such a relationship for test anxiety. Following that line of thought, Martens asserted that a measure of trait anxiety specific to sport competition would be superior to general trait anxiety measures at predicting state anxiety in sport competition. Specifically, Martens proposed the personality construct of *competitive trait anxiety*, which he defined as "a tendency to perceive competitive situations as threatening and to respond to these situations with feelings of apprehension or tension" (Martens, 1977, p. 23).

4. *Competition process.* The final step in Martens' theoretical framework is to consider competitive anxiety within the context of the competition process described at the beginning of this chapter. From an interactionist perspective, we must consider the relevant personality factor, competitive trait anxiety, and the situational factors in the competitive situation that interact to affect behavior and specifically the behavioral response of state anxiety.

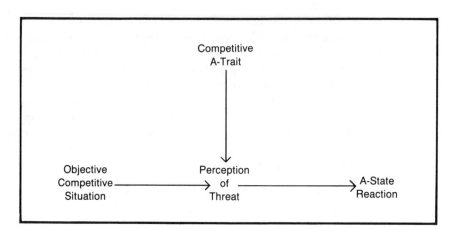

**Figure 5.4** The relationship of competitive anxiety to the competition process. *Note.* From *Sport Competition Anxiety Test* (p. 33) by R. Martens, 1977, Champaign, IL: Human Kinetics. Copyright 1977 by Rainer Martens. Reprinted by permission.

As depicted in Figure 5.4, the objective competitive situation defines the situational factors that affect competitive anxiety. The primary situational source of anxiety in competition is the threat of evaluation. We want to be successful and we worry about performing poorly. Of course, everyone does not worry to the same extent. At this point, competitive trait anxiety affects our perceptions of threat and subsequent anxiety through the subjective competitive situation. The resulting behavioral response is our level of state anxiety.

## Development of the SCAT

To investigate competitive anxiety within the theoretical framework described by Martens, a measure of competitive trait anxiety was needed. Martens thus devoted considerable time and effort to the development of the *Sport Competition Anxiety Test* (SCAT), a self-report measure of competitive trait anxiety. To determine your level of competitive trait anxiety, turn to Appendix A and complete the SCAT. You can then follow the scoring instructions and compare your score to the norms. If you score high (e.g., at the 75th percentile or above), you probably tend to be quite nervous and tense in close competition (just as I do). On the other hand, if you have a relatively low score, you probably control anxiety quite well and seldom choke in competition.

The items on the SCAT are simple and straightforward. You might think that Martens could have developed the scale in an afternoon. Perhaps he could have, but he didn't. The items are simple and straightforward because considerable psychometric testing indicated that those items best identify high and low anxious competitors. The development of the SCAT took approximately five years and, as Martens describes it, "involved testing over 4,000 people and approximately 3,000 man-hours of work" (Martens, 1976a, p. 12). I can personally confirm at least 2,000 man-hours, or, more correctly, woman-hours, of that work. Martens (1977) has discussed the development of the SCAT scale and the data on its reliability and validity elsewhere. In general, the SCAT meets and usually exceeds all generally accepted psychometric standards for psychological tests. The SCAT is reliable, and considerable laboratory and field research demonstrates that the SCAT predicts state anxiety in competition.

The predictive validity of the SCAT is well illustrated in a field study conducted with high school girls' basketball teams. The SCAT was administered to all players on nine teams at a practice session, along with a self-report measure of state anxiety. Later, players completed a precompetition state anxiety measure immediately before a game. (In a few cases the start of the game was delayed while players completed the scale on the court.) Because competitive trait anxiety is the tendency to become anxious about competition, the SCAT should predict state anxiety levels at precompetition. Indeed, the high correlation between the SCAT and precompetition state anxiety ($r = .64$) confirmed that the SCAT is a valid predictor of competitive state anxiety.

In addition to completing the SCAT, the basketball players completed the *Trait Anxiety Inventory* (TAI; Spielberger, Gorsuch, & Lushene, 1970), a measure of general trait anxiety, so that the predictive power of the two trait scales could be compared. If, as Martens proposed, a sport-specific measure of competitive trait anxiety (SCAT) is a better predictor than a general trait anxiety measure (TAI), then the correlation between the SCAT and precompetition state anxiety should be higher than the correlation between the TAI and precompetition state anxiety. It was; the correlation between the TAI and precompetition state anxiety ($r = .30$) was considerably lower than the previously noted correlation between the SCAT and precompetition state anxiety ($r = .64$), confirming the superiority of a situation-specific anxiety measure. Of course, the SCAT is not presumed to predict state anxiety in noncompetitive situations. In fact, the correlation between the SCAT and the practice (noncompetition) state anxiety measure was considerably lower ($r = .25$). Similarly, laboratory experiments of controlled competition situations revealed that the SCAT is an excellent predictor of precompetition and midcompetition state anxiety, but a weaker predictor at postcompetition or in noncompetitive settings.

The extensive research with the SCAT by Martens and colleagues consistently demonstrates the validity of the SCAT as a predictor of competitive state anxiety and its superiority to general trait anxiety measures. Indeed, the relationship between the SCAT and competitive state anxiety is much higher than the usual relationship between a personality measure and subsequent behavior. Thus competitive trait anxiety is one of the most important personality constructs in sport psychology, and the SCAT is one of our few useful personality measures.

The SCAT is a valuable research tool for further investigation of competitive anxiety and has practical value in identifying competitors who tend to become overly anxious in competition and who might benefit from anxiety management training. As good as the SCAT is, however, it is still a personality measure that is most useful when considered along with important situational factors in the competitive situation.

Once competition is underway, the events of the contest often exert powerful influence and override individual differences in competitive trait anxiety. The experience of success or failure is an especially powerful situational factor. Successful performers tend to decrease in state anxiety, and unsuccessful performers typically increase in state anxiety (e.g., Martens & Gill, 1976; Scanlan, 1977; Scanlan & Passer, 1978, 1979). Certainly we all can recognize this effect when we observe the winners and losers after a contest.

Sport psychologists are just now beginning to understand how success/failure and other situational factors interact to influence state anxiety in competition. Now that we have a reliable, valid measure of the personality characteristic of competitive trait anxiety and some relevant situational factors that we can use to predict state anxiety in sport competition, we might consider the implications of state anxiety for sport performance and other behaviors. Actually, the relationship between anxiety and performance is one of the most popular research topics in sport psychology. We will discuss the extensive literature on the anxiety/performance relationship in chapter 8.

## *Summary*

Competitiveness and competitive trait anxiety are closely related sport-specific personality characteristics. Competitiveness is the tendency to seek out and strive for success in sport competition, whereas competitive trait anxiety is the tendency to worry about failure and become anxious in sport competition. Despite the closeness of these constructs, the sport psychology approaches to competitiveness and competitive anxiety are quite different. Sport psychologists approach competitiveness from the perspective of achievement motivation theory and are just beginning to consider sport-specific approaches and measurement techniques, whereas competitive anxiety research focuses on sport-specific issues. Martens developed a reliable and valid sport-specific measure of competitive anxiety (SCAT), and sport psychologists have used the SCAT along with relevant situational factors to investigate competitive anxiety from an interactionist perspective. The continued investigation of competitive and noncompetitive achievement behavior in sport, using sport-specific measures and interactionist approaches, should further our understanding of the role of personality characteristics in sport.

# CHAPTER 6

# *Gender Roles and Sport Behavior*

More girls and women are active sport participants today than ever before. It is no longer shocking to see a 10-year-old girl playing on a local youth baseball team. Even the advertising world now seems to accept females as sport participants. A recent television ad for bathroom tissue pictured a girl stuffing the tissue into her football pads before returning to the backyard to continue the game with the other boys and girls.

Even though girls and women are active sport participants, gender differences in sport behavior are quite evident. Females and males do not necessarily experience sport the same way. For example, a 10-year-old girl and a 10-year-old boy both pitching in a Little League game do not experience the same situation. Parents, spectators, coaches, and teammates treat boys and girls differently, at least to some extent, and gender roles may influence the way the two children respond in the situation. Certainly biological sex is a very salient characteristic that influences much of our behavior and interactions with others. Not surprisingly, then, gender influences sport behavior.

## *Sex and Gender Terminology*

Before continuing the discussion, we should clarify some terms. In this chapter we will adopt the convention used by Deaux (1985) in her review of the psychological literature on sex and gender. *Sex* refers to the biologically based categories of male and female, and *gender* refers to the psychological features frequently associated with these biological states. Within sport psychology, we usually focus on social psychological aspects of personality and behavior, and thus *gender* and *gender role* are the terms typically used to refer to those characteristics and behaviors.

Of course, some research does consider the relationship of sex differences to personality and behavior. The most notable work on sex differences and personality is the classic work of Maccoby and Jacklin (1974). After surveying the literature, Maccoby and Jacklin concluded that sex differences exist in four areas: verbal ability, mathematical ability, visual-spatial ability, and aggressiveness. Their findings indicated that males have greater mathematical ability and greater spatial ability and are more aggressive, whereas females have greater verbal ability. Maccoby and Jacklin's work is highly regarded, but subsequent investigations add qualifications and cast doubts upon even these sex differences.

Although sex differences may exist, those differences are seldom very meaningful. Hyde (1981) used a meta-analysis technique and reported that sex differences accounted for less than 5% of the variance in mathematical and spatial ability. Furthermore, some research suggests that experience or training may alter these differences. Connor, Schackman, and Serbin (1978), for example, found that when girls were given the opportunity to play with "boy" toys, they improved in spatial skills.

Thus even the most documented sex differences are neither universal nor absolute. Most investigators acknowledge that biological factors have some influence on behavior, but not that biological factors are absolute determinants. Even those gender differences with the strongest supporting evidence do not parallel the dichotomous biological sex difference. Instead, the behaviors of females and males overlap considerably. About 40% of females are more aggressive than the average male. Similarly, many females are more competitive than many males. Even if biological sex has some influence on competitive behavior, the social psychological aspects of gender in sport and competition pose more questions and implications for sport participants. The concern of this chapter, then, is not with biologically based sex differences but with the psychological aspects of gender roles and sport behavior.

## Sex and Gender Differences in Sport Behavior

Most people generally think of sport as a male activity and of most sport behaviors as masculine behaviors. If our typical sport behaviors are masculine, we might ask how female behavior in sport differs. In general, females are less competitive, less concerned with and affected by the competitive outcomes of winning and losing, more oriented to social values, and more open to cooperative alternatives than are males.

The reality of those differences hit me several years ago when I was testing fifth- and sixth-grade boys and girls on a competitive motor maze task. Each morning I drove to the schools in a van with my motor maze and an elaborate computer competition set-up. I brought each child into the van, went through my experimental scenario, built up the competition, and ended by asking, "Well, are you all set to really try hard to do well and win this competition?" Boys, without exception, answered affirmatively and eagerly got ready, and so did most of the girls.

Then one day a girl meekly responded, "Well, I don't know. I'm not very good at games like this, and I probably won't do very well." Her response shocked me; I had assumed that Title IX had been passed, that girls played in Little League, that I was in a liberal university community, and that all was well with the female sport world. Like any good scientist, I maintained my objective composure and quietly hoped that this unenlightened female would not ruin the data. As I continued the study, however, I realized that she was not an isolated case; several other girls had similar reactions. I began to realize that girls were seeing the situation differently than boys and that increased formal opportunity for participation did not automatically alter psychological characteristics. I should point out that this hesitant approach was by no means universal. Most girls approached competition in the same way as the boys. One day after I by-passed one young woman because she had a cast on her wrist, she later found me and emphatically stated that she knew she could play my game and do well, even if I didn't. Of course I gave her a chance, and indeed she played the game better than most of the girls and boys.

The reactions of the girls and boys to winning and losing, which I deviously manipulated, were also eye-opening. A few of the losing children were very upset and actually cried. I never let any children leave thinking they were losers, but I did have to stop and wait for several children who broke down and cried during the competition. The surprising thing to me was that all the children who cried were boys. Girls, the supposedly emotional sex, never cried or became visibly upset at a loss. The images of those unexpected reactions, the unconfident approach to competition of some girls and the emotional reaction to failure of some boys, have stayed with me, probably longer and certainly more vividly than the actual results of the study.

Now that the literature on gender differences in achievement and competition has grown, I find that those observed reactions fit with some other findings. When McNally and Orlick (1975) introduced a cooperative broomball game to children in urban Canada and the northern territories (as discussed in chapter 5), they found that girls were more receptive to the cooperative game than were boys. The boys, especially in the south, tried to circumvent the new rules and devise some way to keep score and determine a winner. Duda's (1983) study of competitiveness in male and female Anglo and Navajo children also revealed both gender and cultural differences as male Anglo children were the most win/loss-oriented and placed more emphasis on athletic ability. Duda also reported that gender differences in achievement orientations and attributions were stronger in sport than in academic situations, confirming what we often suspect—that sport competition exaggerates gender differences in achievement behavior.

As mentioned, boys in the maze study were more upset by losing than girls, as well as more concerned with winning. Similar gender differences have been observed in other sport psychology research. Weinberg and Jackson (1979) found that males were noticeably affected by success/failure in terms of interest in the activity and sense of excitement and enjoyment, whereas females were more consistent in their responses. Weinberg and Ragan (1979) found that males were much more interested in a competitive activity than a noncompetitive one and that females were slightly more likely to prefer noncompetitive activity. Vicky Vetere (1977), in her master's thesis, examined the attributions and affective reactions (feelings) of male and female intercollegiate basketball players. Males were more affected by win/loss than were females. Specifically, males were much higher in pride and lower in shame after a win than after a loss, but females had similar reactions regardless of the outcome. Thus females appear to be less oriented to competitive structures, more open to cooperation, and less affected by win/loss outcomes than are males.

The existence of gender differences in sport behavior is not surprising. Gender differences in behavior are documented in nonsport settings, so the extension of those differences to sport is to be expected. From a sport psychology perspective, the next step is to determine the *source* of gender differences in sport behavior and the implications of such differences.

As a prelude to an extended discussion of gender roles and sport, keep in mind that gender roles apply to both males and females. Although much of the research on gender roles in sport psychology as well as general psychology stems from a concern for women's issues and often feminist approaches, gender roles influence the sport behaviors of both females and males.

As Deaux (1985) notes, gender role research is a substantial field but is in considerable flux. Few guiding theories or models exist to provide a research framework. The two theoretical works making the greatest impact are the masculinity/femininity work of Bem and of Spence and Helmreich and the work on achievement motivation stemming from Horner's "fear of success" construct. Both of those research areas have been subject to at least as much criticism as support, and neither is accepted in its entirety. Nevertheless, both sets of investigators stimulated considerable research that has challenged and improved our conceptual models and measures and raised questions that deserve attention in sport psychology.

## Masculinity and Femininity

The most visible body of research on gender roles is the work on masculinity and femininity as personality constructs. Sandra Bem's (1974) theoretical discussion of masculinity, femininity, and androgyny and her development of the *Bem Sex Role Inventory* (BSRI) to measure individual differences in gender role personality characteristics instigated much of this research. At about the same time, Janet Spence and Bob Helmreich (1978) also began theoretical work on masculinity and femininity and developed their own widely used measure, the *Personality Attributes Questionnaire* (PAQ; Spence, Helmreich, & Stapp, 1974). They, along with Bem, are dominant in the field of gender role personality research, and their scales and ideas are the ones most often applied to sport.

## Gender Role Classification

Bem was not the first to discuss masculine and feminine personality characteristics nor the first to criticize the traditional unidimensional model. Bakan (1966) and Constantinople (1973) preceded Bem in suggesting a multidimensional model of gender role classifications. However, Bem's (1974, 1978a) discussion and measurement of masculinity and femininity as separate, independent characteristics and her introduction of androgyny, the construct that refers to the possession of both masculine and feminine personality characteristics, generated the most excitement and is probably the research best known to sport psychologists.

In contrast to traditional approaches, Bem clearly stated that masculine and feminine personality characteristics are neither linked to nor determined by biological sex, nor is there any reason that males should possess only masculine characteristics and females only feminine characteristics. In fact, Bem contended that the most mentally healthy individuals possess both masculine and feminine personality characteristics and engage in both masculine and feminine behaviors depending on the situation.

Bem's constructs and measures of masculinity and femininity were major departures from traditional unidimensional constructs. Traditional measures, such as the masculinity/femininity scale of the MMPI, use a single scale with one extreme indicating high masculinity and the other extreme indicating high femininity. Bem conceived of both masculinity and femininity as positive, desirable sets of characteristics that were separate, independent dimensions rather than opposite extremes of a single dimension. The BSRI contains 60 personality characteristics; 20 are stereotypically feminine (e.g., affectionate, sensitive to the needs of others), 20 are stereotypically masculine (e.g., independent, willing to take risks), and 20 serve as filler items (e.g., truthful, happy). We should note that in response to criticism of the original BSRI, Bem (1978b) now recommends using only 30 of the original 60 items in a revised BSRI. When taking the BSRI, a person is asked to "indicate, on a scale of 1 to 7, how true of you each of these characteristics is." The rating scale and sample items are shown in Figure 6.1.

When Bem first developed the BSRI, one of her primary goals was to assess *androgyny*. According to Bem, androgyny is desirable because androgynous individuals possess two sets of positive characteristics (masculine and feminine) and have greater flexibility of behavior than do individuals who are sex-typed toward either extreme. With the BSRI, androgyny is indicated by high scores on both feminine and masculine characteristics. Thus when scoring the BSRI, Bem recommended a classification procedure rather than simply recording masculine and feminine scores.

Bem originally recommended using the difference between the individual's masculine score and feminine score to determine androgyny. Individuals with similar scores were classified as androgynous, those with feminine

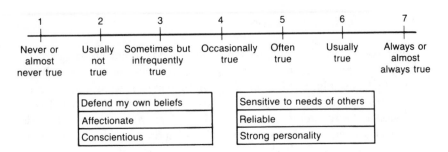

**Figure 6.1**   Sample items from the Bem Sex Role Inventory (BSRI; Bem, 1978b).

scores much higher than masculine scores were feminine sex-typed, and those with masculine scores much higher than feminine scores were masculine sex-typed. Subsequent investigators suggested that simply using difference scores was neither conceptually nor operationally appropriate because individuals who score high on both are not the same as individuals who score low on both. Hence current assessment procedures typically involve a four-way classification system with individuals divided into high and low scorers on each set of characteristics. As shown in Figure 6.2, individuals who score high on both are androgynous; those who score high on masculinity and low on femininity are masculine; those who score high on femininity and low on masculinity are feminine; and those who score low on both are undifferentiated.

Spence and Helmreich followed a conceptual framework similar to Bem's in that they conceptualized and measured masculinity and femininity on two separate, independent dimensions. Their *Personality Attributes Questionnaire* (PAQ) actually has three scales: a masculine scale, a feminine scale, and a third, bipolar scale known as "masculinity/femininity" or M/F. Masculine items on the PAQ are socially desirable for both males and females but are found in greater abundance in males. Similarly, feminine items are socially desirable for both females and males but are found in greater abundance in females. Items on the M/F scale are socially desirable for one sex but undesirable for the other. Sample items for each of the three scales, noting where respondents rated the ideal male and ideal female, are shown in Figure 6.3.

|  | | Masculinity | |
|---|---|---|---|
|  | | Above median | Below median |
| Femininity | Above median | Androgynous | Feminine |
|  | Below median | Masculine | Undifferentiated |

**Figure 6.2**   Four-way classification of individuals on masculinity and femininity used by Bem (1978b).

Scale[a]

| M/F | 1. Not at all aggressive | A | B | C | D | E | *Very aggressive*[b] |
| M | 2. Not at all independent | A | B | C | D | E | *Very independent* |
| F | 3. Very rough | A | B | C | D | E | *Very gentle* |

[a]The scale to which each item is assigned is indicated by M (Masculinity), F (Femininity), and M/F (Masculinity-Femininity).
[b]Italics indicate the extreme masculine response for the M and M/F scales and the extreme feminine response for the F scale.

**Figure 6.3**  Sample items from the three subscales of the Personality Attributes Questionnaire (PAQ; Spence, Helmreich, & Stapp, 1974).

Although the PAQ has three scales, most reports and discussions focus on the feminine and masculine scales and follow approaches similar to those used with the BSRI. As with the BSRI, the PAQ masculine and feminine scores may be used to classify individuals into the four categories. Both Bem and Spence and Helmreich report norms indicating that approximately one third of the respondents fall into the androgynous category, about one third are sex-typed (males fall into the masculine category; females fall into the feminine category), approximately one tenth are reverse sex-typed (females fall into the masculine category; males fall into the feminine category), and the remainder are undifferentiated.

Although both the BSRI and PAQ are widely used, and although considerable literature on gender role classification exists, that research has not fulfilled all the hopes the initial work generated. Both the concepts and measures have been criticized, justifiably (e.g., Locksley & Colten, 1979; Pedhazur & Tetenbaum, 1979). The androgyny construct, particularly, has been of little theoretical or empirical value in gender role research. Although masculinity and femininity relate to some behaviors, and most investigators accept the idea of separate, independent dimensions, the behavioral implications of femininity and masculinity do not seem as far-reaching as originally proposed. In summarizing that literature, Deaux (1985) states that the scales on the BSRI and PAQ

> are best viewed as measures of dominance and self-assertion on the one hand and nurturance and interpersonal warmth on the other. . . . As such, these measures show good predictability for behaviors that require either assertive or nurturant behavior, respectively. Less convincing evidence has been offered to support the assumption that these trait measures are substantially related to other classes of gender-related attributes and behaviors associated with the broader concepts of masculinity and femininity. (p. 59)

Spence and Helmreich (Spence & Helmreich, 1980; Helmreich, Spence, & Holohan, 1979) similarly note the limits of the masculine and feminine personality constructs and propose that the scales and cluster of personality characteristics represented by the scales are more appropriately labeled as *instrumental* (masculine) and *expressive* (feminine). Helmreich et al. further caution that the scales have only a weak relationship to actual gender role behavior and explicitly point out the importance of situational factors in determining whether behaviors that might be considered feminine or masculine are actually carried out.

Thus most researchers working on gender roles now suggest that we can best further our understanding of individual differences and gender role behaviors by adopting an interactionist approach. Individual differences in the personality characteristics traditionally labeled as "masculine" or "feminine," or more appropriately as "instrumental" and "expressive," are important considerations for understanding gender role behavior, including instrumental and expressive behaviors in sport and physical activity. Regardless of how we label them, however, personality characteristics are typically weak predictors of behavior, and the importance of expressive and instrumental personality characteristics varies with the situation.

## Masculinity/Femininity and Sport Participation

Gender role personality characteristics certainly seem to have implications for sport behaviors. Sport activities, especially competitive sports, typically call for behaviors that we would label as masculine or instrumental. Indeed, both the BSRI and PAQ include "competitive" as one of the masculine or instrumental items. Generally, then, we see sport as a masculine activity, and we would expect both female and male sport participants to possess masculine or instrumental characteristics. Several investigators have examined gender role personality orientations and sport participation, and the findings tend to support that expectation.

Helmreich and Spence (1977) reported the PAQ classification distribution of a sample of female intercollegiate athletes along with a sample of female and male academic scientists and a normative sample of female and male college students. As indicated on Table 6.1, most female athletes were classified as androgynous or masculine, indicating highly masculine scores. As Helmreich and Spence note, the female athletes were thus quite similar to the high-achieving female scientists, but different from the female college students who were most often classified as feminine.

Several other studies have examined the masculine and feminine personality characteristics of athletes. In general, the results concur with those of Helmreich and Spence. Harris and Jennings (1977) surveyed female distance runners using the PAQ and found the largest percentage (34%) classified as androgynous, with another 28% classified as masculine, thus replicating Helmreich and Spence's findings. Similarly, Del Rey and Sheppard (1981) used the PAQ with female varsity athletes and also found most participants

**Table 6.1** Distribution in percentage of male and female students, male and female scientists, and female varsity athletes on the four-way PAQ classification.

|  | Undifferentiated | Feminine | Masculine | Androgynous |
|---|---|---|---|---|
| Male Students | 31 | 13 | 27 | 29 |
| Female Students | 21 | 39 | 11 | 29 |
| Male Scientists | 20 | 5 | 43 | 32 |
| Female Scientists | 8 | 23 | 23 | 46 |
| Female Athletes | 20 | 10 | 31 | 39 |

*Note.* From "Sex roles and achievement" by R. Helmreich and J.T. Spence, 1977, in R.W. Christina and D.M. Landers (Eds.), *Psychology of motor behavior and sport—1976*, **2**, p. 42. Copyright 1977 by Human Kinetics Publishers, Inc. Reprinted by permission.

to be classified as androgynous or masculine. Colker and Widom (1980) also used the PAQ to compare female athletes in various intercollegiate sports with female nonathletes. Again, most athletes were classified as androgynous or masculine, and more nonathletes were classified as feminine.

Myers and Lips (1978) used the BSRI in two studies, one with male and female competitive racquetball players and the second with male and female badminton, squash, and handball players. In the first study, most female racquetball players were classified as androgynous, whereas most male racquetball players were classified as masculine. In the second study, players were divided into competitive and noncompetitive categories based on their reasons for entering the tournament. All males were competitive and tended to be androgynous or masculine. Competitive females, like competitive males, tended to be androgynous or masculine, but the noncompetitive females had lower masculine and higher feminine scores and were classified mostly as feminine or undifferentiated.

Overall, the findings indicate that females in competitive sports possess more masculine or instrumental personality characteristics than female nonparticipants. That finding, although logical, has limited impact in sport psychology. First, the findings are limited to selected samples of highly competitive athletes. Similar trends in personality orientations may not hold across different activities, different age groups, or different exercise and recreational programs. Myers and Lips' results, although based on a very small and restricted sample, imply that even within a competitive tournament individuals may have noncompetitive reasons for participating, and those individuals do not necessarily possess masculine or instrumental personality characteristics. It appears likely that varied sport and exercise activities attract individuals with varying instrumental and expressive personality orientations.

The research is also limited to sport participation, but participation is not the only behavior of interest. The more intriguing questions about the relationship of instrumental and expressive orientations to specific sport behaviors have not been addressed. Certainly many situations within sport call for instrumental behaviors. We might consider how expressive and instrumental orientations influence specific tactics, reactions, and behaviors within varied sport situations. Furthermore, not all sport situations call for instrumental behaviors; expressive behaviors are also prevalent in many sport situations. The tendency of many authors to discuss sport as an exclusively masculine activity obscures the fact that many sport activities do not demand instrumental behaviors, and even within competitive sport many expressive behaviors are encouraged. For example, team sport members are expected to be submissive and listen to directions from a coach or captain without assertively questioning decisions in the middle of a game. In addition, creative, expressive actions are often rewarded in sport performances, and certainly coaches and instructors often display nurturant behaviors.

Individual differences in instrumentality and expressiveness are obvious in many sport activities. Some team members quickly step forward and assume a leadership role, whereas others stay back and prefer to follow directions. Some instructors exude warmth and appear very approachable, whereas others appear cold and distant. On the other hand, situational factors in sport exert considerable influence on expressive and instrumental behaviors. Few team members will challenge a coach's decision regardless of how assertive they are outside the sport setting. As with most sport personality issues, we can best understand gender role characteristics and behaviors in sport by considering the interaction of individual differences in masculinity and femininity, or instrumentality and expressiveness, with relevant situational factors in varied sport settings.

## Achievement Motivation and Behavior

As noted at the beginning of this chapter, the two gender role issues that have drawn the most attention and generated the most conceptual and empirical work are the classifications of masculine and feminine personality characteristics and achievement motivation and behavior. Achievement behavior is of special interest in sport psychology because, as discussed in chapter 5, most sport behavior is achievement behavior. Competition or social achievement predominates, but sport also involves considerable noncompetitive or individual achievement. In chapter 5 we discussed individual differences in achievement motivation and the literature on achievement and competitive behavior in sport. In this chapter, we will examine how the consideration of sex and gender qualifies and expands that literature.

## Horner's Fear of Success Construct

Although Atkinson's theory stands as the classic theoretical model of achievement motivation, even the earliest research revealed that the theory does not apply to females exactly as it applies to males. Gender differences were recognized in early achievement research when McClelland, Atkinson, Clark, and Lowell (1953) observed that women's achievement scores did not increase as men's scores increased in response to achievement-arousing instructions. Because of these differences, McClelland, Atkinson, and most subsequent investigators developed their models and reported findings based nearly exclusively on research with males. When females were studied, the findings often were inconsistent or contradictory.

Matina Horner's (1968, 1969, 1972) doctoral work was the premier attempt to resolve gender differences and extend achievement theory to encompass female achievement behavior. Horner proposed the existence of a third motive, the *motive to avoid success* $(M_{as})$, or, as more popularly termed, *fear of success (FOS)*, in addition to the motives to approach success $(M_s)$ and avoid failure $(M_{af})$ presented in Atkinson's model discussed in chapter 5. The motive to avoid success has behavioral implications similar to those of $M_s$ and $M_{af}$. The $M_{as}$, like the $M_{af}$, is a negative or inhibiting motive that detracts from the overall resultant achievement-oriented tendency $(T_a)$. Following the Atkinson model, we could calculate a behavioral tendency to avoid success $(T_{as})$ as

$$T_{as} = M_{as} \times P_s \times I_{as}$$

According to the model, the tendency to avoid success equals the motive to avoid success, times the probability of success, times the incentive value of avoiding success. As with the tendency to avoid failure, the tendency to avoid success is negative. Fear of success involves fear of the negative consequences of success, particularly social rejection. Thus the $T_{as}$ detracts from overall achievement orientation. To determine the resultant achievement behavior, we must consider all three motives and their associated behavioral tendencies as

$$T_a = T_s - T_{af} - T_{as}$$

Horner contends that the addition of the FOS construct and tendency to avoid success to Atkinson's model helps account for previously unexplained gender differences because FOS is much more common in females than in males and is especially evident in women who have the capability of success.

To test her ideas, Horner had females and males respond to cues about Anne or John, a medical student at the top of the class. Horner scored the responses for FOS imagery and found that females included much more FOS imagery about Anne than males included about John. Horner further observed that those females who scored high in FOS did not perform as well as females who scored low in the motive when in a competitive situation. This observation supports the contention that FOS is an avoidance motive with inhibiting effects similar to the motive to avoid failure.

Horner's work inspired considerable debate and research and seemed to account for some apparent gender differences in achievement behaviors. However, subsequent research casts serious doubt on Horner's constructs and measures (e.g., Condry & Dyer, 1976; Tresemer, 1977). Studies conducted after Horner's original work report FOS in men as often as in women, and some findings imply that FOS responses to cues about female achievement may reflect stereotypical attitudes about female success rather than an intrinsic, underlying motive to avoid success. Critics of Horner's work thus argue convincingly that both the FOS construct and the measures used to quantify it are highly suspect. McElroy and Willis (1979) specifically examined the sport literature and concluded that there was no evidence of FOS in female athletes and that the achievement attitudes of female athletes were similar to those of male athletes. Nevertheless, most investigators acknowledge that some successes may carry negative connotations for some people, and research related to fear of success continues. More relevant to this chapter, the issue of gender differences in achievement motivation and behavior continues to be the subject of considerable research, even though FOS and general achievement motives have faded in importance.

## Multidimensional Achievement Orientations

One approach to clarifying gender differences in achievement is to consider achievement motivation as a multidimensional construct. As discussed in chapter 5, Helmreich and Spence (1978) advocated a multidimensional approach and developed the *Work and Family Orientation Questionnaire* (WOFO), which assesses the four dimensions of mastery, work, competitiveness, and personal unconcern. As discussed earlier in this chapter, Spence and Helmreich have conducted considerable research on gender role personality characteristics, and so it is not surprising that they have also investigated gender differences in their achievement orientation work. General norms indicate that gender differences in achievement orientation vary across the four dimensions; males are higher than females on mastery and competitiveness, but females are higher than males on work. With selected high-achieving samples, including varsity athletes, academic scientists, and businesspersons, gender differences in mastery and work diminish, but males remain higher than females on competitiveness.

When comparing gender role personality characteristics (PAQ scores) and achievement orientation, Spence and Helmreich (1983) reported that masculine or instrumental scores for both males and females relate positively to the mastery, work, and competitiveness scales and that feminine or expressive scores relate slightly positively to work and slightly negatively to competitiveness. When the four-way classification was used, androgynous individuals scored highest on both work and mastery, followed by masculine, feminine, and finally, undifferentiated individuals. For competitiveness, however, masculine individuals scored highest and feminine individuals scored lowest, suggesting that the relationship between competitiveness and gender roles differs from the relationship between gender roles and the other achievement dimensions.

My initial work with the *Competitiveness Inventory* (Gill, in press; Gill, Deeter, & Gruber, 1985) suggests that a sport-specific, multidimensional achievement measure may provide insight into gender differences in sport achievement and competitive behaviors. In our work we had college students complete both Helmreich and Spence's WOFO and the *Competitiveness Inventory*. We found gender differences on WOFO scores similar to those reported by Helmreich and Spence; the primary difference was that males scored higher than females on competitiveness. Gender differences on the *Competitiveness Inventory* were much stronger and imply sport-specific considerations. Males scored slightly higher than females on our competitiveness scale (the general tendency to strive for success in sport competition). However, the greater differences were on the other two scales that represent orientation to competitive outcomes rather than striving for success within the competitive process. Females scored higher than males on goal orientation (the tendency to set and strive for personal standards in sport), and males scored much higher than females on win orientation (the desire to win and to avoid losing in competition). Additional research with the *Competitiveness Inventory* and other sport-specific or multidimensional measures of achievement orientation may provide further insight into the relationship of gender roles to achievement orientation and behavior in sport.

## Gender Differences in Achievement Cognitions

Consideration of achievement orientation as a multidimensional construct and the use of sport-specific measures may clarify gender differences in achievement behavior. Current research, however, tends to avoid general achievement motives or personality characteristics and to emphasize individual differences in achievement cognitions. Cognitive approaches to achievement behavior emphasize the individual's thoughts, perceptions, and interpretations as critical mediators of achievement behavior. We will consider cognitive approaches to motivation and specific cognitive theories of achievement in more detail in chapter 10. In this chapter, we will focus on the work examining individual differences in achievement cognitions as an explanation for gender differences in achievement behavior.

From a cognitive perspective, the most notable theoretical work on gender differences in achievement is the recent work of Eccles and her colleagues (Eccles, 1983; Eccles, Adler, & Meece, 1984). Eccles incorporates cognitive constructs into her expectancy x value model of achievement, specifically citing the importance of expectancies. Unlike most cognitive approaches, however, Eccles' work also gives a prominent role to the individual's perception of *task value*. Eccles proposes that task value and expectancies together are the primary, immediate determinants of achievement behavior. The model does not include motives, such as the motive to approach success, but because both task value and expectancies are subjective (i.e., based on the individual's perceptions), individual differences are prominent. Considerable theoretical and empirical work, which we will review in more detail in chapter 10, suggests that expectancies relate to achievement behavior (e.g., Bandura, 1977b; Crandall, 1969). More importantly here, research also reveals gender differences in expectancies (Crandall, 1969; Lenney, 1977), with females typically reporting lower expectancies of success than males. The most recent work qualifies those findings and indicates that gender differences vary with the task and situation (Lenney, 1977).

The task value construct is a more unique aspect of Eccles' model. Unlike the incentive value construct in Atkinson's model, task value in the Eccles model is determined both by characteristics of the task and by the needs, goals, and values of the person. More specifically, Eccles proposes that task value has four components: (a) *attainment value*, which represents the importance of performing the task well; (b) *intrinsic value*, which is the enjoyment inherent in doing the activity; (c) *utility value*, which is the instrumental value of the task for reaching goals; and (d) *cost*, which is what must be given up or suffered because of the activity.

In the complete model, Eccles elaborates on some of the antecedents of both expectancies and task value. Past events and the individual's interpretation of those events (i.e., attributions) influence expectancies. Cultural and social factors, including gender role stereotypes and especially the individual's perception of the attitudes and expectations of others, affect subjective task value.

Eccles et al. (1984) tested her predictions and compared the efficacy of her model with prominent social cognition explanations of gender differences in achievement. The following specific theories were compared to examine the achievement behaviors of male and female students in math and English: (a) *self-concept theories*, which focus on gender differences in confidence or expectancies; (b) *attribution theories*, which focus on the tendency of females to focus on lack of ability as a cause of failure and to take less personal responsibility for success than males; (c) *learned helplessness versus mastery orientation*, which focuses on the tendency of females to exhibit more helplessness or give up, whereas males show more increased persistence and mastery behavior in the face of failure; and (d) *Eccles' expectancy × subjective task value theory.*

The results of two studies supported Eccles' theory and indicated that task value, which is ignored in the other cognitive theories, was the strongest and most consistent mediator of achievement plans and gender differences in academic choices. Some gender differences in ability attributions and expectancies were observed, but they were inconsistent and not applicable to all students. Eccles and her associates noted that expectancies did have predictive value and ability perceptions did affect grades. These findings indicated that free choice behavior, such as voluntary plans or participation, and achievement behavior within a relatively forced or inescapable situation, such as an academic course, are influenced by different motivators. Task value had the strongest influence on plans and choices, but expectancies had stronger effects on grades. In Eccles' study, gender differences were most evident in task value and academic choices and plans.

Similar gender differences would quite likely emerge for achievement choices within sport. Apparently, societal attitudes and gender role stereotypes exist in sport. As we will discuss in chapter 7, people typically hold higher expectations for males and evaluate male performances more favorably than comparable female performances. Those social biases and the individual's perception of the attitudes and expectations of significant others, including parents, coaches, teachers, friends, and spectators, probably differ for females and males in sport and thus probably affect the task value of various sport activities for females versus males. If social standards hold certain activities to be more appropriate for males than for females, then males would likely have higher task values for those activities. If certain activities hold more attainment value or utility value for females, then females would more likely participate in those activities. Once in the activity, however, expectancies may be the stronger determinant of performance and behavior. Research does not indicate consistent gender differences for expectancies and achievement behavior when task value is similar.

Eccles' model and empirical work raise many issues for sport psychology. Her findings suggest that gender differences in task value, probably stemming from social values and stereotypical expectancies for females and males in sport, account for gender differences in sport participation. The model also implies that if the task value is similar for females and males, then expectancies, which are largely influenced by past experiences and attributions, are major predictors of achievement performance and behavior.

Some sport psychology research does suggest that task characteristics mediate gender differences in achievement behavior. Corbin and his colleagues (Corbin & Nix, 1979; Corbin, Stewart, & Blair, 1981) found gender differences in expectancies *only* for masculine tasks. In our laboratory (Gill, Gross, Huddleston, & Shifflett, 1984), we matched male and female competitors of similar ability on a pegboard task. Although males were slightly more likely than females to predict a win, performance expectations were similar, and females actually improved their performance times more than males improved their times in competition. Our findings imply that competition is not necessarily detrimental to female achievement, as some have implied, if the task and situation are appropriate for females. In the real world, however, gender stereotypes and social expectations are much more salient than in the laboratory, and these factors likely exert considerable influence on the achievement choices and behaviors of both females and males.

## Summary

The existing theoretical and empirical work on gender roles and achievement provides a starting point for understanding gender differences in sport behavior. Gender differences in sport behavior clearly do not parallel the dichotomous biological sex difference. Many females are more aggressive, competitive tennis players than many males, and many males are more creative, expressive figure skaters than many females. Research on masculinity/femininity, or, more appropriately, on instrumentality/expressiveness, indicates that those personality characteristics relate to the performance of instrumental and expressive behaviors respectively, and some limited sport psychology research reveals that athletic participants tend to fall into the masculine and androgynous gender role classifications. To date, sport psychologists have not examined the influence of instrumentality and expressiveness or relevant situational factors on the performance of specific instrumental and expressive behaviors in sport.

The literature on gender differences in achievement also suggests personality characteristics that may relate to sport achievement behaviors. More general achievement motives and the related fear of success construct appear to have little value, but multidimensional achievement orientation constructs and sport-specific measures of achievement and competitiveness offer more promise. Even sport-specific achievement measures, however, have limited predictive power. Perhaps the best way to incorporate individual difference measures of achievement orientation and gender roles is to consider how those characteristics influence the cognitive characteristics of expectancies and task value. Although the relationships may be complex, human behavior itself is complex, and interactive models that incorporate individual differences along with situational variables will likely yield the most accurate explanations of gender roles and sport behavior.

# CHAPTER 7

# *Attitudes and Sport Behavior*

Issues related to attitudes and attitude change are common topics within the sport world. If you teach physical education in the public schools, you hope to develop students' appreciation of physical activity and its values as well as their motor skills and physical fitness. If you organize an adult fitness program, you want the participants to hold positive attitudes so that they will stay with the program and maintain desirable levels of health and fitness. If you want to start a wellness program in a large corporation, your first task may be to promote positive attitudes toward the program among the administrators and employees.

Considerable research on attitudes toward sport and physical activity has been conducted. Unfortunately, very little of that research addresses the issues of attitude formation and change or the relationship of attitudes to ensuing sport behaviors. Instead, most of the sport attitude research consists of surveys of various groups about attitudes toward various aspects of physical activity. Research has seldom extended beyond that descriptive work, and sport attitude research contains many of the same conceptual and methodological weaknessess found in sport personality research. Despite the weaknesses of current research, sport attitude issues remain important. Sport psychology research that helps us to understand how attitudes toward sport and exercise are formed and maintained, how attitudes relate to participation and specific sport behaviors, and how positive attitudes can be promoted could be of great value to the field.

## *The Definition and Measurement of Attitudes*

Attitudes are similar to personality characteristics. Indeed, if we adopt a broad definition of personality, attitudes are part of personality. Like personality traits, attitudes are relatively stable, individual difference characteristics that presumably predispose the individual to certain behaviors. Attitudes, however, differ from personality traits such as introversion or dependence in that attitudes are not global predispositions to behave but rather are directed toward specific *attitude objects*, such as classes of people, objects, events, or ideas. Thus if you have a favorable attitude toward fitness, your behavior should reflect that attitude. You might jog three times a week, encourage your colleagues to join the noon aerobics workout, or read fitness publications.

## Defining Attitudes

Allport (1935) presented the classic definition of an *attitude* as "a mental and neural state of readiness, organized through experience, exerting a directive or dynamic influence upon the individual's response to all objects and situations with which it is related" (p. 805). Thus defined, attitudes are internal states that create a readiness or predisposition to respond with certain behaviors. Allport suggests that attitudes are learned or organized through experience and that they direct responses to specific attitude objects. This directive influence in Allport's definition represents what most social psychologists see as the key characteristic of attitudes. Attitudes are *evaluative* and direct behavior positively or negatively in relation to the attitude object. If you have a positive attitude toward running, you might run every morning, encourage others to run, buy running magazines, and exhort the joys of running to your friends and relatives every chance you get. If you hold a negative attitude toward football, you might not play football yourself, discourage others from playing, and turn to another channel when a football game comes on the television.

Triandis (1971) has defined an attitude as "an idea charged with emotion which predisposes a class of actions to a particular class of social situations" (p. 2). Triandis' definition is similar to Allport's earlier definition but more clearly represents the three-component theory of attitudes proposed by some social psychologists. The three-component approach proposes that we study the *cognitive, affective,* and *behavioral* components of attitudes to understand their relationship to behavior.

The *cognitive* component reflects your beliefs, or the information that you have about the attitude object. You might believe that weight training builds muscle bulk, that jogging ruins your joints, or that football players are poor academic students. Whether or not your beliefs are supported by data, if you believe your information is correct, those beliefs form the cognitive component of your attitudes.

The *affective* component consists of your feelings or your positive or negative evaluation of the attitude object. Although beliefs help determine attitudes, two persons can hold the same belief and make different evaluations. Two people might both believe that weight training builds muscle bulk. However, one person might feel that muscle bulk is desirable and that weight training is great, whereas the other person might consider muscle bulk disgusting and thus have a negative attitude toward weight training. The affective component helps to determine the *direction* of your predisposition for behavior.

The third component of attitudes, the *behavioral* component, consists of your intended behaviors toward the attitude object. Depending on the behavioral component of your attitudes, you might plan to attend a football game on Saturday, or you might intend to lift weights at a local gym three times each week.

Although the three-component theory is widely known, many and probably most active social psychologists do not consider all three components to be part of attitudes. Instead, many define "attitude" as only the affective or evaluative component. In a recent text on attitudes, Petty and Cacioppo (1981) stated, "There is widespread agreement among social psychologists that the term *attitude* should be used to refer to a general and enduring positive or negative feeling about some person, object, or issue" (p. 7). Petty and Cacioppo recognize the importance of beliefs and behaviors, but they suggest that the presumed one-way relationship in which beliefs contribute to attitude formation and attitudes then direct behavior may not be representative of the complex ways in which beliefs, attitudes, and behaviors are interrelated.

## Measuring Attitudes

Whether we wish to conduct research on attitudes or assess attitudes as part of the evaluation of an ongoing program, we need reliable and valid attitude measures. We can measure attitudes directly by asking individuals to report their attitudes on some scale or questionnaire, or we can infer attitudes from indirect projective self-reports, behavioral observations, or physiological measures. Behavioral indicators, such as eye contact and body language, and physiological indicators, including galvanic skin response, pupillary response, and facial electromyogram (EMG), have been used in several attitude studies and present some intriguing possibilities. To date, however, the reliability and validity of indirect attitude measures are not well documented.

Direct measurement of attitudes with self-report scales and inventories is standard in most attitude research. The three major types of attitude measures are Thurstone scales, Likert scales, and Osgood's semantic differential scales. Some authors cite scalograms and one-item ratings as additional attitude measures, but neither of these is used to any great extent in general attitude research or sport psychology. A one-item measure may be sufficient in some cases, but of course the reliability and validity of any one-item scale is questionable. Sample items from one-item, Thurstone, Likert, and Osgood's semantic differential scales are presented in Figure 7.1.

**Thurstone Scales.** Thurstone (1928) developed one of the earliest attitude measures by adopting some techniques from perception research to the measurement of attitudes. A Thurstone scale contains approximately 20 statements,

### One-Item Rating Scale

How much do you like jogging for exercise?

not at all _____ _____ _____ _____ _____ _____ _____ very much
(1)    (2)    (3)    (4)    (5)    (6)    (7)

**Thurstone Scale** (the scale values in parentheses are contrived for this example)

Check the statements with which you agree.

_____ 1.  Jogging is the best way to start a day. (10.7)

_____ 2.  Jogging helps a person stay fit and healthy. (7.3)

_____ 3.  Jogging is unnecessary and a waste of time for most people. (3.4)

_____ 4.  Jogging is distasteful and unpleasant. (2.3)

### Likert Scale

For each statement, check the extent to which you agree.

1.  Jogging is a good activity for most people.

_____ strongly agree (+2)

_____ moderately agree (+1)

_____ neutral (0)

_____ moderately disagree (−1)

_____ strongly disagree (−2)

2.  Jogging is boring.

_____ strongly agree (−2)

_____ moderately agree (−1)

_____ neutral (0)

_____ moderately disagree (+1)

_____ strongly disagree (+2)

### Semantic Differential Scale

Rate how you feel about jogging for exercise on each of the scales below:

foolish _____ _____ _____ _____ _____ _____ _____ wise
(−3)  (−2)  (−1)  (0)  (+1)  (+2)  (+3)

good _____ _____ _____ _____ _____ _____ _____ bad
(+3)  (+2)  (+1)  (0)  (−1)  (−2)  (−3)

beneficial _____ _____ _____ _____ _____ _____ _____ harmful
(+3)  (+2)  (+1)  (0)  (−1)  (−2)  (−3)

unpleasant _____ _____ _____ _____ _____ _____ _____ pleasant
(−3)  (−2)  (−1)  (0)  (+1)  (+2)  (+3)

valuable _____ _____ _____ _____ _____ _____ _____ worthless
(+3)  (+2)  (+1)  (0)  (−1)  (−2)  (−3)

**Figure 7.1** Sample items from One-Item, Thurstone, Likert, and Semantic Differential scales assessing attitudes toward jogging.

each representing a different degree of favorableness or unfavorableness toward an attitude object, arranged to present a continuum of equally spaced levels of favorableness.

Construction of a Thurstone scale requires considerable time and effort. First the investigator must gather approximately 100 statements representing varying degrees of favorableness toward the attitude object. Those statements must then be sent to 100 expert judges who eliminate ambiguous and inappropriate items and sort the remaining statements into 11 categories of favorableness. The investigator uses the judges' ratings and retains about 20 items that the judges agree upon and that fall at equally spaced intervals on the favorableness continuum. The average of the judges' ratings becomes the scale value for the statement. To determine an individual's attitude score on a Thurstone scale, the scale values of all the statements that the individual agrees with are totaled.

**Likert Scales.** Constructing a Thurstone scale takes too much time and effort for most researchers, and finding 100 expert judges for a particular attitude area is no easy task. Fortunately, Likert (1932) developed an attitude measure with similar reliability and validity that is easier to construct. As shown in Figure 7.1, Likert scales consist of a series of attitude statements, each rated on a five-point scale (strongly agree, agree, undecided, disagree, strongly disagree). Unlike the Thurstone scale, in which each statement represents a different degree of favorableness, on a Likert scale all statements represent the same attitude, and responses to all items should correlate with each other.

To construct a Likert scale, the investigator must first gather statements and eliminate ambiguous items, but the statements need not be submitted to judges. Instead, members of a sample group rate the statements in accordance with their own attitudes. Those items that best differentiate sample individuals with high and low total scores are retained for the Likert scale.

**Osgood's Semantic Differential Scales.** Semantic differential scales developed by Osgood, Suci, and Tannenbaum (1957) are popular attitude measures. One of the best attitude measures in sport psychology, Kenyon's (1968b) *Attitude Toward Physical Activity Inventory*, is a semantic differential scale. The Osgood procedure requires the individual to rate the attitude object on a set of semantic scales, which are bipolar adjectives generally seven steps apart. Osgood and colleagues reported that three factors account for most of the meaning that we assign to different words or attitude objects: *evaluation* (e.g., good/bad), *potency* (e.g., strong/weak), and *activity* (e.g., active/passive). Keeping in mind the definition of attitudes, usually only the evaluation scales are needed to assess attitudes.

# Attitudes and Behavior

Attitudes, per se, are not very interesting to either sport psychologists or sport participants. Attitudes are important constructs because they presumably influence sport behaviors. The generally assumed attitude/behavior relationship is that attitudes predispose or direct an individual to behave in a positive or negative way toward the attitude object. If we surveyed an adult sample and discovered that some of the individuals held very positive attitudes toward sport activities and physical fitness exercises, whereas others held very negative attitudes, we would assume that those attitudes could predict behavior. Specifically, those who hold the most positive attitudes would be expected to participate in fitness activities more frequently than those who hold the most negative attitudes. If attitudes did not predict participation or some other sport behavior, then attitudes would be of no interest. The attitude/behavior relationship and the related applied question of how to change attitudes in order to change behavior are the central issues of most social psychology attitude research.

In one of the first studies of the attitude/behavior relationship, LaPiere (1934) investigated the prediction of prejudiced behaviors from self-reported prejudiced attitudes. To examine behavior, LaPiere traveled across the country with a Chinese couple and stopped at various restaurants and hotels. The Chinese couple was refused service only once. Six months later LaPiere assessed attitudes at all the places he and the couple had stopped by writing and asking if they would serve Chinese guests. Of the 128 places, 92% said they would *not* serve Chinese guests. LaPiere clearly demonstrated a striking discrepancy between stated attitudes and actual behavior. Social psychologists have pointed out several problems with LaPiere's study, but it still stands as the classic example of a low attitude/behavior relationship. Furthermore, many subsequent studies reported similarly low relationships between attitudes and behaviors on various issues. Because of the inability of attitudes to predict behavior, attitude research declined dramatically through the 1960s and 1970s.

In the mid 1970s some social psychologists, most notably Fishbein and Ajzen (1974, 1975), proposed theoretical models incorporating specific aspects of the attitude/behavior relationship and demonstrated that attitudes *can* predict behavior. First, Fishbein proposed that if we want to predict specific behaviors, we should consider specific attitudes. An individual's general attitude toward physical activity might not predict participation in a specific aerobic exercise program very well, but attitudes toward participating in aerobic exercise should more accurately predict participation in that program.

Even if we assess attitudes toward specific behaviors, prediction of behavior is not perfect. An individual might have a positive attitude toward an aerobic exercise program but still not participate. Perhaps conflicts with other activities, an inconvenient location, or dislike for some of the other participants would discourage participation. Fishbein notes that factors other than attitude affect behavior. In some of his work Fishbein specifically considered the effects on behavior of norms or conventions. According to Fishbein's model, by asking if everyone else at work goes jogging at noon or if friends and relatives think you should join the tennis club, researchers can consider normative behavior or other social situational factors along with attitudes to improve the prediction of behavior.

Although a combination of specific attitudes and social situational factors relates to behavior, Fishbein states that the best predictor of behavior is the individual's *behavioral intention*; that is, to predict participation in an aerobic exercise program, we should ask individuals if they *intend* to participate in the program. Research indicates that behavioral intentions are very strong predictors of actual behavior. Fishbein's model, then, which has been supported with considerable research, proposes that (a) specific attitudes toward the behavioral act must be considered to predict behavior; (b) attitudes toward the behavior, along with normative beliefs, predict behavioral intentions quite well; and (c) behavioral intentions predict actual behavior quite well.

A class assignment that I have used with several sport psychology classes illustrates Fishbein's propositions. For the assignment, each student in the class has three or four people complete a short attitude questionnaire on jogging. The questionnaire includes the semantic differential scale from Figure 7.1 (p. 98) as an attitude measure and two other questions: (a) How many days do you intend to go jogging for exercise next week? (a measure of behavioral intention) and (b) How many days did you go jogging for exercise last week? (a measure of behavior).

In 1979 the class gathered responses from 68 people. Overall, the attitudes were quite positive, averaging 29.8 on a scale with a possible range of 5 to 35. Behavior was less positive, as the average number of days actually jogged was 1.6. The main purpose of the assignment was to examine the relationship between attitudes and behavior. The moderate correlation between the semantic differential attitude score and the behavioral measure of number of days jogged ($r = .44$) indicated that attitude could predict behavior.

As Fishbein's model proposes, the correlation between attitude and behavioral intention ($r = .52$) was even higher, and the correlation between behavioral intention and actual behavior was very high ($r = .81$). I have used this exercise with several classes over several years, and the results have been consistent. Invariably the correlations between attitude and behavior or attitude and behavioral intention are in the moderate range (.35 to .55), with the attitude/behavioral intention correlation slightly higher than the attitude/behavior correlation. The relationship between behavioral intention and behavior has always been over .75.

This class exercise is riddled with poor controls and methodological weaknesses, but a more typical and more methodologically sound study reports the same relationships. Riddle (1980) applied Fishbein's model to examine the attitudes, behavioral intentions, and jogging behaviors of men and women.

Riddle reported a strong relationship ($r = .82$) between behavioral intention and jogging behavior and noted that a combination of attitudes toward jogging and normative beliefs was a good predictor of the behavioral intention (multiple $R = .74$). Riddle concluded that to increase participation in exercise programs we should focus on convincing nonexercisers of the positive effects and refuting their negative beliefs about exercise. Indeed, Fishbein's model and related research do indicate that attitudes toward specific behaviors, such as the attitude toward participation in an aerobic exercise program, can predict behavior. The prediction is stronger if we also consider situational factors, such as the attitudes of family and friends and characteristics of the exercise setting. Thus developing positive attitudes toward exercise activities may increase subsequent participation. However, if we want to predict participation in a specific program, such as a new company fitness program, we should ask employees directly if they *intend* to participate.

# Attitude Change

Riddle's conclusions about changing attitudes and beliefs to increase exercise behavior brings us to a prominent topic for students of attitude research: theories and strategies of attitude change. Most texts on attitudes discuss several theories of attitude change and cite numerous investigations, but here we will consider only two of the most prominent approaches, including the persuasive communication work of Hovland, Janis, and Kelley (1953) and Festinger's (1957) cognitive dissonance theory.

## Persuasive Communication

Hovland and his colleagues at the Yale Communication and Attitude Change Program focused on using *persuasive communication* to change beliefs and attitudes. Any communication is effective only if people attend to, comprehend, accept, and retain it. Most of the research in the Yale program examined various characteristics of the source, communication message, and audience that affect the attention, comprehension, acceptance, and retention processes.

Two major characteristics of the source that influence the effectiveness of a communication are the communicator's expertise and trustworthiness. We are more likely to be persuaded if we believe the speaker has knowledge and does not have ulterior motives. Other characteristics of the source, such as attractiveness and similarity, also may be important in some cases.

Researchers have also examined various characteristics of the message itself, including the order in which arguments are presented (should you make your strongest point first or last?), one-sided versus two-sided arguments (should you refute the opposing arguments or present only your side?), and emotional versus logical appeals. The effectiveness of different types of messages varies a great deal. For example, two-sided arguments seem more effective if the audience already knows both sides of the issue, but one-sided arguments may be more persuasive if the audience already favors your view. Similarly, the effectiveness of presenting your strongest arguments first or last depends on the time between the arguments and the length of time from the last argument until some action is taken. If the action is to be taken immediately, as in a vote to continue a noon fitness program, you should present your strongest arguments last, just before the vote.

Intelligence, self-esteem, and various other social and personality character-istics of the audience have also been studied in the persuasive communication work. Often such characteristics have opposing effects. For example, highly intelligent people may comprehend and retain a message better than less intel-ligent people, but they may be less likely to accept that message. Nisbett and Gordon (1967) assessed self-esteem prior to reading statements about health to students. In some instances the health facts were simple and easily compre-hended but unsubstantiated. In other cases extensive documentation was ad-ded. When the message was simple, people with moderate self-esteem showed the most attitude change, but when the message was complex, people with high self-esteem displayed the most attitude change.

Readers who want more information on the extensive research on persua-sive communication should consult Hovland et al.'s original work and more recent texts on attitudes and persuasion. Persuasive communication research has seldom been put into practice or investigated in the sport area, but persons involved in media campaigns to promote sport and exercise programs or indi-viduals trying to convince others to adopt a program would do well to consult that literature.

## Cognitive Dissonance Theory

Festinger's (1957) *cognitive dissonance* theory has generated more research and discussion than any other theory related to attitudes or attitude change. The basic premise of cognitive dissonance theory is that people like to be consistent in their thoughts, opinions, attitudes, and behaviors. If two cognitive elements conflict, dissonance is created and people are motivated to reduce the dissonance. If you believe everyone should engage in aerobic exercise at least three times a week, but you do not intend to exercise this week, you have dissonance. You might reduce the dissonance in several ways. For one thing, you could change one of the cognitive elements to make the two more consistent. Perhaps you could decide that everyone should engage in aero-bic exercise, but only *if* they have extra time. Another tactic is to reduce the importance of one of the cognitive elements. You might decide that regular exercise is fine but that it's not really very important for a young, healthy person like yourself. A third strategy is to add more consistent cognitions. For example, you might seek out evidence of the negative effects of exercise, tell yourself that running causes muscle and joint injuries, and note that exercise equipment is too expensive for your budget.

According to Festinger, if you want to change attitudes and behavior, you need to create dissonance so that people will be motivated to reduce the dissonance by taking the actions you want them to take. I once knew an elementary physical education teacher who used cognitive dissonance to convince the boys in class that jumping rope was a worthwhile, athletic activity. The boys considered jumping rope an unathletic, "girl's" activity. The teacher made statements such as the following: "Do you know who the best rope jumpers in the world are? Boxers." "The high school wrestling and basketball teams jump rope every day as part of their practices." "Jumping rope is one of the toughest and best training exercises you can do." Because the boys held positive attitudes toward athletic training, the teacher's statements and their negative attitude toward jumping rope created dissonance. The boys quickly reduced the dissonance by becoming enthusiastic rope jumpers.

In one of the few sport attitude studies based on a theoretical model, Al-Talib (1970) applied cognitive dissonance theory to the sport area. Al-Talib had students play a role that was either consistent or inconsistent with their attitudes toward physical education. As cognitive dissonance theory proposes, playing a role that was inconsistent with the students' attitudes yielded attitude change in accordance with the role. Students who held positive attitudes and role-played a negative role changed to less positive attitudes, whereas students who held less positive attitudes and played a positive role changed to even more positive attitudes.

Convincing people to accept beliefs or take actions is not easy. People are quite resistant to ideas that threaten their beliefs. We sometimes reduce dissonance by refusing to accept contradictory information, and we may distort information and perceptions to maintain our beliefs. Fans of intercollegiate and professional athletic teams are quite adept at distorting information so that they can always see their team in a positive light. Hastorf and Cantril (1954) demonstrated this distortion in a provocative study of a 1951 Princeton-Dartmouth football game, the last game of the season. At that time Princeton was undefeated and had a star player, All-American Dick Kazmaier. The game became quite rough, many penalties were called, several players were injured, Kazmaier left the game with a broken nose, and the media featured numerous accusations as well as reports of fights and injuries. Hastorf and Cantril noticed that the interpretations of the game differed at the two schools. Princeton reports favored Princeton, as shown in the following quote from the Princeton student newspaper:

> This observer has never seen quite such a disgusting exhibition of so-called "sport." Both teams were guilty but the blame must be laid primarily on Dartmouth's doorstep. Princeton, obviously the better team, had no reason

to rough up Dartmouth. Looking at the situation rationally, we don't see why the Indians should make a deliberate attempt to cripple Dick Kazmaier or any other Princeton player. The Dartmouth psychology, however, is not rational itself. (Hastorf & Cantril, 1954, p. 130)

Conversely, Dartmouth reports blamed Princeton for all the trouble:

After this incident [Kazmaier's injury], Caldwell instilled the old see-what-they-did-go-get-them attitude into his players. His talk got results. Gene Howard and Jim Miller were both injured. Both had dropped back to pass, had passed, and were standing unprotected in the backfield. Result: one bad leg and one leg broken. The game was rough and did get a bit out of hand in the third quarter. Yet most of the roughing penalties were called against Princeton while Dartmouth received more of the illegal-use-of-hands variety. (Hastorf & Cantril, 1954, p. 130)

Hastorf and Cantril went beyond the surface observations to investigate the actual perceptions of students at the two schools. They visited each school and presented a film of the game. Students, who were typical students and not necessarily football fans, were instructed to be objective as they viewed the film, record any rule infractions that they saw, and indicate which team started the rough play. As expected, students at each school saw more infractions by the other team than by their own team, and responses to the question about who started the rough play revealed a tendency to see one's fellow students as victims rather than perpetrators.

# Sport Attitude Research

As noted at the beginning of this chapter, the bulk of the sport attitude research consists of descriptive studies of various samples' attitudes toward various aspects of sport such as physical education, physical activity in general, women's participation in sport, and competition for children.

## Attitudes Toward Sport

Keogh (1962) reported that students endorsed the social, physical, and emotional values of physical education but not the value of physical education in the school curriculum. This finding prompted Martens (1975) to suggest that perhaps students "like our product, but don't like the way it's packaged" (p. 195). Scott (1953) found that parents, teachers, and administrators all held positive attitudes toward competition for elementary children, and Harres (1968) found generally positive attitudes toward intense competition for women. Selby and Lewko (1976) examined the attitudes toward females in sport of boys and girls who were participants or nonparticipants in a community sport program. As expected, girls held more positive attitudes than boys held. Contrary to expectations, sport participants did not hold more positive attitudes than nonparticipants. Girls who participated in sport held more positive attitudes than girls who did not participate, but nonparticipant boys held more positive attitudes than boys who participated.

Recently, the Miller Brewing Company published the *Miller Lite Report on American Attitudes Toward Sports* (1983), one of the most comprehensive reports of its kind. Overall, the report revealed that sport is pervasive in American society; the majority of respondents were interested in sport and participated at least once a week. The vast majority held positive attitudes toward children's sport participation, but 86% of the parents agreed that children's sports programs place too much emphasis on winning and too little on physical and psychological development. Participants were achievement-oriented; most reported that they always try their best to win, and about half often set high personal goals. However, a surprising 63% of all participants said that at least sometimes they do not really care whether they win or lose. Athletes and nonathletes as well as males and females held similar attitudes, and parents were equally positive toward sport participation for their daughters as for their sons. More males than females were "avid" sport fans, but respondents generally held egalitarian attitudes toward participation. Gender differences appeared to be on the decline.

Those studies are representative of the sport attitude research. The findings vary somewhat with the sample and the measurement technique, but positive attitudes toward sport and physical activity are reported consistently. The research seldom goes beyond that descriptive level to apply more promising theories of attitude change and behavior to relevant sport issues, and many of the descriptive findings are outdated. As with the sport personality literature, although the plethora of research conducted to date has yielded little knowledge, many important questions remain to be researched about the formation and modification of specific attitudes and the relationship of those attitudes to specific behaviors.

One of the most important advances in sport attitude research was Kenyon's (1968a, 1968b) development of an inventory to assess attitudes toward physical activity based on a conceptual model of physical activity as a multidimensional phenomenon. Six dimensions of physical activity were identified, including physical activity as a social experience, as health and fitness, as the pursuit of vertigo (excitement), as an aesthetic experience, as catharsis (relaxation), and as an ascetic experience (physical challenge). With further research, Kenyon developed a set of semantic scales to assess attitudes toward physical activity on each of these six dimensions.

Simon and Smoll (1974) modified the wording of Kenyon's inventory to develop a measure to assess children's attitudes toward physical activity with reliability and validity similar to that of the Kenyon inventory. Both Kenyon's inventory and Simon and Smoll's children's inventory have been used to assess attitudes toward physical activity and the relationship of attitudes to various other factors (e.g., Alderman, 1970; Schutz, Smoll, & Wood, 1981; Smoll & Schutz, 1980; Smoll, Schutz, & Keeney, 1976; Straub & Felock, 1974). In one of the few longitudinal investigations, Smoll and Schutz (1980) used the children's inventory to assess the attitudes of boys and girls in Grades 4, 5, and 6. The general results confirmed earlier findings; girls were more positive than boys were on the aesthetic scale, and boys were more positive than girls were on the vertigo and catharsis scales. These overall gender differences were maintained over time, but individual scores were not stable over time, suggesting that the inventory does not assess an enduring behavioral disposition. Instead, the attitudes of individual children changed a great deal over time. If attitudes themselves are not stable over time, we could not expect consistent predictions of sport behavior based upon those attitudes.

Another attitude measure worthy of note is Sonstroem's (1978) *Physical Estimation and Attraction Scales* (PEAS). Sonstroem's scales assess both attitude toward sport and exercise behavior and perceived sport and exercise abilities. Psychometric testing indicates that the PEAS is reliable and valid, and, more importantly, the PEAS has effectively predicted actual sport participation (Sonstroem, 1978; Sonstroem & Kampper, 1980).

The Kenyon and Sonstroem scales have seldom been used to examine attitudes and behaviors within a theoretical framework. In fact, sport attitude research has been virtually nonexistent over the past 10 years. However, sport psychologists are actively investigating closely related issues within the areas of attribution theory, cognitions, expectations, and behavior. Some of that work is discussed in chapter 10. Next we will consider one cognitive issue that may have relevance for sport attitude research—the issue of stereotyped expectations and behavior.

## Stereotypes in Sport

Considerable research indicates that expectations affect behavior; we tend to see the behaviors that we expect to see. The effects of expectancy apply to both our own expectations and the expectations that others have of us. I am more likely to perform well in an upcoming gymnastics routine if I expect to do well than if I expect to have problems. The literature, most notably Rosenthal and Jacobson's (1968) research on teacher expectations, also suggests that the expectations of teachers and coaches tend to be fulfilled. If a coach expects certain team members to become stars, those players may well develop into better athletes than similarly skilled players in whom the coach sees less potential. Such expectancy effects have implications for sport attitude research because our attitudes, and particularly the stereotypes we hold about certain groups of sport participants, may influence our expectations. For example, if an elementary physical education teacher believes that boys are poor at balance and that strength moves are unsuitable for girls, that teacher may interact differently with boys than with girls in a gymnastics unit and encourage different behaviors. The teacher might give the boys more time and specific instruction on the still rings and encourage the girls to do flexibility exercises and practice intricate moves on the balance beam.

General psychology research confirms the existence of stereotyped expectations for achievement behaviors of males and females, and some research reveals stereotyped expectations specific to sport and exercise. Brawley, Landers, Miller, and Kearns (1979) had both male and female observers rate the performance of a male and a female performing a muscular endurance task. Both male and female observers rated the male performer higher than the female performer even though their performances were identical. In a subsequent study, Brawley, Powers, and Phillips (1980) failed to find similar biases with an accuracy task, implying that stereotyped expectations may be task-specific.

Gender is a very salient and universal category. We immediately recognize an individual as being female or male, and that categorization affects our attitudes and behaviors toward that individual. Gender stereotypes exist in sport and exercise as they exist in the larger society. Recent reviews indicate a trend toward less gender bias. Deaux (1985) notes that research with the *Attitudes Toward Women Scale* (Spence & Helmreich, 1972) documents a shift toward more egalitarian attitudes and away from beliefs in traditional roles for women and men. The *Miller Lite Report* reveals a parallel trend for sport. Generally, males and females hold similar attitudes, parents are equally positive toward the sport participation of daughters and sons, and the trend is toward increasingly egalitarian attitudes toward female and male sport participation.

Gender stereotypes persist, however, and we should keep that in mind as we consider the psychological aspects of sport and exercise behavior. Furthermore, Deaux (Deaux, 1984; Deaux & Lewis, 1984) proposes that the influence of gender stereotypes is more complex than the attribution of personality characteristics to males and females. Deaux advocates a multidimensional conception of gender stereotypes that considers the interactive relationships of various characteristics and the processes through which gender information is presented and acted upon. For example, gender stereotypes may have a stronger influence on an individual's decision to participate in a sport activity than on the individual's behavior within that activity. Eccles' work, which we discussed in chapter 6, revealed such gender differences for academic choices. Once individuals have selected a given activity, gender differences usually diminish and gender stereotypes may operate differently.

Ostrow and colleagues (Ostrow, 1981; Ostrow, Jones, & Spiker, 1981) observed both sex and age biases when individuals were asked to rate the appropriateness of various sport activities for females and males of various ages. Furthermore, the age bias was much stronger than the sex bias. Stereotypes about the appropriate activities and expected performance levels for specific sex and age groups have tremendous implications for the administration of sport programs and whether certain programs will even be offered.

We discussed the effects of gender roles and stereotypes here and in chapter 6. As the number of older adults in the population and concern for the health and fitness of older persons continue to increase, we should also consider the psychological aspects of our attitudes and biases toward activities for various age groups.

Other attitudes may have equally important implications for sport expectations and behaviors. Very little research has been conducted on attitudes toward ethnic minorities or how such attitudes might affect interpersonal and performance behaviors in sport. Provision of sport and exercise activities for individuals with physical and mental disabilities is a prominent professional area within sport and physical education, yet very little research deals with sport issues related to those populations. The attitudes and expectations that instructors and program administrators hold for various groups of disabled individuals and the relationship of such attitudes to specific behaviors and interactions could be a productive research area. Such research could provide practical suggestions, and the investigation of specific attitudes and behaviors within a theoretical framework could also advance our understanding of attitude change and the attitude/behavior relationship within sport. The same statement could be made about sport attitude research in general. Research that addresses relevant questions about specific attitudes and behaviors in sport, conducted within a conceptual framework, may provide information of both practical and theoretical value.

## *Summary*

Attitudes are individual difference characteristics, and, like other personality characteristics, attitudes can influence sport and exercise behaviors. As with the sport personality literature, however, sport attitude research usually involves global attitudes toward sport and physical activity and seldom considers the relationship of specific attitudes to sport behaviors. Assessment of attitudes toward specific sport and exercise behaviors and the consideration of those specific attitudes along with relevant social situational factors, as in Fishbein's model, can provide more insight into sport behavior. As we emphasized in the earlier chapter on personality characteristics, consideration of the interactive effects of specific, relevant attitudes and characteristics, along with relevant situational factors, can best advance our understanding of human behavior in sport.

# PART III

# *Motivation in Sport*

In part III we will examine the sport psychology research on motivation, one of the most basic constructs in psychology. Specifically, information on the two components of motivation, intensity and direction of behavior, is presented in part III. We typically refer to the intensity dimension of behavior as *arousal*. As you will discover in chapter 8, the relationship between arousal and performance is complex. Some arousal benefits sport performers, but overarousal creates problems. Thus chapter 8 also contains a review of the expanding literature on anxiety management skills for sport participants.

Chapters 9 and 10 contain discussions of the second component of motivation, *direction*. Behavioral approaches to directing behavior, particularly reinforcement strategies, are covered in chapter 9, and the diverse literature on cognitive approaches to directing behavior is examined in chapter 10. The relationship of extrinsic rewards to intrinsic motivation, expectations and self-confidence, and the influence of attributions on sport behavior are also included in chapter 10. Although these topics may appear to be diverse and unrelated, they all share an emphasis on cognitive perceptions and interpretations as keys to understanding behavior. Overall, the sport psychology literature on motivation is reviewed in part III to help you understand how we might control arousal and use behavioral and cognitive approaches to direct the behaviors of ourselves and others.

# CHAPTER 8

# *Arousal and Sport Performance*

Motivation is a key construct in psychology, perhaps the most fundamental construct in psychology. Essentially, motivation is *why* people do what they do. As teachers, coaches, and leaders of sport and exercise programs, we are concerned with motivating participants so that they can achieve performance standards and have satisfying and successful experiences. As participants, we want to maintain self-motivation so that we can do our best, achieve desired benefits, and enjoy our activities.

Motivation has two components: *intensity* of behavior and *direction* of behavior. *Arousal*, the general term for the intensity dimension of behavior, is discussed in this chapter. In the following two chapters we will consider behavioral and cognitive approaches to the second component, directing behavior.

## *The Arousal Construct*

Arousal may be defined as the intensity dimension of behavior, the general state of activation or excitation that ranges on a continuum from deep sleep to extreme excitement. Arousal, per se, is neither positive nor negative; arousal increases when we are looking forward to an exciting event as well as when we are in a threatening situation or worried about mistakes.

We all recognize the physiological symptoms of increased arousal. Hans Selye (1956), a noted authority on stress and its effects, refers to the bodily reactions to stress as the *General Adaptation Syndrome* (GAS). The GAS, the physiological or somatic component of arousal, is the "fight-or-flight" response of the autonomic nervous system that we all experience in stressful situations. You know you are anxious when your breathing quickens, your heart pounds, your hands sweat, your stomach feels queasy, your face feels flushed, your knees turn to jelly, and your mouth tastes like cotton.

Increased arousal implies psychological or cognitive reactions as well as physiological responses. A softball player experiencing the physiological symptoms of arousal may also think about the mistakes made last game, worry about everyone watching, and be aware of feeling anxious. Thus arousal is a multidimensional state with both a physiological or somatic component and a psychological or cognitive component.

In sport, the cognitive component of arousal typically involves worrying about performance evaluation or possible failure. Much sport activity involves competition, and, as we noted in chapter 5, competition always involves performance evaluation. In fact, even the calmest sport settings are likely to create some arousal and worry. A child in an elementary physical education class wants to please the teacher and does not want to be the "slowpoke" through an obstacle course, an adult in a noon fitness program does not want to appear out of shape in front of colleagues, and an intercollegiate athlete strives to perform well and avoid errors. In sport, then, individuals typically experience a combination of physiological arousal and cognitive worry, which is state anxiety as defined in chapter 5. Throughout this chapter we will use the terms *arousal* and *anxiety* interchangeably when referring to the typical increased arousal state in sports.

## Arousal Measures

Because arousal is manifested in varied ways, it can be measured in varied ways. Common physiological measures of arousal include heart rate, respiration rate, blood pressure, and galvanic skin response. Behavioral observations are sometimes used, but the most common nonphysiological measures are self-report measures or questionnaires, such as the state anxiety inventory of the *State-Trait Anxiety Inventory* (Spielberger, Gorsuch, & Lushene, 1970) and Thayer's (1967) *Activation-Deactivation Checklist.*

Although arousal can be measured in a variety of ways, researchers find that the measures are not highly related to each other. Physiological measures correlate poorly with self-report measures, and physiological measures in fact often correlate poorly with each other. Individuals apparently have idiosyncratic arousal responses; that is, different people show arousal in different ways. For example, when I am anxious, my face flushes and my muscles tighten up, but my hands do not get sweaty. Another person might become nauseous when anxious but not notice any changes in heart beat or breathing. Yet another person might feel very anxious and worried but show no dramatic increases on any physiological measure. As we discussed in chapter 5, intense competition tends to create at least some anxiety in everyone, but not everyone shows increased anxiety in the same way. Some individuals worry a lot, get distracted, and have trouble concentrating, whereas others experience more problems with muscle tension and coordination.

The recognition of differing anxiety responses has prompted the use of multidimensional anxiety measures. Because anxiety is multidimensional and because individuals manifest anxiety in different ways, a multidimensional approach to anxiety measurement that uses both physiological and psychological measures presents a more complete picture of individual anxiety states and also provides more insight into the nature of anxiety in sport.

If physiological measures are impractical, some recently developed self-report anxiety scales are able to assess physiological (somatic) anxiety and cognitive worry on separate dimensions. The *Worry-Emotionality Inventory* (Liebert & Morris, 1967; Morris, Davis, & Hutchings, 1981), a state anxiety scale, and the *Cognitive-Somatic Anxiety Questionnaire* (Schwartz, Davidson, & Goleman, 1978), a trait anxiety scale, both assess cognitive and somatic anxiety on separate dimensions. Recently, Martens and his colleagues (Martens, Burton, Vealey, Bump, & Smith, 1983) have built upon that work to develop a multidimensional measure of competitive state anxiety unique to sport known as the *Competitive State Anxiety Inventory-2* (CSAI-2). The CSAI-2 assesses cognitive worry and somatic anxiety on separate dimensions and also includes a third dimension, self-confidence. The initial psychometric testing of the CSAI-2 supports the reliability and validity of the scales and further reveals that cognitive worry and somatic anxiety do not follow the same pattern of changes over time. Studies with gymnasts, wrestlers, and golfers suggest that somatic anxiety increases rapidly immediately before competition and decreases during competition. Cognitive worry, on the other hand, does not typically show such a rapid rise prior to competition and may increase during competitive performance. The CSAI-2 should be a valuable tool for examining individual differences in anxiety patterns in sport settings and for investigating the relationship between such patterns and sport behavior.

# Theories Concerning the Arousal/Performance Relationship in Sport

The relationship of arousal to performance is a prominent issue in sport psychology research and practice. We often act as though we assume that arousal affects sport performance. Typical pregame rituals and pep talks aim to increase arousal or get players "psyched-up" for competition. Obviously coaches and others who use psych-up strategies believe that such tactics enhance performance. Are they correct? Does increased arousal improve sport performance? Most of us can recall instances in which a pep talk seemed to help or when an athlete responded to the "big game" with the best performance of the season. The Olympic Games provide a striking example of a situation with high arousal that seems to bring out top performances. For most Olympic athletes, the games are the chance of a lifetime to test their skills with the whole world watching. The pressure and excitement of the games seems to elicit record-breaking performances and personal bests more often than less prominent events.

This is only part of the picture, however. You can probably think of other times when sport performers have "choked" under pressure and performed poorly when overaroused. I once coached a team of seventh-grade girls who, although they would not challenge an NBA team, demonstrated modest basketball skills in intramural games. When faced with competition against a team of seventh graders from another school, those same players completely missed the basket on shots, dribbled off their feet, threw passes into the bleachers, and played with such poor control that they went the entire game without scoring a basket. As a novice teacher I found the obvious overarousal and clear deterioration of skilled performance amazing. Clearly, a "win one for the gipper" speech or similar psych-up tactic would have made the situation even worse for my basketball players.

Coaches who continue to hold the image of a stirring Knute Rockne pep talk as the key to mental preparation may be surprised to learn what Rockne actually said about such tactics. Coleman Griffith, the early sport psychologist we discussed in chapter 2 and a contemporary of Rockne, heard that Rockne did not "key up" the Notre Dame team but instead focused on playing the game "joyously." On December 9, 1924, Griffith wrote to Rockne to ask about his motivational tactics. On December 13, 1924, Rockne replied as follows:*

Dear Mr. Griffith:

I feel very grateful to you for having written me, although I do not know a great deal about psychology.

I do try to pick men who like the game of football and who get a lot of fun out of playing. I never try to make football hard work. I do think our team plays good football because they like to play and I do not make any effort to key them up, except on rare, exceptional occasions. I keyed them up for the Nebraska game this year, which was a mistake, as we had a reaction the following Saturday against Northwestern. I try to make our boys take the game less seriously than, I presume, some others do, and we try to make the spirit of the game one of exhilaration and we never allow hatred to enter into it, no matter against whom we are playing.

Thanking you for your kindness, I am

Yours cordially,

Knute Rockne

Many strange things have been done in the name of psyching-up athletes despite the fact that such tactics often psych them out. As Rockne recognized, sport performers can be *too* keyed up, and psych-up tactics may be counterproductive. As we noted earlier, however, situations and strategies that increase arousal sometimes do improve performance. It is clear that increases in arousal do not *always* help or *always* hinder sport performance. To understand the

---

*Note. From the Coleman Griffith Collection, University Archives, University of Illinois at Urbana-Champaign.

arousal/performance relationship, we must consider how arousal affects motor performance under varying conditions. The influence of arousal on performance has been an issue in psychology for some time, and two major theories have been developed to explain the arousal/performance relationship: drive theory and the inverted-U or optimal level theory.

## Drive Theory

*Drive theory* is one of the most influential theories of motivation in psychology and has played an important role in sport psychology, particularly as an explanation for the effects of an audience on motor performance (see chapter 11). As developed by Hull (1943) and modified by Spence (1956), drive theory is a complex, empirically based, mechanistic explanation of motivation and behavior. For our purposes, however, we will consider a simple version of drive theory.

According to drive theory, the basic relationship between arousal and performance is expressed as

$$P = f (H \times D)$$

Performance (P) is a function of habit (H) times drive (D). Within the Hull-Spence model, *drive* is essentially the same as arousal, a nondifferentiated energizer, or, as defined at the beginning of the chapter, the intensity dimension of behavior. The other main component of drive theory, *habit*, refers to learned responses or behaviors. The more a particular response has been reinforced, the greater the habit strength, and the more likely that response will occur.

Essentially, then, drive theory proposes that as arousal or drive increases (as in intense competition), learned behaviors are more likely to occur. This statement might suggest that any increase in arousal always improves performance. Indeed, the basic arousal/performance relationship is linear; as arousal increases, performance increases (see Figure 8.1). Performance predictions within drive theory, however, are complex. Overall sport or task performance does not necessarily increase as arousal increases. Instead, the performance of the individual's strongest, most dominant response increases. Performance improves *only* if the individual's strongest and most likely response is correct performance. Until an individual becomes proficient at a sport skill, the dominant response is probably not the correct performance. When learning complex sport skills, we are more likely to make mistakes than we are to do everything right.

On a golf swing, for example, many incorrect responses are possible. To perform the swing correctly, one must have the body properly aligned; shift one's weight correctly; keep the body and club in proper alignment throughout the swing; and make the backswing, forward swing, and follow-through

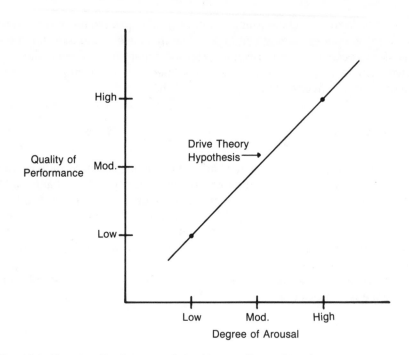

**Figure 8.1** The arousal/performance relationship according to drive theory.

with the correct length, in the correct plane, and at the optimal speed. Unless I am an accomplished golfer with a "grooved" swing, my dominant response is probably not a correct, effective swing. As arousal increases, perhaps in a club match, I am likely to revert to my dominant, error-ridden swing movement even more than usual; perhaps I will swing too fast or swing out too much and slice even more than usual.

A professional golfer, on the other hand, has probably performed each golf shot so often that the correct swing has become the dominant response. We often speak about "grooving" the swing or having a skill learned so well that it becomes automatic. Such comments indicate that the correct response is dominant. When that is the case, as with the pro golfer, increased arousal should improve performance. Thus we can summarize drive theory predictions for sport and motor skills as follows:

- Increased arousal or drive increases the likelihood that the *dominant* response will occur.
- If a skill is relatively simple, or if a skill is very well learned, the dominant response is the correct response, and increased arousal will improve performance.

- If a skill is complex (as most sport skills are) and not well learned, the dominant response is an incorrect response, and increased arousal will impair performance.

The above principles may explain why my seventh graders, who did not have well learned skills, fell apart in competition and why an NBA team might give their best performance of the year in a close, intense play-off game.

## *The Inverted-U Theory*

An alternative explanation of the arousal/performance relationship, and the theory currently favored by most sport psychologists, is the *inverted-U theory*. The inverted-U theory, illustrated in Figure 8.2, proposes that performance is optimal at a moderate level of arousal, and that performance progressively declines as arousal increases or decreases from a moderate level. The inverted-U model makes sense and fits with many of our observations and experiences. Individuals need some arousal to perform at their best; athletes who are too mellow or apathetic give subpar performances. With too much arousal, however, sport performers may be overanxious, tense, and prone to errors.

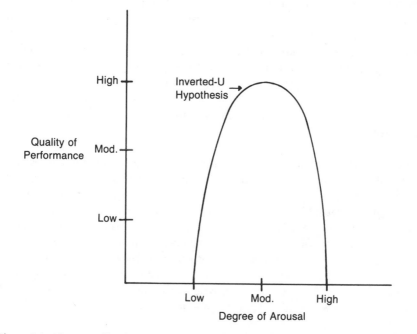

**Figure 8.2** The arousal/performance relationship according to the inverted-U hypothesis.

Although the inverted-U theory makes intuitive sense, controlled tests of the proposed curvilinear relationship are difficult to conduct, and empirical support for the theory is limited. The original inverted-U research of Yerkes and Dodson (1908) involved mice learning a choice discrimination task under weak, moderate, and strong arousal with shock used to manipulate arousal. They found learning to be best under moderate stimulus levels and demonstrated the inverted-U phenomenon, which is sometimes referred to as the *Yerkes-Dodson law.*

Martens and Landers (1970) tested the inverted-U theory in a motor performance situation. Junior high school males performed a tracking task in a controlled experimental setting under low, moderate, or high stress conditions. The stress levels were manipulated by varying the emphasis on performance scores from a relaxed, low-stress setting in which no emphasis was placed on scores to an elaborate, high-stress condition with the researchers dressed in lab coats, subjects hooked up to a bogus shock machine with threatening labels, and instructions indicating that low scores would result in shocks. Additionally, the experimenters inquired about the subject's health and conversed about the dangers of shock in the high-stress condition. The three stress conditions yielded three levels of arousal, as confirmed with both physiological and self-report measures, and performance scores formed an inverted-U pattern with the best performance scores in the moderate stress condition.

More recently, Sonstroem and Bernardo (1982) confirmed the inverted-U theory in a field study with female university basketball players. By comparing each athlete's lowest, median, and highest pregame state anxiety scores with the athlete's composite performance scores for those three games, they found an inverted-U relationship. The best performances were associated with moderate state anxiety levels, and high state anxiety scores were associated with the poorest performances. Furthermore, the inverted-U trend and decreased performance at high state anxiety levels were most pronounced for highly competitive trait anxious athletes (as measured and classified using the SCAT discussed in chapter 5).

**Individual Variations in Inverted-U Patterns.**   Sonstroem and Bernardo's finding that the inverted-U was more pronounced for highly competitive trait anxious athletes illustrates individual differences in optimal arousal levels. The optimal arousal level, the level that yields the best performance, varies from person to person. The highly competitive anxious athlete likely has a lower optimal arousal level than a low competitive anxious athlete has in any competitive situation. Given the same situation, perhaps an intrasquad tennis match to determine rankings for the team, one player might be below optimal arousal and need to psych-up a bit, whereas another player might be overaroused and need to calm down to play in top form.

**Task Differences in Optimal Arousal Levels.**   In addition to individuals differing in optimal arousal levels, optimal levels may differ for different tasks and skills. For example, putting in golf has a low optimal arousal level; golfers perform best with low arousal, and even slight increases may disrupt their concentration and performance. In contrast, weight lifting has a higher optimal arousal level; weight lifters may need more arousal than golfers to perform at their best. Oxendine (1970) offered the following guidelines for determining the optimal arousal levels of various sport tasks:

- A high level of arousal is essential for optimal performance in gross motor activities involving strength, endurance, and speed.

- A high level of arousal interferes with performances involving complex skills, fine muscle movements, coordination, steadiness, and general concentration.

- A slightly above average level of arousal is preferable to a normal or subnormal arousal state for all motor tasks. (p.25)

As Landers (1978) notes, Oxendine's guidelines may have some practical value, but the first and third statements in particular may be questioned on the basis of existing research. No existing research documents that above average arousal yields top performance on any sport or motor task. Most sport tasks that involve speed or strength also involve focusing attention or coordination; for example, a sprinter must get out of the blocks efficiently and avoid distraction throughout the race. Thus sport tasks are not classified as easily as Oxendine's guidelines imply. More precise descriptions of sport tasks might permit better prediction of optimal arousal levels. At present, we can conclude that sport performance is optimal at a moderate arousal level, and we can qualify that relationship by noting that optimal arousal levels vary across tasks and among individuals. Because we cannot predict precise optimal arousal levels for each performer and each task, we might direct our efforts at helping performers recognize and control *their own* arousal levels so that *they* can achieve their own individual optimal states in varying situations. Indeed, some research suggests that the ability to control arousal is the key to successful sport performance.

## Arousal Patterns and Sport Performance

A series of innovative studies by Fenz (1975) examining arousal patterns of parachute jumpers has added further insight into the arousal/performance relationship in sport. Rather than simply taking one measure of arousal, Fenz recorded arousal changes and patterns over time. In his research Fenz has used varied designs and varied arousal measures, including both physiological and self-report measures, but the findings are consistent. Good performers and experienced jumpers do not differ from poorly skilled or novice jumpers in absolute arousal levels, but they do differ in arousal *patterns*. That difference in arousal patterns is illustrated in Figure 8.3.

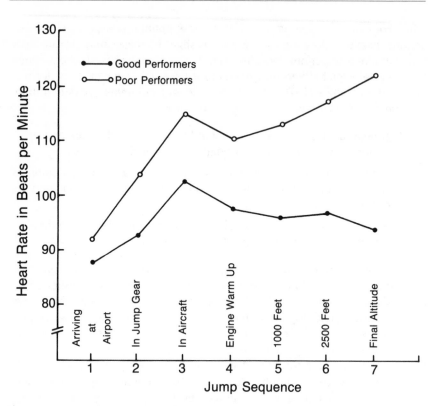

**Figure 8.3** Continuous recordings of heart rate during a jump sequence of good and poor performing parachutists. *Note.* From "Cardiac Conditioning in a Reaction Time Task and Heart Rate Control During Real Life Stress" by W.D. Fenz and G.B. Jones, 1974, *Journal of Psychosomatic Research, 18,* p. 201. Copyright 1974 by Pergamon Press, Ltd. Reprinted by permission.

As shown in Figure 8.3, the arousal of poor performers, as measured by heart rate, continually increases from arrival at the airport and reaches its highest level right at the time of the jump. Good performers increase in arousal at first but peak earlier and gradually decrease in arousal so that they are experiencing *moderate,* near normal levels of arousal at the time of the jump. Fenz has confirmed these differences in arousal patterns between good and poor jumpers across several studies using various measures and procedures.

Fenz's work suggests that the difference between better and poorer performers is not a difference in absolute level of arousal. Good performers do *not* eliminate arousal; they do become anxious, sometimes even more than poorer performers. Instead, the difference appears to be in their ability to *control* arousal. Good performers seem to bring arousal under control so that they are experiencing moderate levels of arousal at the time of performance.

Additional studies suggest that the control of arousal can be disrupted even in experienced, skilled performers. Fenz (1975) reported that one experienced jumper, who demonstrated the controlled pattern of decreased arousal at the time of performance, broke an ankle during a jump. Upon returning to the sport, this jumper reverted to the novice's pattern of continual increases in arousal up to the jump. An examination of the arousal patterns of athletes in other sports returning to competition after absences due to injuries might reveal similar patterns.

Fenz also set up an experiment to see if the arousal patterns of an experienced jumper could be altered by an unusual, threatening situation. After three control jumps, the jumper was told that his chute could malfunction during any one of the next ten experimental jumps. Although the jumper had an emergency chute and was aware of emergency procedures, the threat of malfunction was certainly an extra source of anxiety. Records revealed that the arousal patterns for those ten jumps were similar to the arousal patterns of novices, with continual increases to a peak at the time of the jump.

Perhaps the most encouraging aspect of Fenz's work is a training study in which he attempted to teach arousal control techniques to novice jumpers so that they could exhibit the arousal patterns of experienced jumpers. A comparison of the experimental training group to a control group revealed that the experimental group did indeed demonstrate the controlled arousal pattern of the experienced jumpers even in their first jumps. Although specific performance measures were not taken, Fenz noted that the experimental jumpers had more fun during their training, and several progressed to become experienced skydivers. These initial findings suggest that arousal control training may benefit even novice athletes, but considerable research is needed to determine the effects of varied training programs.

A study of the psychological characteristics and responses of Olympic gymnasts (Mahoney & Avener, 1977) suggests that other athletes share the arousal patterns that Fenz observed in parachute jumpers. Mahoney and Avener compared gymnasts who qualified for the 1976 Olympic team to gymnasts who reached the trials but did not qualify for the team. Retrospective reports of perceived anxiety at various times before and during performance revealed that the qualifiers' anxiety levels were as high or higher than the nonqualifiers' anxiety levels prior to performance, but qualifiers reported lower anxiety than nonqualifiers during performance. As with the parachutists, the better performers seemed to bring anxiety under control and return to moderate levels at the time of performance.

Mahoney (1979) noted that differences in cognitive patterns, and specifically differences in precompetition thoughts, may accompany the differences in arousal patterns. Mahoney observed that the qualifiers seemed to approach competition with a task orientation and to focus their energy and attention on the task, whereas the nonqualifiers worried more *about being anxious*.

Two quotes from the gymnasts in the Mahoney and Avener study illustrate this difference in precompetition thoughts. During an interview, one of the nonqualifiers described his precompetition thoughts as follows:

> When I start chalking up, I feel all queasy and I think to myself, "Oh shit, am I scared! Six thousand people watching! What if I make a mistake? What if I fall off?" I hear myself talking like that and I know I'm not ready. (cited in Mahoney, 1979, p. 436)

In contrast, one of the Olympic qualifiers described similarly high anxiety but then reported a shift in thoughts away from the worry and onto the anticipated performance:

> I get out there and they're waiting for me and all I can think is how scared I am. Twelve years I've worked to lay my life on the line for 30 seconds. Then I try to concentrate—"O.K., this is it; it's now or never. Let's pay attention to your tuck, stay strong on the press-out, and be ready for that dismount." I just start coaching myself. (cited in Mahoney, 1979, p. 436)

Although Fenz did not study thought patterns of parachute jumpers extensively, he suggested similar differences and noted that experienced jumpers were more task-oriented, whereas novices were more likely to ruminate on their own fears.

In general, then, the arousal/performance literature indicates that sport participants perform best at a moderate level of arousal, although that precise optimal level varies across individuals and sport tasks. Further probing of the arousal/performance relationship reveals that the ability to *control* arousal is a key factor that separates better and poorer performers. Better performers are able to control arousal when they must perform in intense competition or other anxiety-provoking situations, and initial work suggests that cognitive factors or thought patterns may play a central role in controlling anxiety.

## Anxiety Management in Sport

As the inverted-U theory suggests, some arousal is helpful. In sport and motor tasks, we need a certain level of activation to mobilize our energies and perform the given activities. An individual might be below optimal arousal levels during a practice session, recreational volleyball game, repetitive aerobic exercise workout, or when competing against an inferior opponent. In most sport settings, however, an optimal or moderate arousal level is reached quickly. Competition or any type of performance evaluation increases anxiety in nearly everyone, and typical warm-up activities increase physiological activity sufficiently. When anxiety increases to a point above the optimal level, however, anxiety control skills are needed. In sport, anxiety control generally implies reducing arousal, and anxiety management strategies usually involve relaxation or calming down.

## The Importance of Anxiety Management

We noted at the beginning of this chapter that arousal in sport typically involves worry about performance. Although a moderate increase in physiological arousal may be useful, increased cognitive worry has no apparent value. In fact, increased worry is associated with lower self-confidence and poorer performance. Even if arousal-increasing tactics are used in nonstressful teaching and practice situations, these strategies need not and should not have anxiety-provoking connotations that increase cognitive worry.

Even considering only physiological arousal, the potential benefits for sport performance are limited. There appears to be no research showing that arousal-increasing techniques enhance performance. The autonomic responses of increased heart rate, respiration rate, blood pressure, and palmar sweating have no apparent functional value in most sport and exercise settings. In fact, the increased autonomic activity could be detrimental. Increased sweating could make handling equipment difficult, and stressing the cardiorespiratory system more than necessary could induce early fatigue and reduce endurance. Increased muscular tension also can create special problems for sport performers.

In a unique investigation of the effects of anxiety on motor performance, Weinberg (1977) used electromyographic (EMG) recordings to examine the muscular activity of high- and low-anxious individuals. High-anxious performers exhibited more unnecessary muscular activity and wasted energy before, during, and after the actual movement. Furthermore, high-anxious individuals exhibited simultaneous contraction of the agonist and antagonist muscles, which interfered with smooth, coordinated muscle action. Such contraction of muscles creates the feeling of paralysis that most sport performers have experienced. Low-anxious individuals exhibited the more efficient sequential pattern with one muscle contracting as the opposing muscle relaxes.

The physiological effects of arousal are not independent of cognitive effects. If I notice my heart beating faster or my knees shaking, I am likely to become more worried. Arousal may be distracting; if I am thinking about my rapid breathing or upset stomach, I cannot be thinking about running the play or performing the routine. In addition to being a general distraction, arousal may narrow a person's attentional field and cause the person to miss peripheral cues.

The narrowing of the visual field with increased arousal is well documented in psychology, particularly in Easterbrook's (1959) cue utilization theory. As arousal increases, the visual field progressively narrows, eliminating more and more peripheral cues. As Landers (1978) notes, this visual narrowing has implications for sport performance. For sport tasks that require a narrow attentional focus, such as putting in golf or batting in baseball, some narrowing of the visual field may be useful to block out distracting stimuli. As the visual field narrows further, however, relevant and important cues may be eliminated. For example, a basketball player leading a fast break may not see a teammate cutting along the sideline. Clearly, then, higher arousal and visual narrowing will create problems for sport tasks that require a broad attentional span, such as leading a play in soccer or quarterbacking in football. Conversely, tasks that require more concentrated attention, such as bowling or weight lifting, may be performed effectively with higher arousal and a narrower attentional field. Considering the relationship between arousal and attentional narrowing may explain the inverted-U relationship between arousal and performance. As arousal increases and attention narrows, irrelevant peripheral stimuli are eliminated and performance is improved. When arousal increases to the point that relevant stimuli are also eliminated, performance is impaired.

Thus some physiological arousal is useful to reach an adequate state of activation and to help focus attention. However, standard warm-up activities and the anxiety-provoking nature of most sport situations probably create sufficient arousal in most participants. Increasing arousal beyond the optimal level may interfere with muscle coordination and attention. Furthermore, initial increases in either physiological arousal or cognitive worry may quickly create a negative thought-anxiety cycle, as described by Ziegler (1978; see Figure 8.4). When confronted with a stressful situation, such as competition or performance evaluation in a physical education class, an initial increase in anxiety occurs that is accompanied by physiological changes associated with the stress response. Even slight changes, such as increased muscle tension, may interfere with coordination. Perhaps you are playing shortstop and bobble the first ball hit to you because you are a bit tight and are thinking about the last time this opponent hit one past you. Making that error increases your cognitive worry and further heightens physiological arousal, decreasing your concentration and increasing the probability of more errors. Unless you can break out of

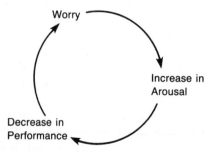

**Figure 8.4** A negative cycle is created by worry, increases in arousal, and the accompanying decrease in performance.

the cycle by controlling your worry and physiological arousal, you may be in for a long afternoon. Thus effective anxiety management skills are the key to breaking the negative cycle and achieving successful, satisfying performance.

## Anxiety Management Techniques

Experienced, highly skilled athletes, such as the experienced parachute jumpers in Fenz's studies or the Olympic gymnasts studied by Mahoney, are able to bring anxiety under control when they need to perform. Some athletes easily control their anxiety with simple techniques and have few problems. Other sport performers, however, including some professional athletes, have considerable difficulty controlling anxiety. Some athletes resort to elaborate techniques to control anxiety, such as hypnosis or biofeedback, or seek help from psychological therapists or counselors.

At this time, research on anxiety management techniques in sport is limited. We do not know very much about which techniques are most effective for different individuals in different situations or the best ways to help sport participants develop anxiety management skills. With this caution in mind, let's examine the anxiety management techniques developed thus far. Some of the initial work on anxiety management in sport offers practical suggestions for sport performers and persons who interact with sport participants as teachers, coaches, or trainers.

**Educational Techniques.** One of the most effective anxiety management techniques is to educate performers about the nature of anxiety and its impact on performance. Many sport participants mistakenly believe that high arousal is necessary and that the way to prepare for performance is to "psych-up." The optimal psychological state for most sport tasks, however, is a state of relaxed concentration. Carl Lewis, whose incredible four gold medal performance at the 1984 Olympics certainly demonstrated peak performance under pressure, described his running like this:

> When I run like Carl Lewis, relaxed, smooth, easy, I can run races that seem effortless to me and to those watching. (Callahan, 1984a, p. 52)

Of course, Carl Lewis put in tremendous effort and worked hard to develop his skills. But at the time of his competitive performance, he reduced his arousal and tension to achieve a controlled, relaxed state. Performers must be alert and attentive to the task, but they should also be free of excess muscle tension. In other words, they should be in control, yet relaxed. Most anxiety management techniques used with athletes aim to achieve this controlled and relaxed state.

Sometimes simply telling athletes about the importance of relaxation and control is enough to eliminate some ineffective psychological approaches. For example, an athlete may try to deal with a performance problem, such as a batting slump, by increasing psychological tension and arousal. Or perhaps a coach, with the best of intentions, will put extra pressure on such an athlete, thereby aggravating the negative thought-anxiety cycle. Information about the negative effects of increased anxiety and the importance of concentration and muscle relaxation may help many performers by creating an awareness of the desired psychological state for competition and by providing alternative tactics.

**Cognitive Techniques.**    Many specific anxiety management techniques are applicable to sport. Techniques usually focus on physiological relaxation, cognitive control, or a combination of the two. Simple cognitive techniques that help the individual to reduce worry and negative thoughts and to focus on the *task* are often quite effective.

Mahoney and Fenz reported that successful performers who were able to control arousal were more task-oriented. Those findings suggest that helping an individual to focus on specific actions and tasks to be performed might enhance performance. A simple thought-stopping technique could be applied in many sport situations. Whenever the individual recognizes a negative thought such as "My feet are rooted to the floor" or "I don't want to strike out again like last time," that individual should immediately and clearly think *"STOP."* The individual should not allow the negative thought to persist but instead should substitute a positive statement, such as "I'm relaxed and ready to move" or "I'm going to watch the bat contact the ball."

A more general but related approach is to use attentional control to direct the individual's attention away from worry and onto something else, preferably cues relevant to the task. For example, a basketball substitute waiting to enter the game might focus on the movement of an opposing forward along the baseline. Attentional directions and cues used in practices and warm-ups might help performers to use similar attentional control techniques in competition. For example, an instructor might direct a tennis student to notice where the racquet contacts the ball on the stroke. Providing specific attentional directions may start a positive, task-oriented thought pattern and also prevent the individual from worrying about errors.

The cognitive technique that is probably the most popular with athletes at the present time is *imagery*. As we discussed in chapter 4, many athletes use imagery to mentally practice specific moves or routines. Some athletes, such as high jumper Dwight Stones, are such obvious imagers that spectators can almost see the performance as the athlete mentally rehearses. Imagery can also be used as a relaxation technique without adding the skill rehearsal component. Simply imagining a calm, peaceful scene may allow an individual to transcend a stressful situation mentally and gain control. In addition, as in the process of counterconditioning when one response is substituted for another, it is impossible to be in a relaxed state and feel anxiety at the same time.

**Relaxation Exercises.** Individuals may also use relaxation exercises that work directly on physiological arousal. One of the simplest but most effective relaxation techniques is slow, deep breathing. Increased respiration rate is an autonomic response associated with increased arousal. However, respiration is one of the physiological responses most easily brought under conscious control. For example, you would have much more difficulty controlling your heart rate than your breathing rate. In his work with parachute jumpers, Fenz (1975) reported that respiration rate tends to decrease or come under control earlier in the jump sequence, whereas other physiological responses, including heart rate and palmar sweating, remain at high levels for longer periods. These trends suggest that bringing respiration under control might be an effective way to start the relaxation process.

Progressive relaxation, an anxiety management technique originally developed by Jacobsen (1938), is one of the most common relaxation techniques used today. Progressive relaxation is relatively simple to use, although practice is needed to become proficient and effective. As its name suggests, progressive relaxation involves the progressive tensing and relaxing of various muscle groups. An example of a progressive relaxation exercise that I have used in teaching psychological skills for sport appears in Appendix B.

Progressive relaxation has been used extensively with athletes. Typically a psychologist, sport psychologist, or coach will conduct several sessions with the athlete, giving cues to tense and then relax specific muscle groups. The first sessions may take 45 minutes to an hour, but as individuals become more proficient, sessions are shortened. The goal is for the individual to learn to recognize subtle levels of muscle tension and to relax those muscles at will. Individuals can learn progressive relaxation on their own with the aid of handouts or initial instructions. In fact, many athletes already use versions of progressive relaxation. A basketball player preparing to shoot a free throw often shrugs the shoulders and then drops them; that is a form of progressive relaxation. Readers who wish to know more about progressive relaxation should read *Progressive Relaxation: A Manual for the Helping Professions* by Bernstein and Borkovec (1973), which provides excellent background information and practical advice.

As an anxiety management technique, progressive relaxation involves relaxing the muscles and assuming that the mind follows. Varied meditation techniques work in the reverse direction; the individual relaxes the mind and lets the body follow. Meditation generally involves a relaxed, passive focusing of attention; tension and strain are avoided. Often the meditator simply focuses on breathing with no analytic thought or special effort. Benson's (1976) relaxation response is one of the easiest and most popular meditation techniques. To use the Benson technique, the individual finds a quiet setting without distractions and simply focuses on breathing. Benson suggests silently repeating the word "one" or any other nonstimulating word with each exhalation to help maintain attention. Meditation involves a *passive* attention. Neither the mind nor the body is active; the individual simply attends to breathing and focuses attention back on breathing when it wanders without straining or worrying about it.

**Cognitive-Behavioral Anxiety Management Programs.** All the cognitive techniques and relaxation exercises mentioned so far are fairly simple techniques that most sport participants could use without special training. More elaborate anxiety management techniques may be appropriate in certain cases, especially when a sport psychologist or counselor is working with an individual athlete. For example, some athletes use hypnosis to help them relax and concentrate, and some use biofeedback to learn to control anxiety responses. Currently, the anxiety management techniques that psychologists use most often with athletes are cognitive-behavioral programs. Such programs combine relaxation exercises with cognitive techniques.

Suinn (1976, 1983) uses a combination of progressive relaxation and imagery in his *Visuo-Motor Behavioral Rehearsal* (VMBR) technique, a program he has used successfully with Olympic skiers. Ron Smith (1980), a clinical psychologist who has worked extensively with sport participants, has developed a cognitive-affective approach to stress management training that combines progressive relaxation with cognitive coping skills. Specifically, Smith incorporates the cognitive skills of cognitive restructuring, which involves changing irrational, negative thoughts to positive ones, and self-instruction or self-coaching. Smith has used the program successfully to help both athletes and individuals in nonsport settings to deal with anxiety. By combining relaxation techniques that focus on the physiological component of anxiety with techniques that focus on the cognitive component, these cognitive-behavioral programs take a multidimensional approach to a multidimensional phenomenon. Thus they are often more complete and effective than the simpler techniques.

Although cognitive-behavioral programs are effective clinical techniques that have been used successfully with athletes, they should be used *only* by persons with extensive psychological training and experience. The coach who must deal with a high school swimmer who becomes nauseous before every meet or the physical education teacher who must work with a 12-year-old who hides at the back of the line will find the simpler cognitive techniques and relaxation exercises more appropriate.

## Summary

To summarize the arousal/performance relationship in sport, nearly all sport settings increase arousal, although individuals vary greatly in terms of how they react and to what extent their performance is affected. Some increase in arousal may be beneficial for *some* individuals performing *some* activities. However, arousal that increases beyond a moderate level may impair performance, especially in complex skills that are not well learned. Furthermore, the cognitive worry that accompanies increased arousal further impairs performance. Sport participants who can eliminate worry and concentrate on the task while controlling their physiological arousal responses will be more comfortable and perform better than those who cannot regulate or control their anxiety. Instructors and coaches who can help participants learn to recognize arousal states and develop anxiety management skills to control their arousal will be more effective than those who emphasize pep talks and arousal-inducing strategies.

**CHAPTER 9**

# Behavior Modification in Sport

The previous chapter focused on arousal, the energizing or intensity aspect of motivation. This chapter considers the other motivational component of behavior, the *direction* of that aroused energy. Reinforcement and other behavioral approaches that teachers and coaches can use to direct behavior and help participants develop desired skills are discussed in detail.

## Behavior Modification Terms and Concepts

Behavioral theories and reinforcement constructs are among the most widely researched and accepted principles of modern psychology. These theories are based on the fundamental assumption that behavior is determined by its consequences; behaviors are strengthened when they are rewarded and weakened when they are punished or unrewarded.

Teachers and coaches spend a great deal of time keeping scores, evaluating performance, providing feedback, and generally reinforcing and punishing behaviors of sport participants. As Siedentop (1978) states, they can apply these reinforcement techniques systematically and effectively by learning to manage behavioral contingencies to improve athletic productivity. B.F. Skinner (1968), the most widely known and probably most outspoken behavior theorist, takes the extreme position that teaching consists entirely of contingency management.

> Teaching is the arrangement of contingencies of reinforcement under which students learn. They learn without teaching in their natural environments, but teachers arrange special contingencies which expedite learning, hastening the appearance of behavior which would otherwise be acquired slowly or making sure of the appearance of behavior which might otherwise never occur. (pp. 64-65)

Teachers and coaches must understand the basic principles of contingency management to use reinforcement effectively in their work with sport participants. Some authors (e.g., Dickinson, 1977; Rushall & Siedentop, 1972) stress behavioral techniques in sport and physical education to the exclusion of other methods, and even sport psychologists with other orientations recognize that behavioral contingencies play an important role in sport instruction.

When reinforcers are used effectively, the results can be striking. Skinner demonstrated some remarkable effects in his classic work with laboratory rats and pigeons. Among other things, Skinner's techniques were used to train pigeons to identify defective drug capsules on an assembly line and, during World War II, to monitor and correct missile flight paths. As recently as 1979, newspapers reported that the Coast Guard had trained pigeons to spot orange life rafts and to signal a helicopter pilot. The reports noted that the pigeons were at least as accurate as humans in spotting survivors of maritime disasters. Skinner even got his pigeons into sport by using reinforcement techniques to teach them to play a passable version of ping-pong.

Of course, pigeons are not heavy sport participants, and we are more concerned with the effects of contingency management techniques on humans. Various reports indicate that behavioral techniques are often highly effective at modifying human behaviors. Behavioral programs have been used successfully in various institutional settings, programs for mentally handicapped individuals, health-oriented programs such as weight control and substance abuse treatments, and standard teaching settings.

To understand behavior modification, we need to establish some basic terminology. First, the primary tool of most behavioral programs is *reinforcement*. Reinforcement is any operation that increases the likelihood, or *strength*, of the behavior that it immediately follows. Anything could act as a reinforcer as long as it increases the likelihood of a behavior. Common reinforcers in sport include tangible rewards such as trophies, certificates, and scholarships and nontangible, social rewards such as cheers from the crowd or praise from a coach. Successful performance itself often acts as a reinforcer in sport; seeing the ball go through the basket or serving an "ace" may reinforce specific moves or actions.

In the examples just cited, behaviors are reinforced by providing something positive such as praise or awards; this is termed *positive reinforcement*. Behaviors also can be strengthened by eliminating something negative, which is termed *negative reinforcement*. For example, in some of the experiments with rats in a Skinner box, the floor of the box was a shock grid that continually shocked the rat unless a bar was pushed. When the rat pushed the bar, the shock stopped. Stopping the shock acted as a negative reinforcer and strengthened the behavior of pushing the bar.

Negative reinforcement is less obvious than positive reinforcement in sport, but it does occur. If you learned to dive into the water the way most people do, you probably took quite a few painful belly flops. When you finally did the dive correctly and did not flop down on the water, you did not feel the usual pain. Removal of the pain negatively reinforced the correct diving technique. Or perhaps you have played for a very critical coach who went over every mistake you made each time you came off the field. If you came off the field one time and that coach said nothing to you, the absence of criticism could negatively reinforce your previous play.

People unfamiliar with reinforcement terminology often find the definition of negative reinforcement confusing because in everyday conversation the term is often used incorrectly. People often say "negative reinforcement" when they mean "punishment." Remember, negative reinforcement, like positive reinforcement, is *reinforcement,* an operation that *strengthens* behavior.

*Punishment* is any operation that *decreases* the strength of a behavior. Punishment can occur either by presenting something negative or by taking away something positive. Critical comments for poor play, penalties for improper behavior, and being faked out by an opponent are negative events that may punish or weaken the preceding behaviors. We also punish behaviors by taking away something positive. Parents often take away privileges, such as use of the telephone or car, as a form of punishment. In sport, coaches might bench starters for breaking training rules.

To summarize, *reinforcement* is any operation that *strengthens* a behavior, and *punishment* is any operation that *weakens* a behavior. Reinforcement may occur in two ways: by presenting something positive (positive reinforcement) or by taking away something negative (negative reinforcement). Similarly, punishment may occur by presenting something negative or by taking away something positive.

## *Behavior Modification in Teaching and Coaching*

Even those who do not accept Skinner's extreme position that teaching is entirely contingency management recognize that the effective application of reinforcement and punishment is a critical component of successful teaching. Teachers and coaches can structure the environment to ensure that desired behaviors are rewarded. Kauss (1980) states that positive reinforcement is the most powerful reinforcement technique and strongly advocates the extensive use of positive reinforcement by teachers and coaches.

Positive reinforcement is more than standing off to the side and remarking "nice job" as each student in line performs a skill. Reinforcement is effective only when it is applied immediately and consistently and only when both the teacher and the student know what specific behaviors are being reinforced. Kauss (1980) lists the following five guidelines to keep in mind to use reinforcement effectively:

1. *Reinforce immediately.* The more immediate the reinforcement, the stronger its effect will be. Reinforce correct moves and behaviors

*immediately* after they occur; do not wait until the next play, the next practice, or after several others have performed.

2 . *Maintain consistency.* Try to reinforce correct behaviors every time they occur, especially when teaching new skills. When learning new skills, performers often change tactics and styles until something is reinforced. If instructors do not reinforce the specific desired behaviors, students may turn to easier moves or ones that attract some type of attention.

3 . *Respond to effort and behavior, not to performance outcome alone.* When first learning a complex skill, individuals seldom perform all components of the skill correctly. Instructors should not wait for the complete skill to be performed perfectly but should reinforce efforts and behaviors that are moving toward the desired performance. Responding to behavior rather than performance outcome is critical in teaching sport skills. Most sport skills have specific desirable outcomes such as getting in a serve, scoring a basket, or stopping an opponent. Successful outcomes are powerful reinforcers. Often beginners can achieve some success with techniques that are less than ideal. For example, a tennis player trying to learn the slice serve often has control problems and sometimes resorts to a flat serve that allows more accuracy. Instructors must ensure that students focus on the proper technique rather than on where the ball lands, and they must reinforce correct moves and techniques even when the outcome is not perfect.

4 . *Remember that learning is not entirely cumulative; it has its ups and downs.* Perhaps the main point here is that neither performers nor instructors should panic when occasional mistakes or performance slumps occur. Unless a performer has slipped into an incorrect performance pattern, instructors should continue to reinforce correct skills and behaviors, even if the total performance is not perfect, and be careful not to put undue pressure on the individual. As we noted in chapter 8, extra pressure may increase anxiety and further aggravate performance difficulties.

5 . *Use reinforcement to maintain desired behaviors once they are learned.* Frequent and consistent reinforcement is critical in early learning, and reinforcement remains important even after a skill has been well learned. Instructors need not praise every performance of a simple skill, but occasional or *intermittent* reinforcement will help maintain desired behaviors. Failure to reinforce correct behaviors may lead to the *extinction* of those behaviors. Teachers and coaches are often guilty of focusing on incorrect skills and behaviors and ignoring the students who create no problems or the performers who do not make obvious mistakes. As a result, many times those students change their behaviors, perhaps to improve their skills or perhaps simply to gain

attention. Sometimes those changes result in the deterioration of desirable skills and behaviors. Teachers and coaches who rely on positive reinforcement as the main teaching technique are likely to have fewer problems maintaining desirable behaviors than those who focus on misbehaviors and performance errors.

Of course, behaviors that do not occur cannot be reinforced. If you wait for a beginning high jumper to do the Fosbury flop correctly before giving any reinforcing comments, you will wait a long time. Obviously, some modifications are needed to reinforce complex skills effectively. Let's consider Skinner's ping-pong-playing pigeons. How do you think Skinner used reinforcement to teach pigeons to play ping-pong? Did he wait for the pigeons to walk onto the table and rally back and forth for a few strokes before providing a reward? Of course not. To teach pigeons to play ping-pong, Skinner used the reinforcement technique of *shaping*. Shaping refers to the reinforcement of successive approximations of the final desired performance. To shape behavior, you reinforce small changes or steps toward the desired behavior. With the pigeons, you might first reinforce the pigeon for going toward the ping-pong ball. Next you would reward the pigeon for hitting the ball, and then eventually reward it for hitting the ball over the net.

Shaping is a key teaching technique in sport because most sport skills, plays, and routines are developed gradually through a series of *progressive* steps. Effective teachers and coaches are masters at recognizing these successive steps and reinforcing performers as they move closer to the correct performance. To help develop your shaping technique, consider a specific skill or move that you would teach. Write down the successive steps that an individual would go through from the beginning stage to the final accomplished performance, including as many steps and details as possible. When you work with learners, determine their present ability and provide instructions to help them move to the next step without overloading them with unnecessary information about steps and skills beyond their present ability. Then reinforce any efforts and behaviors that help the performers move closer to the final goal. Humans learn much faster than pigeons, but shaping is still a gradual process. Learners will not move through all steps like clockwork, and some individuals will progress much faster than others. However, if several of your students seem to be stuck at the same stage, you might reconsider your plans and perhaps incorporate additional intermediate steps.

You may be wondering why I am stressing reinforcement and ignoring punishment. Reinforcement and punishment appear to be equally prominent techniques; if reinforcement enhances learning, will punishment of the alternative undesirable behaviors double the rate of learning? Generally, punishment will not accelerate learning. Punishment has a role in teaching and coaching, but its role is limited. Most experts are cautious about the use of punishment because of its undesirable effects and advocate emphasizing reinforcement.

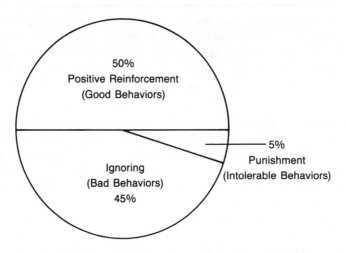

**Figure 9.1** Suggested distribution of reinforcement and punishment for effective teaching and coaching. *Note.* From *Peak Performance* (p. 99) by D.R. Kauss, 1980, Englewood Cliffs, NJ: Prentice-Hall. Copyright 1980 by David R. Kauss. Reprinted by permission.

Kauss (1980) proposes the diagram in Figure 9.1 as a guide for developing effective reinforcement techniques.

Kauss' diagram assumes that individuals perform correctly or execute acceptable behaviors about half of the time and perform undesirable behaviors the other half of the time. Good behaviors should be positively reinforced as often as possible. In contrast, bad behaviors should be *ignored* most of the time. Punishment should be applied only to behaviors that are intolerable, such as behaviors that are dangerous or disruptive to the entire group.

In principle, punishment of undesirable behaviors should reduce those behaviors. In practice, punishment seldom works as intended and can create problems in the teaching process. We have all witnessed incidents in which punishment actually reinforced an undesirable behavior by drawing attention to it. Perhaps criticism is the only attention an athlete gets from a coach, or perhaps singling out the student who disrupts a skill demonstration enhances that student's reputation with classmates. Such punishment may strengthen the very behavior it was intended to discourage.

Even when punishment does not draw attention to and reinforce undesirable behaviors, it may create other problems. In typical skill instruction, a teacher might point out the errors in a particular move or skill by saying, "Don't try to throw before you've caught the ball; you're picking your head up too soon." Such negative statements are made to punish or reduce undesirable behaviors but do not provide alternative behaviors; the performer knows what to avoid, but not what to do. The individual who wants to avoid the error may continue to think about the error, and that attention itself may increase the likelihood of the error. Instead of making negative statements that may call attention to the error, instructors should use positive, action-oriented statements that tell the individual what to do, such as "Look the ball into your glove."

If undesirable behaviors are not replaced by desirable behaviors and skills, the undesirable behaviors may not be eliminated but only suppressed when the threat of punishment is present. The class clown, for example, may be restrained when the teacher is watching but create a disturbance when the teacher is not watching. Often we do not teach individuals correct alternative behaviors but only teach them to avoid punishment. For example, if a physical education student is embarrassed when an instructor draws attention to poor skill with critical comments, the student may learn to avoid punishment by avoiding the activity, perhaps by skipping class or staying at the back of the line rather than by trying to improve his or her skills. In most sport situations, individuals learn skills faster and exhibit more positive behaviors if positive behaviors are reinforced as often as possible and all but absolutely intolerable behaviors are ignored.

When punishment is necessary, instructors should be careful not to inadvertently reinforce undesirable behaviors with attention or another reward. If punishment is necessary, many psychologists recommend a *time-out* procedure. A time-out procedure involves taking the individual out of the situation and away from all possible reinforcers. No negative comments or events are used, but the time-out space or activity must *not* offer any potential rewards. Sometimes benching an athlete or sending a student to a quiet area to work away from everyone else will eliminate attention and potential reinforcers.

The following points summarize the guidelines for effective modification of sport behavior. First and most importantly, positively reinforce correct skills and desirable behaviors as often as possible. Ensure that participants know which specific behaviors are being reinforced, and try to provide reinforcers immediately and consistently. Ignore most incorrect skills and undesirable behaviors. Do not call attention to an error or ineffective technique but instead state comments in a positive way that tells the performer what to do. Use punishment as a last resort for behaviors that must be stopped immediately. Punishment must be swift and sure, specific to the undesirable behavior, and not a source of attention or reinforcement. When using punishment, also be sure to provide the performer with a positive alternative behavior.

## Behavior Modification in Sport

In theory, the systematic use of behavior modification should be a powerful instructional approach to motivating sport participants. Reinforcement techniques have successfully modified behaviors in a variety of nonsport settings. We will now examine actual studies and instances that have put behavior modification theory into practice in sport. Although sound, controlled studies are lacking, some evidence indicates that behavior modification is effective for some sport behaviors in some sport settings.

Several investigators have applied behavioral techniques and reportedly modified both performance and nonperformance behaviors in sport. Readers who want more information on that research should consult Rushall and Siedentop (1972), who discuss the application of behavior modification in sport at length, and Donahue, Gillis, and King (1980), who present a more recent and comprehensive review of sport psychology research on behavior modification. Donahue and her associates conclude that behavioral principles and strategies can be used effectively to develop, maintain, or change target sport and physical education behaviors, but they caution that the existing research is limited in its scope of behaviors, sport activities, and reinforcement techniques. Furthermore, many of the studies reviewed by Donahue et al. are theses or unpublished papers that are not readily available for examination, and several published papers are methodologically weak. Although more sound, controlled studies are needed, the evidence suggests that behavioral techniques may effectively modify coaching/teaching behaviors, specific performance skills, and nonperformance sport behaviors such as attendance.

Some of the strongest effects are reported in investigations of nonskill behaviors. For example, McKenzie and Rushall (1974) used public records and token rewards to increase attendance, reduce tardiness, and increase work output at swimming practices. Siedentop (1978) and Donahue et al. (1980) also cite several other instances in which behavioral techniques have been used to modify attendance, disruptive practice behaviors, interpersonal communication within teams, and the academic behaviors of athletes.

Few studies have examined behavioral techniques with specific sport skills, but some evidence suggests that behavior modification may improve performance. Donahue and her colleagues (1980) cite studies demonstrating the effective modification of jogging and exercise rates, sport behaviors at a basketball camp, batting performances of professional baseball players, swimming practice times, and running performances in a basketball preseason conditioning program.

One of the best research-based examples of the effective modification of sport performance is Komaki and Barnett's (1977) use of behavioral techniques with a Pop Warner football team. The investigators used a multiple baseline design to examine the effect of a behavioral intervention on the performance of five players (center, quarterback, and running backs) on three specific plays. Each play was broken down into five stages, and the correct behavior for each player at each stage was specified clearly. Observers used a checklist to record correct execution of each stage by each player at practices and games.

The intervention was introduced after baseline observations of 10 days for Play A, 14 days for Play B, and 18 days for Play C. It included an explanation and demonstration of the correct behaviors for each player at each stage, as well as immediate feedback and recognition for performing each stage correctly after each play in practices and games. The intervention improved performance, assessed as the percentage of stages performed correctly on all three plays. Performance on Play A improved from 61.7% at baseline to 81.5% after the intervention, Play B improved from 54.4% to 82%, and Play C improved from 65.5% to 79.8%. In each case performance improved dramatically *only* after the intervention was introduced for that particular play.

Behavioral techniques have been used not only with sport performers but also with physical education teachers and coaches themselves. Research on the modification of teaching and coaching behaviors is of interest not only as an illustration of behavior modification but also because few studies of any kind have been conducted on teaching and coaching behaviors in sport. Donahue et al. (1980) cite several studies in which behavioral techniques successfully modified the behaviors of physical education teachers and coaches. Rushall and Smith (1979), for example, used self-monitoring to increase the reward and feedback behaviors of a swimming coach.

In addition to directly reinforcing teaching and coaching behaviors, several investigators have taught practicing teachers and coaches behavioral techniques to incorporate into their ongoing sport situations. Allison and Ayllon (1980) developed and evaluated a behavioral approach to coaching that consisted of systematic use of (a) verbal instructions and feedback, (b) positive and negative reinforcement, (c) positive practice, and (d) time-out. They reported that the coaches easily applied the method and effectively increased correct skills and reduced errors in tennis, football, and gymnastics.

More recently, Rush and Ayllon (1984) used the same behavioral method in youth soccer. Instead of the regular coach applying the technique, a highly skilled team member served as a peer coach and used behavioral coaching to work with nine boys with deficient skills. The results of the study using a multiple baseline with reversal design revealed that all nine players improved in specific soccer skills with behavioral coaching but not with standard coaching techniques.

Rush and Ayllon noted that for one of the skills, the throw-in, the basic behavioral coaching method with positive reinforcement was ineffective for two of the three boys. They therefore introduced the shaping technique, starting with a shorter distance and gradually increasing to the target distance of 20 feet (6.06 meters). Shaping improved the two boys' performances, confirming the importance of successive steps and progressive reinforcement for developing complex motor skills. To date, very few studies have examined shaping, which may well prove to be one of the most important and valuable behavior management techniques in sport. Further research is needed to explore how and when shaping techniques can effectively modify sport skills.

In fact, most of the behavior modification research conducted to date does not tell us much about *how* and *when* behavioral techniques affect skill performance. Most of the effective behavioral techniques used thus far are complex programs that involve many variables in addition to reinforcement. The Komaki and Barnett (1977) study, for example, singled out key players and included a skill breakdown, detailed individual instructions to each player, demonstrations, and checklists to provide feedback as well as positive reinforcement after each play. Any one component of the overall program could be the critical factor affecting performance.

Perhaps the particular combination of techniques used by Komaki and Barnett is the most effective approach. On the other hand, perhaps simply providing clear, step-by-step instructions is sufficient to improve performance; perhaps positive reinforcement does not significantly enhance skill development. Indeed, a series of studies conducted in the 1970s specifically examined the influence of social reinforcement on motor performance and yielded few notable effects.

## Social Reinforcement and Motor Performance

The influence of social reinforcement on motor learning and performance was a prominent issue in sport psychology during the early 1970s when sport psychology was following an experimental social psychology model and building a data base. *Social reinforcement* is that subset of reinforcement that consists of nontangible, positive or negative evaluative comments and actions from others. Social reinforcement can take the form of verbal praise and criticism or nonverbal smiles, frowns, and subtle gestures. Often a teacher can communicate a positive or negative evaluation through the tone of voice used regardless of the actual content of the statement. Indeed, nonverbal information often overrides verbal statements as when a negative evaluation is communicated through a half-hearted or sarcastic positive statement. Because positive and negative evaluations, both verbal and nonverbal, are so common in sport and motor activities, the influence of social reinforcement on motor learning and performance presented a logical research topic.

A series of studies, conducted mainly by Martens and his colleagues, followed an experimental social psychology model to isolate social reinforcement effects within controlled laboratory investigations. The tasks studied were primarily novel and complex motor tasks that required an extended learning period. The experimental manipulations consisted of positive and/or negative comments given in a controlled, systematic manner.

Two of the earlier experiments involved college males performing a coincident timing task (Roberts & Martens, 1970) and preschool children rolling a ball up a ramp to a target (Martens, 1970). Roberts and Martens used positive comments, negative comments, and a no-comments control condition, whereas Martens added a combination of positive and negative comments and a nonevaluative conversation condition to the original three conditions. None of the social reinforcement conditions improved performance in either study.

To determine whether specific mediating variables might have obscured social reinforcement effects, Martens conducted two subsequent studies examining internal-external control (Martens, 1971) and socioeconomic status (Martens, 1972). These studies again revealed no social reinforcement effects on motor performance.

Martens (1975) posed some explanations for the disparity between the social reinforcement effects demonstrated in extensive nonsport research and the lack of social reinforcement effects in his motor performance studies. Most of the prior research had used relatively simple speed and quantitative tasks such as card sorting and marble dropping. Apparently the performance of more qualitative, complex motor skills is less easily modified by social reinforcement. First, Martens noted that the social reinforcement provided in his experiments did not give the performers any additional helpful information. In all of Martens' studies, performers received better, more specific information through seeing their performance, being told their scores, and receiving kinesthetic feedback. Thus, as a source of information, social reinforcement was redundant and of no value toward improving skill performance.

The absence of any informational value does not, however, explain the lack of motivational effects in the Martens experiments. Some insight in this area was provided by Stevenson (1965), who reviewed the psychology literature on social reinforcement and suggested that social reinforcement has little motivational influence if the task itself has a clear product or high level of intrinsic interest. The motor tasks used in the Martens studies, and indeed most sport tasks, have a clear performance product. In the roll-up task, for example, children were trying to hit a target, and success at reaching that goal was obvious without social reinforcement. Furthermore, most sport and motor tasks, even the experimental tasks of the Martens studies, are intrinsically motivating. Individuals want to perform well and to do their best on such tasks even without social reinforcement. Unless they have been doing the task long enough to become bored, social reinforcement will not add to their already high level of motivation. Until a complex motor skill is mastered, individuals cannot control and modify their performance at will, even if their motivation to do so is high.

Some subsequent experiments examined some of Martens' suggestions. Harney and Parker (1972) proposed that the administration of social reinforcement must be frequent and intense to affect motor performance. Their results confirmed this hypothesis. When both positive and negative social reinforcement were administered "enthusiastically" after every trial, significantly better performance was achieved than in the control condition. Studies by Wankel (1975) and Martens, Burwitz, and Newell (1972) examined the influence of social reinforcement during later performance stages when individuals could become bored and less intrinsically motivated. Both studies found some indications that social reinforcement has motivational effects in these later performance stages.

My own master's thesis work (Gill & Martens, 1975) attempted to separate the informational and motivational effects of social reinforcement by controlling other sources of information feedback. By eliminating vision and controlling feedback on the roll-up task, I created four conditions: (a) a social reinforcement condition in which individuals received praise for good scores and negative comments for poor scores, (b) a knowledge of results (KR) condition in which participants received precise error scores, (c) a combination of both social reinforcement and KR, and (d) a control group that received neither social reinforcement nor KR. Both social reinforcement and KR improved performance over the no-feedback condition, and the group that received both social reinforcement plus KR performed best. Surprisingly, the group that received only social reinforcement performed better than the KR-only group, which suggests that social reinforcement information was sufficient for performance improvement and possibly had a motivational influence.

All of these studies together suggest that social reinforcement may have an informational effect on motor performance when other sources of information are absent and that social reinforcement may also have a motivational effect when the task or activity is not intrinsically motivating. However, none of the identified effects of social reinforcement were very dramatic, and many of the experimental situations were quite artificial. Most sport tasks present a clear goal and are intrinsically motivating. Also, various sources of information feedback that are clearer and more precise than social reinforcement are available to most sport performers. Thus the effects of social reinforcement on the immediate performance of motor tasks is limited at best.

The limited influence of social reinforcement on motor skill performance does not mean that social reinforcement is undesirable or useless. Certainly none of the studies cited, nor any other research that I know of, has shown social reinforcement to have any detrimental effects on motor performance. More importantly, social reinforcement may have other beneficial effects. Social reinforcement is a primary component of teaching and coaching behavior. The way an individual uses social reinforcement is a key element of communication and interpersonal style. Some work on coaching behaviors (Smoll & Smith, 1984), which we will discuss in more detail in chapter 11, indicates that the relative use of positive, reinforcing behaviors versus punitive behaviors affects players' attitudes toward the coach and toward the activity itself.

Communication styles and the use of social reinforcement may affect interpersonal relationships, participation, and both performance and nonperformance behaviors over the long term, even if immediate performance effects are not evident. The behavior modification work discussed in the earlier sections of this chapter indicates that social reinforcement is a component of most effective behavioral programs. Additional research, especially long-term studies, may further clarify the role of social reinforcement in motivating performance and nonperformance behaviors of sport participants.

# *Summary*

Behavioral approaches are powerful teaching and coaching strategies. We should positively and frequently reinforce correct skills and behaviors. In contrast, we should not call attention to incorrect behaviors but rather give corrective instructions in a positive way and use punishment only as a last resort. With complex sport skills, we may need to break the skill down into specific steps and shape the performance by reinforcing successive improvements toward the final desired performance. Some research supports the effectiveness of such reinforcement strategies for sport, but to date that research does not tell us *how* behavioral approaches work.

Experiments reveal that social reinforcement has little effect on motor performance when other feedback is available or when performers are already motivated to do their best. On the other hand, social reinforcement may be an important component of teaching and coaching styles and interpersonal relationships in sport. To understand the role of social reinforcement in sport, we must go beyond simple reinforcement effects and consider the individual's *interpretation* of behavioral techniques as well as the relationship of extrinsic reinforcement to intrinsic motivation, an issue that is discussed in the next chapter.

# CHAPTER 10

# Cognitive Approaches: Intrinsic Motivation in Sport

The behavior modification approaches discussed in chapter 9 assume that all behavior is determined by past reinforcements and contingencies in the present environment. Skinner, the most extreme behaviorist, claimed that to understand behavior we need only observe the behavior and the environment while ignoring thoughts, feelings, and other inner processes. In contrast, cognitive approaches not only accept inner processes but in fact focus on them. Because cognitive theorists see the individual as an active perceiver and interpreter of information, they consider those cognitive processes to be the key to understanding motivation and behavior.

In cognitive theories, the primary source of motivation is not *extrinsic* rewards and reinforcers but *intrinsic* motivation. According to Deci (1975), "Intrinsically motivated behaviors are behaviors which a person engages in to feel competent and self-determining" (p. 61). Seeking out challenges and striving to meet those challenges are the primary intrinsically motivated behaviors. People engage in intrinsically motivated behavior when no extrinsic rewards or reinforcers are present. In fact, the absence of extrinsic rewards is often the measure of intrinsic motivation; the more a person engages in an activity in which no extrinsic rewards are present, the higher the intrinsic motivation for that activity.

Extrinsic rewards are common in sport, but they do not account for all sport participation and activity. If asked why they participate in sport, most people will give intrinsic reasons, such as for the excitement, challenge, or sense of accomplishment. The *flow* experience is sometimes considered the definitive intrinsic reason for participation in an activity. Csikszentmihalyi (1975) defined flow as the conditions under which participants experience fun and enjoyment. He studied the flow phenomenon by asking individuals involved in various activities, including rock climbing, chess, dance, basketball, and music, to describe those conditions. Many described flow as a sense of total involvement with "everything coming together" for a peak performance in their activity. A comment by Billie Jean King (1974) about the perfect tennis shot represents the type of response he received.

> I can almost feel it coming. It usually happens on one of those days when everything is just right, when the crowd is large and enthusiastic and my concentration is so perfect it almost seems as though I'm able to transport myself beyond the turmoil on the court to some place of total peace and calm. (p. 199)

A sense of flow can involve an entire team. Bill Bradley (1976) described a game in which his New York team trailed Milwaukee by 19 points with only 5 minutes remaining to play.

> Suddenly, we "caught fire." Everything we shot went in and our defense held Milwaukee scoreless for 5 minutes. We won by 3 points, accomplishing what came to be known as "a believer feat." Those who saw it believed in our invincibility. I even think we did. (p. 92)

After analyzing reports similar to these, Csikszentmihalyi concluded that the flow experience includes the following characteristics: (a) total involvement in and concentration on the task, (b) loss of self-consciousness, (c) clear and unambiguous task demands and feedback, (d) a feeling of being in control, and (e) the absence of extrinsic goals and rewards. The flow experience is also *intrinsically* rewarding. When the individual's skills are equal to the challenges and the preceding six conditions are met, the flow experience occurs and intrinsic satisfaction is greatest. If task demands are greater than the individual's capabilities, the individual becomes anxious and worried, and if the challenges do not meet the individual's skills, the individual becomes bored.

The flow state described by Csikszentmihalyi, with control and competence as key characteristics, is a state of intrinsic motivation as defined by Deci. This focus on feelings of competence and self-determination is central to most cognitive approaches. Although the cognitive theories and research discussed in this chapter cover a wide range, all emphasize cognitive processes, intrinsic motivation, and the individual's sense of perceived control and competence. In this chapter, we will examine the relationship between extrinsic rewards and intrinsic motivation, theories and research related to expectations and self-confidence, and attribution theory and its application to achievement behavior in sport.

## Intrinsic Motivation and Extrinsic Rewards

Both intrinsic and extrinsic motivation are prominent in sport. Most individuals participate in sport for intrinsic reasons. They enjoy the competition, they like the action and excitement, they feel good when they perform well and demonstrate skills, and they just have fun. Extrinsic rewards are also common. We give awards and trophies to winning teams and individuals, we give T-shirts to runners in a local race, and we award scholarships to highly skilled intercollegiate athletes. The practical question concerns what happens when we *combine* extrinsic rewards and intrinsic motivation.

At first glance, the obvious answer is the more motivation the better. As we noted in chapter 9, extrinsic rewards and reinforcers can be powerfully motivating. If we add extrinsic rewards to an activity that is already intrinsically motivating (e.g., giving special awards to all children who compete in an intramural track meet), those rewards should simply increase the total motivation in an additive manner. We tend to assume that, at worst, extrinsic rewards would have no effect and that they certainly could do no harm.

Such conventional wisdom was accepted in theory and practice until the mid 1970s when researchers sent a shock wave through the psychological community with studies on the effects of rewards on intrinsic motivation (Greene & Lepper, 1974; Lepper & Greene, 1975; Lepper, Greene, & Nisbett, 1973). In one study appropriately subtitled "Turning Play Into Work," Lepper and his colleagues proposed and demonstrated that extrinsic rewards can actually *undermine* or *decrease* intrinsic motivation. To test their ideas, the investigators selected an activity that was intrinsically motivating for nursery school children: drawing with felt pens. They observed the amount of free time that the children spent using the pens over a baseline period and then introduced a reward manipulation.

Each child was asked to draw with the felt pens under one of three reward conditions. In the "expected reward" condition, an experimenter promised the child a "Good Player" certificate for drawing with the pens and gave the certificate to the child after the session. In the "unexpected reward" condition, a second group of children were not told about the certificates before drawing for the experimenter but received the unexpected reward after the session. In the final, "no reward" condition, the children were not promised rewards and did not receive certificates. One week later, Lepper's group again observed the children to see if the reward manipulation affected their intrinsic motivation for the drawing activity. As predicted, the children who drew for the expected rewards showed a drop in intrinsic motivation, whereas the other two groups continued to use the felt pens just as much as they had before the experiment.

Many other studies confirm the finding that extrinsic rewards can undermine intrinsic motivation. Deci's (1971, 1975) considerable research on rewards and intrinsic motivation has demonstrated that working for rewards reduces intrinsic motivation and that working under surveillance or threat of punishment similarly reduces intrinsic motivation.

The research of Deci and of Lepper and Greene stirred considerable interest among psychologists and educators. Previously, critics had questioned the value of extrinsic rewards and reinforcers, but no one had hypothesized that extrinsic rewards could have detrimental effects. If rewards actually reduce intrinsic motivation as this research suggests, then many educational practices—and certainly many sport practices—must be questioned. Should we award patches or certificates when students reach physical fitness test standards? Should we award trophies in the local softball tournament? Should we give T-shirts to everyone who finishes the 5K run-walk at the Fitness Fair? Such questions do not have simple yes or no answers. Rewards may undermine intrinsic motivation, but, as we noted in chapter 9, rewards can also modify sport behaviors and performance in positive, desirable ways.

## Cognitive Evaluation Theory

Deci's (1975) cognitive evaluation theory provides a useful conceptual framework for sorting out the relationships between extrinsic rewards and intrinsic motivation. According to Deci, the person's interpretation of the reward, rather than the reward itself, is the critical factor in motivation.

Deci suggests that two aspects of rewards can affect intrinsic motivation: the *controlling* aspect and the *informational* aspect. The controlling aspect conflicts with the need for self-determination. If the controlling aspect of a reward is high, then the individual perceives the reward as controlling behavior. If you run in a race to get a T-shirt or use certain strategies and skills in a tennis match so that you can win the trophy, those rewards have high controlling aspects. On the other hand, if the controlling aspect of the reward is low, the participant does not see the reward as affecting his or her behavior, and self-determination is high.

According to cognitive evaluation theory, when the controlling aspect of a reward is high, or *salient*, rewards undermine intrinsic motivation. In the Lepper et al. study, the controlling aspect of the expected reward was high; the children were drawing with the pens in order to get the certificates. Prior to the experiment, the children played with the pens because it was *intrinsically* motivating. The expected rewards, however, caused a shift in the children's sense of control from personal control and intrinsic motivation to the rewards. Because the control of drawing behavior shifted to the rewards, the children in the "expected reward" group had no motive to draw during the later free-time observation period when rewards were no longer present, and thus their drawing activity decreased. Because the children receiving unexpected awards did not perceive their rewards as controlling, the unexpected rewards did not undermine intrinsic motivation.

Rewards can also affect intrinsic motivation through their informational aspect. Whereas the controlling aspect of rewards affects intrinsic motivation by changing the individual's sense of self-determination, the informational aspect affects intrinsic motivation by changing the individual's feelings of competence. A reward with high informational value can provide either positive or negative information. Positive information about skills, abilities, and behaviors enhances the individual's feelings of competence, and negative information detracts from such feelings. For example, receiving a patch for attaining a certain level on a physical fitness test provides positive information that can enhance your feelings of competence. In most sport situations, however, rewards are given to a select few (e.g., trophies for the first- and second-place finishers in a tennis tournament), and those who strive for but do not receive rewards may receive negative information that decreases their feelings of competence.

Most rewards have both controlling and informational aspects, but the two aspects vary in salience. Tangible rewards, such as trophies and money, tend to have a very salient controlling aspect, whereas verbal feedback seems less controlling. Rewards given for specific performance standards have more informational value than rewards distributed randomly or on the basis of ambiguous criteria. When the controlling aspect of a reward is emphasized and made more salient, the reward is likely to undermine intrinsic motivation. For example, if a basketball coach continually talks about winning the championship trophy and stresses that all team and player actions are for the single goal of winning the trophy, the reward is likely to become very controlling and undermine the players' intrinsic motivation for participating on the team and playing well.

When the informational aspect of a reward is salient, the reward may either enhance or detract from intrinsic motivation depending on whether the reward gives positive or negative information about the individual's competence. For example, if a basketball coach sets clear, specific goals for each player, provides feedback on progress, and verbally praises players who reach their goals, the players may see the feedback and praise as primarily informational. Players who receive positive information may experience increased feelings of competence and enhanced intrinsic motivation. Similarly, players who receive negative feedback may feel incompetent and less intrinsically motivated.

As these examples suggest, most rewards in sport can be either highly controlling or highly informational depending on how they are presented and how they are interpreted. Cognitive evaluation theory implies that coaches and instructors should minimize the controlling aspects of rewards, use rewards for informational purposes, and ensure that all participants have a reasonable chance to earn positive feedback.

## Research on Rewards and Intrinsic Motivation in Sport

Recent reviews by Ryan, Vallerand, and Deci (1984) and Weinberg (1984) indicate that the undermining effect of rewards is quite robust. Not only have many studies in psychology confirmed Deci's and Lepper and colleagues' original findings, but several studies show that extrinsic rewards can undermine intrinsic motivation in sport and motor tasks (e.g., Halliwell, 1978; Orlick & Mosher, 1978; Thomas & Tennant, 1978).

In one of the more thought-provoking sport studies, Ryan (1977, 1980) compared the intrinsic motivation of scholarship and nonscholarship athletes. In the first study, Ryan sent a questionnaire assessing intrinsic motivation to a group of male athletes, some of whom were on athletic scholarships and some of whom were not. The scholarship athletes reported *less* intrinsic motivation than the nonscholarship athletes. Specific scores from one of the questions are reported in Table 10.1. Responses to other questions assessing enjoyment and liking of the sport followed the same pattern. Scholarship athletes reported less intrinsic motivation than nonscholarship athletes, with the difference between the two groups increasing over the four class years.

Ryan (1980) next conducted a larger survey of both male and female athletes in several sports at several schools. The basic finding of the first study was replicated as scholarship football players reported less intrinsic motivation than nonscholarship football players. However, further comparisons revealed more complex relationships. Among male wrestlers and female athletes in all sports, scholarship athletes reported *greater* intrinsic motivation than nonscholarship athletes. Ryan suggested two possible reasons for these varying results. First, if virtually "all" good football players receive scholarships, then the scholarships provide no competence information to their recipients. However, if only the top wrestlers and top female athletes receive scholarships, then the scholarships provide positive information about competence and are more intrinsically motivating. Secondly, Ryan notes that football coaches may use scholarships in a more controlling manner than coaches in other sports.

Another issue that has recently emerged in the intrinsic motivation literature is the relationship of competition to intrinsic motivation. This issue is

**Table 10.1** Intrinsic motivation of scholarship and nonscholarship athletes[a]

| | Freshman | Sophomore | Junior | Senior | Average |
|---|---|---|---|---|---|
| Are college athletics as "much fun" as you had expected?[b] | | | | | |
| Scholarship | 3.6 | 4.8 | 4.6 | 4.8 | 4.45 |
| Nonscholarship | 3.7 | 3.6 | 3.8 | 2.8 | 3.48 |

[a]From "Attribution, intrinsic motivation, and athletics" by E.D. Ryan, 1977, in L.I. Gedvilas and M.E. Kneer (Eds.), *Proceedings of the NAPECW/NCPEAM National Conference—1977*, p. 351. Reprinted by permission.
[b]Responses are on a 1 to 7 scale, with 1 indicating much more and 7 indicating much less.

obviously of special concern to sport psychologists. Some authors suggest that competition, and especially a focus on *winning* in competition, can act as an extrinsic reward to reduce intrinsic motivation. Deci, Betley, Kahle, Abrams, and Porac (1981) compared individuals who competed with one another to those who competed against a standard of excellence. Those in face-to-face competition later exhibited decreased intrinsic motivation in a noncompetitive free-choice period. This effect was especially strong for females.

Weinberg and Ragan (1979) compared individuals in two competition conditions (success and failure) and a no-competition condition. In contrast to Deci et al.'s findings, Weinberg and Ragan reported that competition enhanced intrinsic motivation for males and had no effect on females. It should be noted that the free-choice activity in Weinberg and Ragan's study involved competition, whereas Deci et al. used a noncompetitive free-choice setting. Thus the results of these studies may not be comparable, and the question of how competition affects intrinsic motivation is still unsettled.

The effects of competitive success and failure on intrinsic motivation are much clearer. A series of studies by Weinberg and colleagues (Weinberg, 1979; Weinberg & Jackson, 1979; Weinberg & Ragan, 1979) consistently indicated that individuals exhibited greater intrinsic motivation after success than after failure. This influence of success/failure on motivation is logical because of the high informational value of competitive success/failure. Vallerand and colleagues report similar informational effects in sport settings. Vallerand (1983) observed that positive comments about performance enhanced the intrinsic motivation of youth hockey players, and in a second study Vallerand and Reid (1984) reported that intrinsic motivation on a stabilometer task increased with positive and decreased with negative feedback. Further analysis revealed that the feedback affected perceived competence, and that perceived competence in turn affected intrinsic motivation. The findings on feedback and the effects of success/failure on intrinsic motivation demonstrate clear informational effects that fit with Deci's cognitive evaluation theory. Rewards or events that provide positive information enhance perceived competence and intrinsic motivation, whereas negative information about competence detracts from intrinsic motivation.

The intrinsic motivation literature on the controlling effects of rewards is less consistent, but considerable psychology research and theory indicate that a sense of *perceived control* is a powerful motivating factor. Numerous studies demonstrate that even minor changes that give a person a bit more choice and control can have strikingly positive effects on motivation and behavior. In one of the few studies conducted in a sport setting, Thompson and Wankel (1980) investigated the influence of choice on women's participation in a local fitness program. Women in the experimental choice condition believed that their choices were used to select exercises for the program. Actually the exercises were selected so that both the experimental and control groups liked the exercises equally. Over a six-week period, the choice group had significantly higher attendance, especially during the last two weeks, and questionnaire responses revealed greater intrinsic motivation for the choice group. Thus strategies that allow personal choice or control seem to enhance self-determination, a key component of intrinsic motivation.

A decade of research on rewards and intrinsic motivation has taken us quite far. Prior to the early work of Deci and Lepper and Greene, both psychologists and educators often stressed extrinsic rewards as primary motivational tools. Demonstrations of the detrimental effects of rewards on intrinsic motivation disrupted this trend in psychological thought and practice. These findings indicate that we should no longer award medals, championship rings, and all-star plaques without first considering possible negative consequences. On the other hand, continued research indicates that rewards do not *automatically* undermine intrinsic motivation any more than they automatically enhance motivation. The practical question, then, is not *whether* we use extrinsic rewards and reinforcers, but *how* they should be used. As cognitive theorists stress, the individual's interpretation of the reward is critical. Rewards that increase the individual's feelings of competence and self-determination enhance intrinsic motivation, and rewards that take away control or detract from perceived competence tend to decrease intrinsic motivation.

Many of the guidelines for using reinforcement presented in chapter 9 fit well with cognitive approaches. We should use small rewards that are not too salient or controlling, and we should phase out rewards as intrinsic motivation develops. Rewards cannot undermine intrinsic motivation if no intrinsic motivation exists. Carefully chosen rewards may encourage people to participate in new activities in which they can develop a sense of competence and intrinsic motivation. Rewards may also provide valuable competence information in ongoing activities, especially if rewards are given for the attainment of clearly specified goals that are perceived as within reach of all participants. Coaches and instructors who rely on encouragement and reinforcement, emphasize the process rather than the outcome, and use rewards as symbols of accomplishments rather than to coerce and control behavior may find extrinsic rewards to be useful tools that help to develop a sense of competence and personal control in sport participants.

## Expectations and Self-Confidence

Self-confidence may be the most critical cognitive factor in sport. Many top athletes exude confidence. Muhammad Ali and Joe Namath were known for their colorful and convincing boasts. Prior to the Los Angeles Olympic Games, eventual gold medal gymnast Mary Lou Retton said, "The competition is worried about me this time around. I welcome the added pressure. It makes me fight even more" (Callahan, 1984b, p. 63). Flamboyant two-time Olympic decathlon champion Daley Thompson once fantasized about meeting Jim Thorpe, Bob Mathias, Bruce Jenner, and other champions in an all-time decathlon contest: "Then we'd see who's best. I know, of course, but it would be great fun" (Leo, 1984a, p. 65). Sport participants recognize the value of a positive attitude, and as coaches and instructors we tell performers to "think like a winner" or "believe in yourself." As we noted in chapter 4, research indicates that the most consistent difference between elite and less successful athletes is that elite athletes profess greater self-confidence (e.g., Gould, Weiss, & Weinberg, 1981; Mahoney & Avener, 1977).

Is self-confidence really that important? If self-confidence helps sport performers, can we do anything to enhance a sport participant's confidence? If we could help individuals increase their confidence, would they perform better, enjoy the activity more, or experience any other benefits? At this time a number of psychologists and sport psychologists are just beginning to address some of these questions.

## Bandura's Self-Efficacy Theory

Albert Bandura (1977b, 1982) proposed a clear and useful conceptual model of self-efficacy and the relationship of self-efficacy to performance and other behaviors. As defined by Bandura, *self-efficacy* is a situation-specific form of self-confidence, or the belief that one is competent and can do whatever needs to be done in a specific situation. *Self-confidence* is a more global and stable personality characteristic. Self-efficacy, which is specific to a given time and setting, may fluctuate greatly. For example, a high school wrestler in a tournament might feel very confident or efficacious going into the first match. But if the wrestler goes into the final period behind on points and feeling tired and sees the opponent looking fresh and eager for action, he may quickly feel much less confident.

Bandura asserts that self-efficacy predicts actual performance when necessary skills and appropriate incentives are present. He suggests that efficacy expectations are the primary determinants of choice of activity, level of effort, and degree of persistence. Self-efficacy theory implies that various techniques and strategies used by coaches, instructors, and performers affect performance and behavior because they affect self-efficacy, the critical mediating variable. Efficacy expectations develop and are changed through four major types of information: performance accomplishments, vicarious experiences, verbal persuasion, and emotional arousal. Changes in self-efficacy, in turn, influence actual behavior. The role of self-efficacy in athletic performance is diagrammed in Figure 10.1.

*Performance accomplishments*, or actual success experiences, provide the most dependable information and have the most powerful effects on self-efficacy. For example, if you are learning the topspin serve in volleyball class,

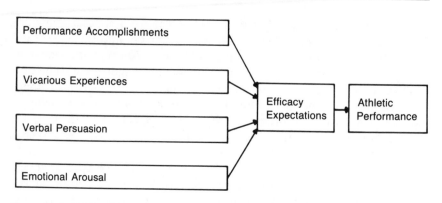

**Figure 10.1** Relationships among sources of efficacy information, efficacy expectations, and athletic performance. *Note*. From "Self-Efficacy as a Cognitive Mediator of Athletic Performance" by D.L. Feltz, 1984, in W.F. Straub and J.M. Williams (Eds.), *Cognitive Sport Psychology* (p. 192), Lansing, NY: Sport Science Associates. Copyright 1984 by William F. Straub and Jean M. Williams. Reprinted by permission.

actually practicing the serve correctly more effectively leads you to believe that you can perform the serve than the instructor simply telling you that you can do it. In sport we use many tactics to help individuals get the feeling of successful performance. We might have a football team walk slowly through an offensive play, physically guide a gymnast through a complex move, or have young basketball players use a smaller ball and a lower basket.

Studies by Feltz, Landers, and Raeder (1979) and McAuley (1985) demonstrated the effectiveness of techniques to increase efficacy and improve performance. Feltz and her colleagues compared participant modeling (demonstration plus guided performance), live modeling, and videotaped modeling techniques of presenting the back dive. McAuley used participant modeling, live modeling, and a control condition to teach participants a dive roll mount onto the balance beam. Both studies found participant modeling to be the most effective technique for increasing self-efficacy, reducing anxiety, and improving performance. Further analyses with both studies (Feltz, 1982; McAuley, 1985) supported Bandura's causal predictions; that is, modeling treatments affected self-efficacy, and self-efficacy affected performance.

Self-efficacy can also be increased through *vicarious experience*, or watching another person accomplish the skill. We often use demonstrations when teaching sport skills, and sometimes watching another student do a task reduces worry and enhances confidence. For example, seeing one member of a beginning swim class go underwater or watching a classmate do a scary tumbling move often reduces anxiety and induces other participants to follow suit. Although vicarious experience is not as effective as actual experience, several sport psychology studies confirm that modeling enhances self-efficacy (Gould & Weiss, 1981; McAuley, 1985; Weinberg, Gould, & Jackson, 1979).

*Verbal persuasion* is the third technique used to enhance self-efficacy. Verbal persuasion is less powerful than actual or vicarious experience, but teachers and coaches often encourage performers with statements such as "You've got the talent; I know you can do it." Sometimes coaches and instructors even resort to deception to persuade performers that they can accomplish certain tasks. Ness and Patton (1979) compared the weight-lifting performance of individuals who thought the weight was less than it actually was, those who thought the weight was greater, and those who were unaware of the weight. Performers lifted more weight when they believed it was less than its actual value. However, Mahoney (1979) could not replicate those findings. Furthermore, using deception with your students and athletes may undermine your credibility and trustworthiness.

The role of the fourth source of efficacy information, *emotional arousal*, is less clear and less well established. Bandura suggests that arousal, or, more precisely, perceptions of arousal, affect behavior through efficacy expectations. If you notice your heart pounding and your knees shaking prior to a game, you are likely to feel less confident. Relaxation training and other arousal reduction techniques should increase self-efficacy, but the individual's interpretation of arousal must also be considered.

In a test of Bandura's self-efficacy model, Feltz (1982) failed to find a relationship between self-efficacy and arousal as measured by heart rate. A subsequent study (Feltz & Mugno, 1983), however, revealed a negative relationship between self-efficacy and perceived arousal. Feltz (1984) suggests that if an athlete's interpretation of arousal as fear or anxiety can be changed to an interpretation of arousal as a state of being psyched-up or prepared, self-efficacy should be enhanced. But in a study in our lab (Lan & Gill, 1984), we were unable to change competitors' perceived anxiety or self-efficacy by telling them that increased arousal is a typical response that is beneficial to good competitors. Our findings suggest that stronger tactics are needed to change an individual's interpretation of arousal and self-efficacy.

Self-efficacy theory is quite influential in current sport psychology research and practice, and the initial work confirms much of Bandura's model. However, the model does not account for all sport performance and behavior change. Both Feltz and McAuley found that self-efficacy alone cannot predict performance. Bandura himself emphasized the importance of considering necessary skills and incentives as well as other cognitive processes, including causal attributions, which will be discussed later in this chapter.

## Goal Setting

Goal setting is one technique that may help ensure adequate incentives to enhance performance in sport settings. In an excellent review, Locke, Saari, Shaw, and Latham (1981) describe the positive effects of setting appropriate, challenging, and specific goals on task performance, and Bandura's research (Bandura & Schunk, 1981; Schunk, 1983) indicates that appropriate goals can enhance self-efficacy. Several authors have discussed the importance of goal setting in sport (e.g., McClements & Botterill, 1979, 1980; O'Block & Evans, 1984), but specific research findings are limited. In general, goals appear to be most effective when they are specific, immediate, and challenging but realistic and stated in behavioral or action-oriented terms so that progress can be measured. General goals such as "try harder," "play well," or "have a successful season" sound nice but have little motivational value; such goals do not tell the person *what to do.*

Hayden Fry, a highly successful football coach at the University of Iowa, illustrated the importance of specific, short-term performance goals in a recent statement to the press. Despite a continuous losing streak of about 20 years, the Iowa football team quickly became successful under Coach Fry. The team broke into the top half of the Big Ten conference in Fry's first year, continued to improve, and has played in bowl games for the past four years. When asked how this turnaround was accomplished, Fry stressed that success is a series of small steps toward improvement.

> Our objective is to strive each day to improve. That's the key to our turnaround and how you maintain consistency. It seems very simple, but when you take out all the garbage, all the things that go with life, the one objective should be to improve. The dumbest guy on our team understands that explanation. We tell them that if you pick one little-bitty segment of your play, and work on that day after day, that'll really show up on game days. (Zavoral, 1984, p. 1)

Hayden Fry's approach demonstrates an astute application of the psychological principles of goal setting and building upon small performance accomplishments to improve his players' confidence and performance.

Specific models may be used to set performance goals in sport. McClements and Botterill (1979, 1980) developed a mathematical model that uses typical performance curves to help set performance goals. O'Block and Evans (1984) advocate *interval goal setting* (IGS), which allows more flexibility than the McClements and Botterill model but still helps the performer to focus on immediate, specific goals. Following the steps outlined in Figure 10.2, IGS uses the athlete's last five performances to predict an interval or range as the goal for the next performance. In the example illustrated, O'Block and Evans used IGS to set a performance goal for a 12-year-old swimmer doing the 50-yard freestyle.

To calculate the interval goal, follow these steps:

1. Find A—the average of the last five performance times (A = 26.91).
2. Find B—the previous best time (B = 26.43).
3. Find C—the difference between the average and previous best (C = A − B = .48).

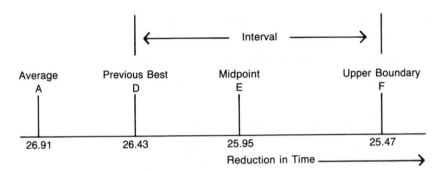

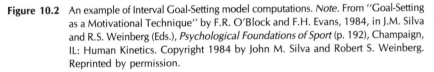

**Figure 10.2**  An example of Interval Goal-Setting model computations. *Note.* From "Goal-Setting as a Motivational Technique" by F.R. O'Block and F.H. Evans, 1984, in J.M. Silva and R.S. Weinberg (Eds.), *Psychological Foundations of Sport* (p. 192), Champaign, IL: Human Kinetics. Copyright 1984 by John M. Silva and Robert S. Weinberg. Reprinted by permission.

4. Find D—the lower boundary of the interval, which is the previous best (D = B = 26.43).

5. Find E—the midpoint of the interval, which represents a realistic performance improvement (E = D − C = 25.95).

6. Find F—the upper boundary of the interval, which represents an exceptional performance improvement (F = E − C = 25.47).

IGS sets a goal that is realistically higher than the athlete's previous best with an interval that allows for some variation. To remain effective, interval goals should be adjusted based on new performances as the performer progresses.

The IGS technique of O'Block and Evans and McClements and Botterill's computational models are useful guides for setting performance goals for events that are measured with standard, quantitative scores such as time or distance. Setting goals for aspects of performance and sport behaviors that are not typically measured quantitatively requires some creativity. Nevertheless, coaches and instructors should help performers to set goals in specific, measurable terms, even if mathematical computations are not feasible. Specific, measurable goals guide the individual's actions, and realistic, attainable goals appear to enhance self-efficacy. Furthermore, as the individual continues to reach progressively more difficult short-term goals, those performance accomplishments should develop a stronger sense of self-efficacy. Harris and Harris (1984) offer the following practical guidelines to develop effective performance goals:

1. When establishing goals, make sure the goals are ones that you established or that you and your coach established together.

2. Put the goals in writing.

3. Goals must be challenging but attainable, measurable, realistic, and manageable.

4. When two or three goals are established, they must be compatible.

5. Goals should be flexible enough to allow for revision and change.

6. Goals should have structured time frames or target dates.

7. Priorities should be structured for goals.

8. All factors related to goal attainment should be taken into account.

9. Goals must be stated to allow for evaluation of effort as well as performance.

10. Goals should be related to the overall aim of performance. (pp. 144-145)

## Expectations of Others: The Self-Fulfilling Prophecy

The influence of the expectations of others on individual performance was demonstrated dramatically in Rosenthal and Jacobson's (1968) classic work on teacher expectations and student achievement. Rosenthal and Jacobson induced false expectations by telling teachers that some of their students were "intellectual late bloomers" who should show large gains in academic performance. In reality, the "late bloomers" did not differ from control children, but the stated expectations became a self-fulfilling prophecy when the late bloomers indeed improved academic performance more than the other children.

Those striking findings prompted considerable research, and many studies confirmed the original results. Rosenthal (1976) reviewed over 300 studies using meta-analysis and concluded that the pooled results supported the self-fulfilling prophecy: 37% of the studies reported significant differences consistent with the self-fulfilling prophecy, most nonsignificant results were in the predicted direction, and no results were in the opposite direction. In another review, Brophy (1982) found support for the self-fulfilling prophecy but cautioned that findings were not totally consistent and that the extent of the effect on behavior was quite limited. As Brophy noted, however, even a small effect may be important in considering the educational implications of the self-fulfilling prophecy phenomenon.

How do teacher or coach expectations affect student performance? Brophy and Good (1970) proposed a four-stage process, and Martinek (1981) applied that model to sport as follows: (a) Teachers form expectations using impression cues such as sex, race, handicap, intelligence, past record, and previous interactions; (b) teachers' expectations affect the quality and quantity of student/teacher interactions; (c) expectations and interactions influence students' physical and social psychological outcomes; and (d) student outcomes reinforce teachers' initial expectations.

Rosenthal (1974) suggested, and research supports, four areas of teacher behavior that can influence student/teacher interaction and subsequent student behavior: climate, input, output, and feedback. Climate refers to the general class atmosphere; teachers tend to be warmer to high-expectancy children. Teachers also give more input to high-expectancy children by using more complex, time-consuming methods and providing more difficult material. Teachers also increase high-expectancy students' output by giving them more time to respond, ask questions, and solve problems. Finally, teachers give high-expectancy students more feedback about performance.

Brophy and Good (1970) examined teacher behaviors and confirmed that teachers systematically discriminate in favor of high- over low-expectancy students in demanding and reinforcing quality of performance. Their findings indicated that teachers demanded better performance from children for whom they had higher expectations and were more likely to praise their good performances. Conversely, teachers were more likely to accept poor performances from low-expectancy children and less likely to praise their good performances.

Babad, Inbar, and Rosenthal (1982) observed similar differences in student/ teacher interaction in physical education. High-expectancy students received more affirmation and praise, were treated more warmly, were given more opportunity to respond, and received less criticism for errors. Martinek and Johnson (1979) likewise found that elementary physical education teachers treated students in the top 10% and bottom 10% of the class on expected achievement differently. Teachers approached the top students more frequently, accepted their ideas more readily, and gave them more praise and encouragement. In contrast, Rejeski, Darracott, and Hutslar (1979) found that basketball coaches in a youth league gave more instruction to *low-expectancy* players. Horn (1984a) similarly reported that junior high school softball coaches gave low-expectancy players more instruction and praise for success. Thus in at least some situations teachers may provide more opportunity and feedback to poorer students and players.

As Horn (1984b) notes in a comprehensive review of the expectancy literature related to sport, differential treatment and individual instruction is often desirable, and teacher expectations that are performance-based, accurate, and flexible may help guide such individual instruction. Expectations are most damaging when they are based on inaccurate stereotypes and biases. As noted in chapter 7, we often hold stereotyped attitudes about the motor abilities of and appropriate activities for individuals based on biases regarding sex, age, race, ethnic background, or disability. Scheer and Ansorge (1975, 1979) demonstrated that the expectations and performance ratings of gymnastics judges were influenced by the gymnasts' order of performance. Such expectations are not based on accurate, objective information about the individual's past performance and capabilities. If such inaccurate expectations are maintained rigidly, they may become self-fulfilling causes of behavior. Based on her review, Horn (1984b) made the following recommendations for teachers and coaches to reduce the negative effects of expectancies and enhance positive instruction:

- Strive to keep judgments or assessments of children's ability both accurate and flexible.
- Be aware that differential expectations for individual children within a class or team are certainly appropriate due to variation in their actual skill abilities.
- Emphasize children's progress in skill development or their improvement rates rather than using absolute performance measures to evaluate their competence.
- Provide children with feedback that is primarily informational rather than evaluative.
- Be persistent in teaching following a child's failure to perform a particular skill.
- Develop a strong belief in the ability to teach each child.

## Attributions and Sport

The study of *attributions*, or the perceived causes of events and behaviors, is one of the most active research areas in both social and sport psychology. Currently, the issue of attribution formation and the relationship of attributions to performance, interpersonal behaviors, and feelings are especially prominent. Attribution theories are cognitive approaches that focus on people's perceptions and interpretations of the reasons for both their own behaviors and the behaviors of others. The attributions we make about our successes and failures affect the effort and persistence we devote to an activity as well as our thoughts and feelings about our performance. If you are unable to do the shotput in your physical education class, you behave differently depending on *why* you think you cannot do it. If you think you need practice, you might stay at the shotput area and keep trying. If you think you need instruction, you might ask the teacher for guidance. If you think you are just too weak and uncoordinated, you might give up and try the long jump for a while.

The attributions we make about others also affect our behaviors and interactions. If you go up for a rebound and get elbowed by an opponent, you react differently depending on whether you think the elbowing was intentional or accidental. A teacher who thinks you cannot put the shot because you are not strong enough responds differently than a teacher who thinks you are lazy and not paying attention. Coaches think about the reasons their teams win and lose, and they act on the basis of those attributions in preparing for future contests.

Sometimes we try to change attributions to change behavior. Teachers and coaches often say, "You can do it if you try," to encourage performers to keep working at skills. Several years ago I attended the basketball games at a major university. One player, a 7-foot, rather hefty center who was particularly slow with almost no vertical height on his jumps, was continually chided by the fans for his sluggishness and lack of intensity. In a statement to the media, the coach decried the crowd's unfairness and pointed out that "Joe" was not lazy, but in fact worked especially hard on his rebounding and really needed some support. The coach's attempt to change the fans' attributions worked; from then on the fans no longer booed but cheered enthusiastically whenever "Joe" made any decent play.

## Weiner's Model of Achievement Attributions

Although he was not the first—and certainly not the only—person to propose major theoretical models about attributions, Weiner (1974, 1979; Weiner, Frieze, Kukla, Reed, Rest, & Rosenbaum, 1972) has done the most to bring attribution constructs to prominence, especially in relation to achievement behavior. Using Heider's (1958) original attribution work on the "naive" analysis of behavior and other early cognitive motivational approaches as a base, Weiner developed an attributional theory of achievement behavior. Weiner suggested that individuals make attributions about their successes and failures in achievement situations and that those attributions affect achievement situations and that those attributions affect achievement motivation and behavior. Specifically, Weiner proposed that the essential difference between high and low achievers is a difference in attributional patterns.

In studying attributional patterns, first we should determine the types of attributions that people actually make. What reasons do people give for success and failure in sport? For example, try the following exercise:

> Think about your favorite sport activity. Now think about the last time that you won or had a very successful performance in that activity. *Why* did you win? What was the main reason for your success? Now think about the last time that you lost or had a very unsuccessful performance. What was the main reason for your lack of success?

Your reasons will probably fall into one of four categories: ability, effort, luck, or task difficulty. According to Weiner, these four categories cover most of the reasons people give for success or failure in achievement situations. *Ability* includes attributions such as "I'm not very good at tennis" or "Our team has the best athletes." *Effort* might include statements such as "We were really up for the game" or "I never gave up when it got tough." *Task difficulty* includes attributions to the opponent, such as "They were a ranked team," and attributions to the task itself (e.g., "The moves were just too complicated"). *Luck* attributions include chance, random events, and environmental factors (e.g., "We got the breaks" or "They had the ref on their side").

The four attributions themselves are not the critical consideration in Weiner's theory. Instead, attributions are classified along two dimensions, *locus of causality* and *stability,* and the attribution dimensions have various effects. Figure 10.3 illustrates Weiner's two-way dimensional classification of attributions. The *locus of causality* dimension refers to whether the attribution is to something internal or external to the performer. Ability and effort are characteristics of the individual and are hence internal attributions, whereas luck and task difficulty are external. The *stability* dimension refers to whether the attribution is relatively stable and unlikely to change over time or unstable and changeable. Ability and task difficulty are stable; your tennis ability does not change much from one match to the next, your opponent will stay just as strong, and the height of the net will not change. On the other hand, effort and luck may change; you might be more up for the next match and try harder, or you might get the breaks on line calls. Considering both dimensions, ability is an internal, stable factor; effort is internal and unstable; task difficulty is external and stable; and luck is external and unstable.

Now go back to the reasons you gave for your last win and loss and see where your attributions fit in Weiner's classification. Often individuals make internal attributions for success and external attributions for failure. If you classify all the reasons given for success or failure, invariably more of the success attributions than failure attributions fall into the internal category (ability and effort). If you pay attention to the comments of winning and losing players and coaches for a while, you will notice that external attributions (lucky/unlucky breaks, officials' calls, weather) almost always come from the losing side. I cannot recall ever hearing a winning coach state that a team won because of a particular referee's decision, but I have often heard that comment from losing coaches. This tendency to attribute success internally and failure externally is usually interpreted as a *self-serving bias,* meaning that those attributions somehow serve or help us. For example, you probably will feel better about winning the 800-meter run if you think you won because you gave your best effort than if you think you won because your chief rival had the flu.

According to Weiner, the internal/external dimension relates to affect, or feelings of pride and shame. Internal attributions elicit stronger feelings. You

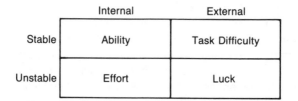

|  | Internal | External |
|---|---|---|
| Stable | Ability | Task Difficulty |
| Unstable | Effort | Luck |

**Figure 10.3** Weiner's 2 × 2 classification scheme for causal attributions.

take more pride in successes that you earn yourself than in those due to external factors. You also feel greater shame when failure is your fault than when you fail because of external factors. It does not feel as bad to lose because of poor officiating as it does to lose because you gave up at the end. Thus making internal attributions for success and external attributions for failure is self-serving because it maximizes feelings of pride and minimizes feelings of shame. The tendency to give more internal attributions for success than for failure is one of the most consistent findings in the attribution literature, and the self-serving bias is reported in several sport psychology studies (Bird & Brame, 1978; Gill & Gross, 1979; Iso-Ahola, 1977; Lau & Russell, 1980; Roberts, 1978; Scanlan & Passer, 1980).

The *stability* dimension also has implications for achievement behavior. Specifically, stability relates to our expectations for future success and failure. Stable attributions lead us to expect the same outcomes again, whereas unstable attributions allow us to expect different outcomes. If you think your team won the volleyball match because it is the best team in the league, you will expect to keep on winning. If you think you failed to do the high jump because the skill is too complicated for you, you will expect to continue failing. Conversely, if you had to play over your head to win the match, you cannot be confident of future victories. If you think you were unable to do the high jump because you were tired and did not concentrate enough before starting your approach, you can change your behavior and maintain hope for future success.

Although Weiner's model provides the theoretical base for most current attribution research, that model and research findings, including the self-serving bias, have been refined and expanded in recent years. Weiner himself has made several modifications. Researchers often interpreted the four basic attributions of ability, effort, luck, and task difficulty as the *only* attributions. But Weiner (1979) has pointed out that those were never intended to be the only attributions. Sport psychology research clearly demonstrates that those four attributions alone are not adequate. Bukowski and Moore (1980), Gill, Ruder, and Gross (1982), and Roberts and Pascuzzi (1979) all found that sport participants gave many attributions that did not fall into the four basic categories. Furthermore, luck and task attributions are rare, and attributions to the team (e.g., teamwork) are not easily classified but are quite common. In any case, the specific attributions themselves are not of primary importance. As Weiner and several reviewers of the sport attribution literature (Brawley, 1984; Brawley & Roberts, 1984; Rejeski & Brawley, 1983) note, the *dimensions* of attributions are the critical theoretical considerations.

Attribution research during the 1970s indicated that the two dimensions of locus and stability were insufficient, and Weiner (1979) proposed a third dimension called *controllability*. Controllable attributions are under the control of the individual or others, and uncontrollable attributions are not under anyone's control. Effort is the only one of the four original attributions that is controllable.

Just as the locus and stability dimensions affect feelings and expectations, the controllability dimension affects behavior. Weiner suggests that controllability affects our moral judgments and reactions to others. We tend to reward and punish people on the basis of controllable attributions. This is reflected in our tendency to praise athletes and students who give extra effort and to criticize those who do not try. We are more apt to criticize a student who is lazy or slacks off than one who performs poorly due to poor coordination or physical disability.

In general, then, the attributional dimensions affect behavior as follows:

- *Locus of causality* (internal/external) relates to feelings of pride and shame. We experience stronger feelings with internal attributions than with external attributions.

- *Stability* relates to future expectations. We expect similar outcomes with stable attributions and changeable outcomes with unstable attributions.

- *Controllability* relates to our moral judgments and responses to others. We reward and punish others on the basis of controllable attributions. We praise people for effort and controllable successes, and we criticize lack of effort and controllable failures.

Researchers in both social and sport psychology continue to actively investigate attributions and the relation of attributions to expectations, feelings, and interpersonal behaviors. For example, controllability was not part of Weiner's original model, but subsequent work indicates that controllability may have implications for both individual achievement behavior and our responses to others. Abramson, Seligman, and Teasdale (1978) discuss learned helplessness, which we will consider later in this chapter, in terms of uncontrollable attributions. Specifically, Abramson and colleagues propose that individuals who perceive outcomes as uncontrollable have motivational, cognitive, and emotional deficits. These deficits are evidenced by the fact that such individuals are unlikely to initiate responses, are likely to have difficulty later learning that responses do make a difference, and are likely to feel depressed. Weiner's original model has been refined and expanded, and continued research, especially research specific to sport, will yield further modifications.

## Attributional Approaches to Achievement Behavior

As noted earlier in this section, Weiner's attributional theory of achievement behavior, like Atkinson's theory discussed in chapter 5, considers differences between high and low achievers in choice, effort, and persistence on achievement tasks. Atkinson's theory uses a personality characteristic, the need to achieve, to account for individual differences within a drive or need reduction framework, whereas Weiner adopts a cognitive approach and asserts that high and low achievers differ in their attribution patterns and that those attribution differences account for behavior differences. Specifically, high achievers, as compared to low achievers, tend to attribute success to internal factors and failure to unstable factors. Because high achievers attribute success to internal factors, they experience more pride in their successes and seek out achievement situations because those situations are rewarding to them. Achievement situations are less rewarding to low achievers, who do not attribute successes internally. Because high achievers tend to attribute failure to unstable factors, they are more likely to persist and try harder, whereas low achievers attribute failure to poor ability and give up.

Carol Dweck (1978) describes a cognitive model of achievement behavior that combines many of the ideas we have already discussed about expectations, attributions, and behavior. In Dweck's model, illustrated in Figure 10.4, initial expectancies (expectations) affect behavior or performance. As noted earlier in the section on self-efficacy, higher expectations lead to superior

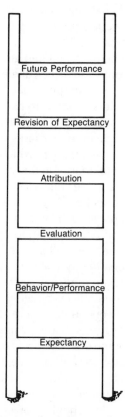

**Figure 10.4** Dweck's conceptualization of cognitions and achievement behavior.

performance and greater persistence on achievement tasks. That performance is evaluated with a score, as a win or loss, or perhaps with verbal feedback from a teacher or coach. The performer then makes an attribution about the performance, and that attribution leads to revised expectancies for future performances.

**Learned Helplessness.** Dweck is best known to sport psychologists for her work on *learned helplessness* (Diener & Dweck, 1978, 1980; Dweck, 1975, 1980; Dweck & Goetz, 1978; Dweck & Reppucci, 1973). Learned helplessness is the acquired belief that one has no control over negative events or that failure is inevitable and one cannot do anything about it. Learned helplessness is an attributional interpretation of extreme low achievement that fits into Dweck's model. According to Dweck, learned helpless individuals differ from mastery-oriented individuals (high achievers) in their expectancies and attributions in achievement situations, and especially in their failure attributions. Helpless individuals attribute failure to stable, uncontrollable factors, especially lack of ability, and give up after initial failure because they see no hope of future success. In contrast, mastery-oriented individuals tend to see failure as a temporary setback and challenge due to unstable, controllable factors. Thus mastery-oriented individuals persist in the wake of failure, often with extra effort; they try and try again.

Dweck reasoned that if helpless children give up because they perceive failure as inevitable and uncontrollable, then altering the children's attributions for failure should help them persist in spite of failure. To test her ideas, Dweck worked with extremely helpless children in two treatment conditions. Half of the children experienced only successes—a treatment often used with low achievers in which they are given easier tasks that guarantee success. The other half received attribution retraining in which they were successful most of the time but failed on several trials. On the failure trials, the experimenter explicitly attributed the failure to the child's lack of effort. Overall, the attribution retraining was much more effective in changing children's responses to failure and improving performance. Children in the "success only" group did not improve performance and did not learn to cope effectively with failure.

Certainly we encounter learned helpless individuals in sport. The most obvious cases are the children in physical education classes and youth sport programs who "know" they are too slow, uncoordinated, and unathletic to ever do well at sports. Occasionally even highly skilled athletes can become helpless when they suddenly encounter failure after continual success up to that point. Dweck's work suggests that we can best help those individuals by encouraging them to attribute their failures to unstable, controllable factors, including not only effort but strategies, practice, techniques, or anything that could be changed. Of course, we should not tell a 10-year-old girl who has poor balance, flexibility, and strength that she can do a back flip on the balance beam if she only tries harder. We should, however, encourage her to persist in achieving *attainable* goals. Helpless individuals believe that they will always fail, and thus they give up even at tasks within their capabilities. Those are the situations we should address. We must encourage helpless individuals to strive for reasonable achievement goals that they can reach with appropriate effort and practice.

**Teacher Feedback and Achievement Behavior.** Teachers and coaches can do much to help individuals develop mastery-oriented achievement cognitions and behaviors. As noted earlier in this chapter, the expectations of others can affect interactions and performance. Within her model, Dweck emphasizes the effect that the evaluations of others can have upon students' achievement cognitions and behaviors. In a provocative study on teacher evaluations and student achievement, Dweck (1978) monitored teacher feedback to elementary children, noting differences between feedback to girls and feedback to boys. As mentioned in chapter 6, considerable research demonstrates gender differences in achievement cognitions. Females report lower expectations of success than males report in most achievement situations (Crandall, 1969; Lenney, 1977). Similarly, females take less responsibility for success and more often attribute failure to lack of ability, whereas males more often make achievement-oriented attributions (Dweck, 1978; Frieze, Parsons, Johnson, Ruble, & Zellman, 1978). Dweck's observations of teacher feedback provide some insight into how those gender differences in achievement cognitions develop.

In Dweck's study, teacher feedback was coded as positive or negative and in terms of whether it was for intellectual aspects of work or for nonintellectual aspects, such as neatness and conduct. Overall, boys received more negative feedback, but not for their work. Most of the negative feedback to boys was for conduct and other nonintellectual aspects of behavior. Almost all of the negative feedback to girls related directly to their work. Dweck also recorded the specific attributions made by teachers and observed that failures were attributed to lack of effort eight times more frequently for boys than for girls.

These differences in teacher feedback parallel gender differences in achievement cognitions. Because girls receive negative feedback from teachers for their *work*, they interpret such failure feedback to indicate lack of ability. Boys, on the other hand, could easily attribute negative feedback to lack of effort or a generally negative attitude of the teacher. Perhaps the most promising aspect of Dweck's work is a follow-up study in which either the typical "girl" feedback pattern or the typical "boy" feedback pattern was given to *both* boys and girls. The findings indicated that the "girl" pattern elicited more typically female achievement responses from both girls and boys, and the "boy" pattern likewise elicited more achievement-oriented cognitions and behaviors from both girls and boys.

Of course, the teacher feedback patterns that Dweck found in elementary classrooms may not apply to sport and exercise settings. Nevertheless, the findings suggest that teachers and coaches can have considerable impact on the achievement cognitions of sport participants.

## Summary

Cognitive motivation is one of the most active and prominent areas in sport psychology. Considerable research indicates that cognitive perceptions and interpretations are critical to understanding sport participation and behavior. Individuals participate in sport for intrinsic reasons, and intrinsic motivation is a key influence on sport performance and behavior. Cognitive constructs, particularly self-efficacy or confidence and attributions, appear to be critical mediators between our teaching and coaching strategies and the participant's behaviors. In general, the collective work on intrinsic motivation, expectations, and attributions suggests that we should help participants to set challenging, realistic goals and should encourage performers to stress effort and personal control in reaching their goals. With the use of these approaches, participants' accomplishments will elicit feelings of competence, personal control, and the desire to continue achieving in sport activities.

# PART IV

# *Social Influence and Sport*

In part IV we will shift our emphasis away from individual characteristics and motivation and onto the social environment. Sport psychology research on social influence and motor performance is reviewed in chapter 11. Specifically, we will discuss the influence of spectators, competitors, coaches, and instructors on sport performance and behavior.

The sport psychology literature on aggression, a form of social interaction that sparks considerable interest among sport participants, is reviewed in chapter 12. We will consider explanations of aggression, including instinct theories, drive theories, and the more strongly supported social learning theories, as well as research on the relationship of aggression to sport performance and behavior. Finally, we will discuss the equally important but less researched topic of prosocial or moral behavior in sport.

# CHAPTER 11

# *Social Influence and Motor Performance*

The influence of other people on sport and motor performance was the central issue in the early sport psychology research of the 1960s and 1970s. Social influence remains an important concern because virtually all sport activity is social activity. Much sport activity involves competition, which is by definition a social situation. Even activities that do not involve competition usually involve social interaction. Physical education classes, adult fitness programs, and noncompetitive recreational sports all involve several people performing skills and interacting with one another. Similarly, instructors and sport leaders exert considerable social influence as they give directions and guidance, evaluate performance, provide feedback, and respond to behaviors.

The key aspect of sport that creates a powerful social influence situation is *social evaluation*. Performance is evaluated by others, and that social evaluation affects behavior. Coaches and teachers give instructions, watch us perform, and tell us how we are doing. We win or lose in competition, often in front of family, friends, coaches, opponents, spectators, and even the media. Even when fellow participants do not evaluate directly, sport activities usually involve some evaluation of individual performance. You know, for example, that your classmates will see how well you do the handstand and that your colleagues in the noon aerobic exercise group may see you as uncoordinated and out-of-shape.

In this chapter we will consider the main types of social influence that have been researched and discussed in sport psychology. First we will consider social facilitation, or the influence of the presence of others on performance. Next we will turn our attention to the influence of others who are not simply passive spectators but competitors. In the third section we will look at the spectator/performer relationship in the reverse direction—the influence of a performer on the observer—as we examine the modeling process. Finally, we will consider the general influence of coaching behavior on sport participants.

# Social Facilitation: Audience Effects

*Social facilitation*, or the influence of the presence of others on performance, includes two subareas: audience effects and coaction effects. In the social facilitation literature, *audience* refers to passive spectators who simply observe and make no comments or overt evaluations. *Coaction* means that other people are doing the same thing at the same time without competition or interaction among the coactors. A line of students in a golf class, all practicing the chip shot, is an example of coaction.

## Early Social Facilitation Research

Social facilitation is one of the oldest and most studied topics in social psychology. In fact, as mentioned in chapter 2, the first social psychology experiment (Triplett, 1898) was an investigation of social facilitation and motor performance. Competitive cycling was popular around the turn of the century, and Triplett was a cycling enthusiast as well as a psychologist. Using cycling records, Triplett compared unpaced performance times to paced and competitive times. As Triplett suspected, paced times were about 35 seconds per mile faster than unpaced times, and competitive times were fastest of all. Like most careful scientists, Triplett set up a controlled experiment to test his observations and found that children performed the task of winding a fishing reel faster when in pairs than when alone. Triplett proposed the principle of *dynamogeny* to explain his findings, asserting that the presence of others arouses competitive drive, releases energy, and increases speed of performance.

Subsequent research on social facilitation continued to expand upon Triplett's findings and ideas. Allport (1924) conducted several experiments and first used the term *social facilitation* to refer to performance improvements due to the presence of others. Actually, however, the growing body of research revealed that the presence of others did not *always* improve performance. Some studies confirmed Triplett's findings, reporting that people performed better with an audience or coactors on tasks such as the pursuit rotor, monitoring a light panel, and simple vowel cancellation and multiplication problems. Some enterprising investigators even observed that chickens ate more in the presence of other chickens and that ants exhibited more nest-building activity in the presence of other ants. On the other hand, some researchers reported that people were less accurate, made more errors, and had more trouble learning nonsense syllables and following a finger maze in the presence of others. Reviews by Landers and McCullagh (1976) and Wankel (1984) provide more detailed analysis of the social facilitation research for readers who want more information.

## Zajonc's Interpretation of Social Facilitation

Social facilitation research appeared to be on the wane and stalled by contradictory findings when Zajonc (1965) created new impetus for research into the topic with his clarifying interpretation of the literature. Specifically, Zajonc proposed that the equivocal findings could be explained by applying drive theory, which we discussed in chapter 8. As outlined in Figure 11.1, Zajonc proposed the following conclusions:

- The presence of others, either as an audience or as coactors, creates arousal or drive.

- Increased arousal increases the likelihood that the individual's dominant response will occur.

- If the skill to be performed is simple or well learned, the dominant response is the correct response and performance improves.

- If the skill is complex and not well learned, the dominant response is an incorrect response and performance is impaired.

Zajonc's proposals inspired considerable research, much of which confirmed his observations. Of most interest to us is Martens' (1969) test of Zajonc's predictions for the learning and performance of a motor task. Martens divided his study into separate learning and performance phases of a relatively complex coincident timing task that required practice before performance became consistent. Male college students performed the coincident timing task either alone or with an audience of 10 other male students. Using the palmar sweat index to assess arousal, Martens found that the audience condition did indeed elicit more arousal than the alone condition during both the learning and performance phases. During the learning phase, individuals performed better when alone (mean error of −69 milliseconds) than in the audience condition (mean error of −103 msec). In the performance phase, those performance differences were reversed. The audience condition elicited greater arousal and better performance (mean error of −36 msec) than the alone condition (mean error of −59 msec).

Martens' findings confirmed Zajonc's predictions that the presence of an audience created arousal, impaired learning of a complex skill, and facilitated later performance after the task was well learned. Several subsequent sport psychology studies added further support for Zajonc's views. For example, coactors elicited faster running times (Obermeier, Landers, & Ester, 1977) and better performance on a simple muscular endurance task (Martens & Landers, 1969) but impaired performance on more complex motor tasks (Burwitz & Newell, 1972; Martens & Landers, 1972).

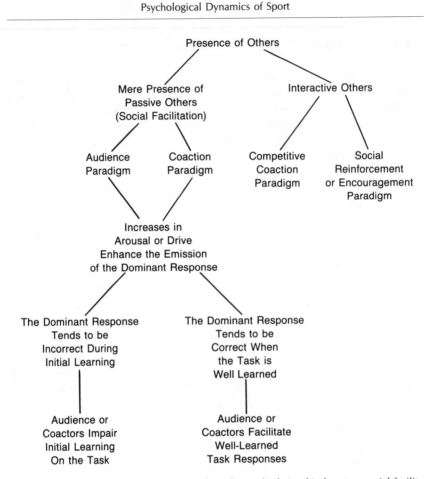

**Figure 11.1** Schematic outline of Zajonc's hypothesized relationship between social facilitation paradigms and drive theory predictions. *Note.* From "Social Facilitation of Motor Performance" by D.M. Landers and P. McCullagh, 1976, *Exercise and Sport Science Reviews,* **4,** p. 140. Permission to reprint granted by Journal Publishing Affiliates.

## *Alternative Explanations of Social Facilitation*

According to Zajonc, the *mere presence* of others creates arousal that in turn affects performance. Cottrell (1968) challenged Zajonc's contention that the mere presence of others was sufficient to elicit arousal. Cottrell pointed out that the presence of others does not always create arousal and in fact sometimes has a calming effect. According to Cottrell, the presence of others creates arousal only when the others can evaluate performance. Thus it is *evaluation apprehension,* or the perception that others can observe and judge one's performance, that creates arousal. Cottrell's own research and later studies with motor tasks (Burwitz & Newell, 1972; Martens & Landers, 1972) support the role of evaluation apprehension in social facilitation.

More recently, some authors have suggested that simply adopting drive theory, or looking at arousal as the only source of social facilitation effects, is limiting. These researchers argue that instead we should consider cognitive processes. In a comprehensive review, Geen and Gange (1977) concluded that drive theory appears to be the best explanation for social facilitation thus far, but they advocated more attention to cognitive processes in future research. Baron, Moore, and Sanders (1978) have suggested that distraction, rather than the mere presence of others or evaluation apprehension, accounts for performance changes. Landers (1980) proposed that sport psychologists should take a more cognitive approach to social facilitation with more specific focus on attentional processes. In any event, neither drive theory nor evaluation apprehension has stirred much interest in sport psychology research in the last 10 years, and sport psychologists have not yet applied cognitive theories and concepts to the social influence area.

## Audience Effects and Sport Performance

Perhaps the main reason sport psychologists have abandoned social facilitation research is the failure to demonstrate any notable effects in real-life sport settings. Although many social facilitation experiments were conducted in the 1960s and 1970s, the experimental variables were often trivial (e.g., putting the audience in red shirts), and the results of the few field investigations were disappointing. Paulus and colleagues, for example, looked at audience effects on gymnastics and on batting performance in professional baseball (Paulus & Cornelius, 1974; Paulus, Judd, & Bernstein, 1977). Crowd size was not related to batting performance, and, contrary to predictions, better gymnasts were less facilitated by an audience than were poorer gymnasts.

Landers, Bauer, and Feltz (1978) pointed out several problems with the social facilitation research in a critique and replication of Martens' audience study. Both Landers et al. and Martens (1979), in his reply, noted that even though some laboratory experiments support Zajonc's predictions, the findings have not been generalized to actual sport settings, and the practical value of the research is limited.

One practical issue involving audiences and sport performance that has been studied is the widely held belief in the "home advantage." Schwartz and Barsky (1977) documented the home advantage with professional baseball, football, and hockey teams and with college basketball and football teams. Teams won games more often at home than away for all sports, and the home advantage was greatest for the indoor sports of hockey and basketball. Further analyses revealed that the home advantage held for offensive play (e.g., hits, goals, shots, points) but that defensive statistics (e.g., errors, saves, fouls) did not differ for home and away games.

In a more recent study, Varca (1980) probed further into the home advantage phenomenon with basketball teams. Varca observed that home and away teams did not differ on field goal percentage, free throw percentage, or turn-overs. Instead, the home team demonstrated more of what Varca termed "functionally aggressive behavior" (steals, blocked shots, rebounds), whereas the away team exhibited "dysfunctionally aggressive behavior" (fouls). The descriptive findings of Schwartz and Barsky's and Varca's studies document a home advantage and suggest that playing at home or away creates differences in aggressive behavior as one explanation. At this time, however, the findings are merely suggestive; we do not yet know the extent and limits of the home advantage or its underlying processes.

In fact, recent work (Baumeister, 1984; Baumeister & Steinhilber, 1984) documents a home field *disadvantage*. Baumeister demonstrated that directing attention to the internal performance process, or increased self-consciousness, can disrupt the performance of well-learned, automatic skills. Professional athletes perform sport skills automatically with minimal conscious attention. Baumeister reasoned that the opportunity to win a championship before a home crowd increases self-consciousness and disrupts skilled performance. Data from World Series baseball games and professional basketball games confirmed Baumeister's views; home teams tended to choke in final, decisive games. Thus competing on the home field can be a disadvantage in some circumstances. Certainly the mere presence of others does not explain the home advantage, although audience presence may play an important role. Perhaps attentional factors, such as distraction or self-consciousness, are critical mediators. Further investigations considering various cognitive processes and social influence factors operating in different sport settings may give us more insight into the effects of social facilitation on sport and motor behavior.

## Competition and Motor Performance

Because it involves the presence of others, competition is in one sense a form of social facilitation. Competition, however, is characterized by a more direct social evaluation process than the standard audience or coaction situation. Because the associated social evaluation is so clear and intense, competition would be expected to increase arousal and affect performance just as the presence of others does. If anything, competition should create even greater arousal and stronger performance effects. Surprisingly, sport psychologists have not researched the effects of competition as much as audience effects. Nevertheless, existing studies suggest that competition effects on performance parallel audience effects.

Research indicates that competition improves performance on simple or well-learned skills and on speed, strength, and endurance tasks. Specific studies demonstrate that competition improves performance on a dynamometer task (Berridge, 1935), elicits faster reaction times (Church, 1962; Gaebelein & Taylor, 1971), and facilitates endurance performance on a bicycle ergometer (Wilmore, 1968). With more complex motor tasks, Gill (1978b) reported that competition improved performance on a well-learned motor maze task, and Wankel (1972) found that competition improved the performance of high-ability individuals, whereas low-ability individuals performed better under noncompetitive conditions. Research showing detrimental effects of competition on motor performance is sparse, but some early studies reported that competition impaired accuracy while facilitating speed (Church, 1968; Dashiell, 1935; Whittemore, 1924).

A recent experiment (Gross & Gill, 1982) implies that the influence of competition is more complex than the improvement of speed and impairment of accuracy. In our study, we varied the instructions on a dart-throwing task across five conditions ranging from complete emphasis on speed, to equal emphasis on both speed and accuracy, to complete emphasis on accuracy. We found that competition did improve speed over noncompetition, but only when the instructions emphasized speed. When the instructions emphasized accuracy, performers were slower in competition than in noncompetition. However, competition did not affect accuracy at all, even when the task instructions emphasized accuracy.

Starkes and Allard (1983) recently took a different approach to investigating the effects of competition on performance with their study of perceptual processes in volleyball. Starkes and Allard followed a signal detection paradigm to see how quickly and accurately individuals could detect a volleyball in slides that were rapidly flashed on a screen. Both volleyball players and nonplayers attempted the task under both competitive and noncompetitive conditions. Overall, players were faster than nonplayers, confirming the findings of an earlier study by Allard and Starkes (1980) that we discussed in chapter 4.

The more important concern here, however, is the effect of competition. Competition increased arousal (assessed as increases in heart rate) and elicited faster times from both players and nonplayers; however, the increase in speed was much greater for nonplayers. Competition also decreased accuracy on the detection task, but Starkes and Allard asserted that the increased speed in competition was more striking than the decreased accuracy and that volleyball players may purposely choose a strategy of sacrificing a small degree of accuracy for a very fast response. The Starkes and Allard and the Gross and Gill results imply that performers can adopt varying speed/accuracy strategies depending on the task demands and that competition may further modify or intensify the speed/accuracy components of performance. Further research may help to clarify the influence of competition and other social influence factors on speed, accuracy, and other more specific components of motor control and performance.

Some initial research suggests that the influence of competition on sport and motor performance may be quite complex. To complicate matters even more, we must also consider the possible influence of winning and losing or success and failure. Success/failure affects competitors' anxiety levels, as we noted in chapter 5, and winners not only report lower anxiety than losers, but also greater satisfaction and higher perceived ability (Gill, 1977). If success/failure affects feelings and cognitive responses, perhaps success/failure also affects performance in competitive situations.

In a well-controlled experiment, Martens and White (1975) systematically varied the win/loss ratio over several sessions on a motor maze task. They reported that individuals performed better when the win/loss ratio was 50% than when the ratio was either higher or lower. The finding that a 50% win/loss ratio elicited top performance fits well with the achievement motivation literature, particularly Atkinson's theory. As discussed in chapter 5, Atkinson asserts that achievement situations with a 50% chance of success represent maximum challenge and elicit the strongest achievement efforts. On the other hand, a 50% win/loss situation might elicit debilitating worry and arousal from some competitors, especially those with low achievement motivation or high competitive anxiety. Although the existing evidence suggests that challenging games and situations provoke achievement strivings that improve performance, that research is quite limited and we should not assume that a 50% win/loss ratio always elicits top performance.

## Modeling: The Demonstration Process

Earlier in this chapter we described social facilitation as the influence of an audience on a performer. In the modeling process, social influence is reversed; the performer influences the audience. Modeling occurs any time we learn by demonstration or change our behavior to imitate behaviors we have observed. Modeling can facilitate or inhibit behaviors. For example, seeing office colleagues go out jogging every noon hour might encourage a fellow employee to join them. When a coach benches a starter for breaking training rules, the coach not only intends to punish that player's inappropriate behavior but also hopes that other team members will learn by example.

The most prominent role of modeling in sport is in the process of observational learning; we learn sport and motor skills by observing others. As instructors, we teach most sport skills by modeling. I cannot recall ever seeing an instructor teach someone to dribble a soccer ball or do a dance step without some type of demonstration. The pervasiveness of observational learning in sport raises many questions. How does modeling provide information or motivation to change motor performance? When and how often should we demonstrate skills during the learning process? Who should demonstrate the skills? Should we demonstrate parts of complex skills and common errors or only complete, correct skills? How much time should we spend modeling versus using other methods or actual practice? What skills or characteristics of skills are most appropriate for modeling? Despite the obvious importance of the modeling process in sport and exercise, sport psychologists and other motor behavior researchers have only begun to answer some of these questions.

## *Bandura's Analysis of Observational Learning*

According to Bandura's (1977a) social learning analysis, modeling affects the learning and performance of skills and behaviors through the four component processes illustrated in Figure 11.2. The first two processes, attention and retention, relate to the learning or acquisition of the modeled skill. The motor reproduction and motivation processes determine actual performance of the skill that has been acquired.

**Attentional Processes.** To learn any skill through modeling, people must first pay attention to the model. More specifically, the observers must attend to and perceive accurately the significant features of the modeled behavior. For example, if your tennis instructor demonstrates a backhand return, but you are watching the ball, then you may not pick up the key elements of the stance, swing, and follow-through. A number of factors, including characteristics of the model, the observer, and the skill, can affect the observer's attentional processes while watching a modeled behavior. For example, young athletes clearly attend to and imitate the skills and behaviors of their favorite professional players, even when we prefer that they would not. A youngster not only imitates an effective technique but may pick up an awkward stance or learn to throw tennis racquets and temper tantrums. Models usually present

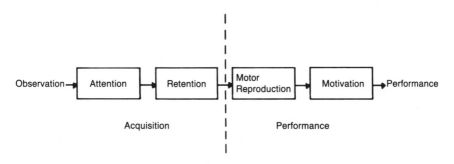

**Figure 11.2** Component processes in Bandura's social learning analysis of observational learning. *Note.* Adapted from Bandura (1977a).

more information than an observer can process effectively, especially when the observer is just beginning to learn a complex skill. Thus observational learning can be enhanced by channeling attention to critical features of the demonstrated skill (Minas, 1980). Generally, students and athletes are attentive because they like their instructors and coaches, trust their instructor's knowledge, and want to improve their skills. As a result, the instructor may use special cues or techniques to direct the learner's attention to key elements of the skill.

**Retention Processes.** The second component of Bandura's formulation implies that even if people attend to the model, they must remember the modeled behavior to learn the skill. Retention involves the development of symbolic representations of the skill that serve as internal models for later action. Activities that aid in the development of such internal representations, particularly imagery and verbal or symbolic coding, can improve observational learning (Bandura & Jeffery, 1973). For example, mentally rehearsing the serve immediately after a demonstration may strengthen the performer's image of the skill. Good instructors are masters at giving just the right cues or phrases to help performers code the skill in memory. For example, we usually remember dance steps with phrases such as "step-together-step," and ski instructors typically code the unweighting motion of a parallel turn with the phrase "down-up-down."

**Motor Reproduction Processes.** After attending to and retaining a modeled skill, the performer must match his or her actions to the internal representation of correct performance. Matching actual behavior to ideal behavior, or doing what you want to do, is not easy with complex sport and motor skills. I can watch Dr. J do the slam dunk and retain a clear image of how to perform that skill, but I will never do the slam dunk at a normal 10-ft-high basket. Of course, we usually do not demonstrate sport skills unless we believe observers have the basic capabilities needed to do them. On the other hand, even a capable student does not immediately imitate a complex golf swing or complicated gymnastics move. Modeling sets up an internal image and symbolic representation of the skill, and, through practice with feedback from an instructor and self-correction, the performer can gradually match his or her performance to that image. Physical capabilities, the ability to retain appropriate responses, and accurate feedback are important considerations in the motor reproduction phase.

**Motivational Processes.** The final component of Bandura's model focuses on motivation to perform the observed behavior. We do not imitate everything we learn through observation. External reinforcement, vicarious reinforcement (reinforcement to the model), and self-reinforcement all help determine which behaviors we will imitate. When you see a teammate elude a defender with a particular dribbling move, you have some incentive to imitate that move. Likewise, if your instructor praises you for "getting the idea" of the demonstrated serve, you will probably keep trying to do it.

## Modeling and Motor Performance

Although sport psychologists have only begun to investigate the modeling process, the limited existing research suggests that models provide information that aids in the learning of sport skills, especially those that are complex or involve several procedural steps or alternative strategies. Studies by Feltz and Landers (1977) and Martens, Burwitz, and Zuckerman (1976) indicate that modeling improves performance by providing information about how to perform complex motor skills. Gould (1978) compared the effectiveness of modeling across several motor tasks and reported that modeling was more helpful for a complex task with several steps than for a relatively simple task.

Research by Weiss (1983) suggests that the age or developmental level of the observer also influences the effectiveness of the modeling process. Older children (ages 7–8) performed equally well after observing either a silent or a verbal model, but the performance of younger children (ages 4–5) was enhanced only by observing the verbal model. Weiss' findings confirm the role of developmental factors, particularly verbal-cognitive abilities, in the observational learning process.

As Bandura's model indicates, models may play a motivational role as well as an informational role. Some initial research indicates that characteristics of the model may affect the modeling process through motivational effects. Gould (1978) observed that the sex of the model affected observational learning, and Gould and Weiss (1981) found that models similar to the observer elicited greater endurance performance than dissimilar models elicited.

In a study of model characteristics with implications for teaching motor skills, Landers and Landers (1973) compared the effectiveness of teacher and peer models who were skilled or unskilled on the Bachman ladder task, a novel balancing task. Landers and Landers reasoned that modeling would facilitate the performance of fifth- and sixth-grade girls and that skilled models and teacher models would be more effective than unskilled and peer models. Modeling did facilitate performance; all groups who observed a model performed better than a control group who did not see a model. Model characteristics did not, however, influence performance as expected. The skilled teacher model did elicit better performance than all other groups, but the unskilled peer model did not elicit the poorest performance. Students who observed the unskilled peer performed better than students who saw either the skilled peer or the unskilled teacher.

Many explanations could be posed for these unexpected findings. Perhaps students imitate their teacher whether the teacher is competent or incompetent at the task; perhaps students assume that if the teacher cannot do the skill, then surely they cannot do it either; perhaps students do not want to show up the teacher; perhaps seeing an unskilled peer sets up a competitive standard that challenges and motivates students. The Landers and Landers findings might suggest that teachers should only demonstrate if they can perform the skill. If they are unable to perform effectively they should have a student demonstrate, even if the student is not highly skilled. These findings, however, are from only one study, with one task, one sample, one set of procedures, and one combination of model characteristics. Further research may clarify the role of model characteristics and other motivational factors, such as instructional techniques and reinforcement patterns, and how those motivational factors interact with task characteristics and informational factors within the modeling process.

## Modeling Nonperformance Behaviors

Although the influence of the modeling process on the learning and performance of motor skills is our main concern, models also influence nonperformance behaviors in sport. According to Bandura's self-efficacy theory, vicarious experiences are a major source of self-efficacy. As Feltz, Landers, and Raeder (1979) and McAuley (1985) demonstrated, modeling can enhance self-efficacy and reduce anxiety on fear-provoking sport tasks as well as facilitate performance. One of the most notable roles of modeling is in the development of aggressive and prosocial behaviors. Bandura is widely recognized for his "Bobo doll" experiments demonstrating the influence of models on the learning and performance of aggressive behaviors. As we will discuss in more detail in chapter 12, modeling probably plays a major role in violent or aggressive behaviors in sport. In fact, research by Bryan (Bryan, 1969; Bryan & Walbek, 1970) implies that our actions speak louder than our words when communicating social behaviors.

Bryan compared the relative importance of words and deeds on the generosity behaviors of elementary school children. After playing a miniature bowling game, the children received certificates that they could either redeem for prizes or donate "to the poor." The model in the study either acted generously and donated the certificates or acted greedily and kept the certificates. At the same time, the model either preached generosity by extolling the values of charity or preached greed by pointing out that the certificates were earned and need not be donated. Bryan used all combinations so that the model might both preach and practice greed or generosity, might hypocritically preach generosity but keep the certificates, or, strangely, might preach greed but actually donate the certificates.

Bryan's findings confirmed that actions did indeed speak louder than words. Children did as the model *did* regardless of what the model *said*. Hypocrisy had no effect on the children's decisions. Children were just as generous when the model preached greed but donated the certificates as when the model both preached and practiced generosity. Preaching generosity while keeping the certificates did not elicit any more generosity from the children than both preaching and practicing greed. Bryan did suggest that words might provoke thoughts and have long-term effects on behavior even if they did not affect immediate actions. Nevertheless, his findings imply that out-of-shape instructors advocating fitness exercises and coaches who talk about being good sports while storming up and down the sidelines may be wasting their breath.

## Coaching Behavior as Social Influence

In chapters 9 and 10 we discussed reinforcement techniques and cognitive instructional approaches, and in this chapter we have considered various social influence processes, including modeling, which is probably the most common instructional strategy in sport. So far we have discussed these various techniques and approaches in isolation. Teachers and coaches do not, however, use positive reinforcement, goal setting, feedback, or demonstrations in isolation. Instead, when interacting with students or athletes they use various techniques as part of an overall coaching or instructional style. Research on coaching behavior suggests that the relative use of different techniques, such as how often coaches encourage athletes versus how often they criticize them, influences the behaviors and reactions of sport participants.

One of the first attempts to assess coaching behavior was Tharp and Gallimore's (1976) systematic observation of John Wooden. As you probably know, John Wooden was one of the most successful, and probably *the* most successful, coach in college basketball. Before retiring in 1975, Wooden coached UCLA basketball teams to 10 national championships in 12 years, a record unapproached by any other coach. The investigators observed Wooden's coaching behavior over the 1974–1975 season in an attempt to determine the methods and behaviors of a highly successful master coach and teacher. Tharp and Gallimore's coding system incorporated standard teaching behavior categories such as reward, punishment, and modeling and a few categories created especially for Wooden's behavior, such as "hustles." After developing the coding scheme, Tharp and Gallimore observed 2,326 teaching behaviors over 30 hours of practice sessions. The percentage of behavioral acts falling into each category is listed in Table 11.1.

This study's most striking finding was the predominance of instructional acts in Wooden's coaching behavior. Despite the experience and high skill level of the UCLA team, more than 50% of Wooden's behaviors were specific instructions to players about what to do or how to do it. Considering the other

**Table 11.1** Distribution of John Wooden's coaching behaviors.

| Code | Category | Description | Percent of Total Communications |
|------|----------|-------------|---------------------------------|
| I | Instructions | Verbal statements about what to do or how to do it | 50.3 |
| H | Hustles | Verbal statements to activate or intensify previously instructed behavior | 12.7 |
| M+ | Modeling-positive | A demonstration of how to perform | 2.8 |
| M− | Modeling-negative | A demonstration of how *not* to perform | 1.6 |
| V+ | Praises | Verbal compliments, encouragements | 6.9 |
| V− | Scolds | Verbal statements of displeasure | 6.6 |
| NV+ | Nonverbal reward | Nonverbal compliments or encouragements (smiles, pats, jokes) | 1.2 |
| NV− | Nonverbal punishment | This infrequent category included only scowls, gestures of despair, and temporary removal of a player from scrimmage, usually to shoot free throws by himself | Trace |
| W | Scold/reinstruction | A combination category: a single verbal behavior which refers to a specific act, contains a clear scold, and reasserts a previously instructed behavior; e.g., "How many times do I have to tell you to follow through with your head when shooting?" | 8.0 |
| O | Other | Any behavior not falling into the above categories | 2.4 |
| X | Uncodable | The behavior could not be clearly heard or seen | 6.6 |

*Note.* From "What a coach can teach a teacher" by R.G. Tharp and R. Gallimore, 1976 (January), *Psychology Today*, **9**(8), p. 76. Copyright 1976 by the American Psychological Association. Reprinted by permission.

acts that conveyed information, such as modeling and scold/reinstruction, about 75% of Wooden's behaviors provided instruction. Furthermore, most of the instruction involved basic, fundamental basketball skills.

Tharp and Gallimore also reported that Wooden seldom used praise but actually scolded his players more often than he praised them. Scolds and nonverbal punishment were, however, only a small portion of Wooden's behaviors.

It is also relevant to consider that the UCLA basketball players of Wooden's coaching era received tremendous praise from both inside and outside the basketball world. Certainly their many successes were quite rewarding. The students and athletes that most coaches work with do not have the history of extraordinary success and many rewards that Wooden's players received. Thus we should not assume that limiting praise is necessarily an effective coaching technique. In fact, the most extensive, systematic research on coaching behavior indicates that effective coaches devote considerable time to praise and encouragement and rarely use punitive behaviors (Smoll & Smith, 1984).

## Coaching Behavior in Youth Sports

Ron Smith and Frank Smoll's seven years of work with youth sport coaches stands out in sport psychology as a model of systematic, progressive research culminating in the application of results in training programs. Prior to Smoll and Smith's work, many people talked about youth sports and vocally criticized youth sport coaches. Researchers seldom delved, however, into the world of youth sports, and certainly no one attempted to investigate such a nebulous topic as coaching behavior.

Smith and Smoll took the first step toward understanding the coaching process by developing a systematic observational system, the *Coaching Behavior Assessment System (CBAS)*, to quantify coaching behaviors (Smith, Smoll, & Hunt, 1977). After observing and analyzing the behaviors of coaches in several sports, Smith and his colleagues generated the twelve categories of coaching behaviors listed in Table 11.2.

Coaching behaviors fall into two major categories: *reactive* behaviors, which are responses to players' behaviors, and *spontaneous* behaviors, which are initiated by the coach. To use the CBAS, observers simply check the appropriate category for each observed behavior. The relative proportions of behaviors in the twelve categories are used as the measure of coaching style. Smith et al. demonstrated that the CBAS is easy to use, includes most coaching behaviors, has good reliability, and shows individual differences among coaches. In general, coaches use a good deal of reinforcement and instruction, but coaching styles differ, most notably in their amounts of instruction and the relative proportions of positive behaviors (reinforcement and encouragement) and punitive behaviors.

The development of the CBAS was an important research advance that enabled researchers to investigate more intriguing practical questions: "Do differences in coaching behaviors affect the players?" and, if they do, "Can coaching behaviors be changed to enhance the sport experience for participants?" In a two-phase research program, Smith and Smoll and their colleagues addressed those issues. In Phase I, the behaviors of Little League coaches were compared to players' attitudes toward the coach, the activity, and teammates

**Table 11.2** Response categories of the Coaching Behavior Assessment System.

| Classification | Definition |
| --- | --- |
| *Class I. Reactive Behaviors* | |
| *Responses to desirable performance* | |
| Reinforcement | A positive, rewarding reaction, verbal or nonverbal, to a good play or good effort |
| Nonreinforcement | Failure to respond to a good performance |
| *Responses to mistakes* | |
| Mistake-contingent encouragement | Encouragement given to a player following a mistake |
| Mistake-contingent technical instruction | Instructing or demonstrating to a player how to correct a mistake |
| Punishment | A negative reaction, verbal or nonverbal, following a mistake |
| Punitive technical instruction | Technical instruction that is given in a punitive or hostile manner following a mistake |
| Ignoring mistakes | Failure to respond to a player mistake |
| *Response to misbehavior* | |
| Keeping control | Reactions intended to restore or maintain order among team members |
| *Class II. Spontaneous Behaviors* | |
| *Game-related* | |
| General technical instruction | Spontaneous instruction in the techniques and strategies of the sport (not following a mistake) |
| General encouragement | Spontaneous encouragement which does not follow a mistake |
| Organization | Administrative behavior which sets the stage for play by assigning duties, responsibilities, positions, etc. |
| *Game-irrelevant* | |
| General communication | Interactions with players unrelated to the game |

*Note.* From "Leadership research in youth sports" by F. Smoll and R. Smith, 1984, in J.M. Silva and R.S. Weinberg (Eds.), *Psychological foundations of sport* (p. 375), Champaign, IL: Human Kinetics. Copyright 1984 by John M. Silva and Robert S. Weinberg. Reprinted by permission.

(Smith, Smoll, & Curtis, 1978). Researchers observed and recorded behaviors with the CBAS, asked coaches what they thought their behaviors were (self-perceptions), asked players what they thought the coaches' behaviors were (player perceptions), and interviewed players to assess their liking for the coach, the activity, and teammates, as well as self-esteem.

In general, the coaches took a positive approach, using a great deal of reinforcement, technical instruction, and general encouragement. The players appeared to perceive coaching behaviors quite accurately. But the coaches' perceptions of their own behaviors were not at all accurate; coaches did not know which behaviors they used most often. The low correlation between CBAS results and coaches' self-perceptions implies that the first step in any coach training program should be to make coaches aware of their actual behaviors. In fact, that knowledge alone may be sufficient to positively modify the behaviors of many well-intentioned coaches who do not realize how much reinforcement or instruction they actually provide.

Before suggesting that coaches adopt particular behaviors, however, we should demonstrate that coaching behaviors affect the players. Smith et al.'s findings confirmed that coaching styles do indeed relate to player attitudes. As you might expect, coaches who used more reinforcement and encouragement and less punitive behaviors were better liked. Contrary to the belief that children just want to have fun and do not care about skill development, coaches who used more instruction were also better liked. A generally positive approach that combined instruction and encouragement related not only to participants' liking for the coach but also to their liking for the activity and teammates and to a greater increase in self-esteem over the season.

Perhaps you are wondering if coaching behaviors affected win/loss records. Perhaps coaches who used the positive approach won more games and it was winning or success that led to more positive player attitudes. In fact, coaching behaviors were not related to win/loss records, and players did not like winning coaches any better than losing coaches. The best liked coaches actually had slightly poorer win percentages (.422) than the least liked coaches (.545), but that difference was not significant. Although win/loss records were not related to the players' liking for the coach or the activity, players on winning teams felt that their parents liked the coach more and that the coach liked them more than did players on losing teams. As Smoll and Smith (1984) commented, winning apparently made little difference to the children, but they knew it was important to the adults.

Based on their findings, Smoll and Smith developed behavioral guidelines for youth sport coaches. Those guidelines, presented in Figure 11.3, advocate a positive approach that stresses frequent reinforcement and encouragement.

I. Reactions to player behaviors and game situations:

A. Good plays

*Do: Reinforce!!* Do so immediately. Let the players know that you appreciate and value their efforts. Reinforce effort as much as you do results. Look for positive things, reinforce them, and you'll see them increase. Remember, whether the kids show it or not, the positive things you say and do stick with them.

*Don't:* Take their efforts for granted.

B. Mistakes, screw-ups, boneheaded plays, and all the things the pros seldom do

*Do: Encourage* immediately after mistakes. That's when the kid needs encouragement most. Also, give *corrective instruction* on how to do it right, but always do so in an encouraging manner. Do this by emphasizing not the bad thing that just happened, but the good things that will happen if the kid follows your instruction (the "why" of it). This will motivate the player positively to correct the mistake rather than motivate him/her negatively to avoid failure and your disapproval.

*Don't: Punish* when things go wrong. Punishment isn't just yelling at kids; it can be any indication of disapproval, tone of voice, or action. Kids respond much better to a positive approach. Fear of failure is reduced if you work to reduce fear of punishment.

C. Misbehaviors, lack of attention

*Do:* Maintain order by establishing clear expectations. Emphasize that during a game all members of the team are part of the game, even those on the bench. Use reinforcement to strengthen team participation. In other words, try to prevent misbehaviors from occurring by using the positive approach to strengthen their opposites.

*Don't:* Constantly nag or threaten the kids in order to prevent chaos. Don't be a drill sergeant. If a kid refuses to cooperate, quietly remove him or her from the bench for a while. Don't use physical measures (e.g., running laps). The idea here is that if you establish clear behavioral guidelines early and work to build team spirit in achieving them, you can avoid having to repeatedly *keep control*. Remember, kids want clear guidelines and expectations, but they don't want to be regimented. Try to achieve a healthy balance.

II. Getting positive things to happen:

*Do:* Give *instruction*. Establish your role as a teacher. Try to structure participation as a learning experience in which you're going to help the kids develop their abilities. Always give instruction in a positive fashion. Satisfy your players' desire to become the best athletes they can be. Give instruction in a clear, concise manner; if possible, demonstrate how to do it.

*Do:* Give *encouragement*. Encourage effort; don't demand results. Use it selectively so that it is meaningful. Be supportive without acting like a cheerleader.

*Do:* Concentrate on the game. Be "in the game" with the players. Set a good example for team unity.

*Don't:* Give either instruction or encouragement in a sarcastic or degrading manner. Make a point, then leave it. Don't let "encouragement" become irritating to the players.

**Figure 11.3** Behavioral guidelines for youth sport coaches. *Note.* From "Leadership Research in Youth Sports" by F. Smoll and R. Smith, 1984, in J.M. Silva and R.S. Weinberg (Eds.), *Psychological Foundations of Sport* (pp. 385-386), Champaign, IL: Human Kinetics. Copyright 1984 by John M. Silva and Robert S. Weinberg. Reprinted by permission.

One effective way to implement a positive approach in your teaching and coaching is to follow the three-step *sandwich approach*: sandwich a positive, action-oriented instruction between two encouraging statements. For example, after your shortstop has bobbled a grounder, you should immediately give a sincere, encouraging statement such as, "Nice try; you got into position well." Then give a corrective instruction: "Next time, lay your glove on the ground and look the ball into it." Finally, finish off with another encouraging statement such as, "Hang in there; you'll get it."

In Phase II of their research, Smith, Smoll, and Curtis (1979) used their behavioral guidelines in a training program for youth sport coaches to see if training would induce more positive behaviors and affect player attitudes. The training program included discussion of the Phase I results, presentation of the behavioral guidelines, modeling, role-playing and practicing the positive approach, and a two-week period of observations with self-monitoring and feedback of CBAS results to the coaches.

In the Phase II experiment, differences in coaching behavior and player attitudes between the coaches in the training program and a control group of coaches paralleled the findings of Phase I. Trained coaches used more reinforcement and encouragement and less punitive behaviors than control coaches, and players perceived the trained coaches as using more positive behaviors. Children who played for the trained coaches reported more positive attitudes, specifically liking for the coach, perception of the coach as knowledgeable, liking for teammates, enjoyment of the activity, and self-esteem, than did children who played for the control coaches. In summary, the training program was effective in increasing positive, supportive coaching behaviors. Those behaviors in turn elicited more positive player attitudes.

Smith and Smoll's work has made an impact in sport psychology. Many youth sport programs have adopted the behavioral guidelines and positive approach generated by their research. The CBAS is a valuable research tool that sport psychologists have used to study the relationship of coaching behaviors to other factors. Horn (1984a), for example, used the CBAS in investigating teacher expectancies and sport behaviors. More studies using the CBAS and applying sound research methods may further elucidate the social influence of teachers and coaches on sport performance and participants' reactions to the sport experience.

## Summary

Social influence is pervasive in sport; virtually all sport and exercise activities involve some type of social interaction. Sport psychology research reveals that social interaction, even the simple presence of others as passive spectators, affects sport performance and behavior. In general, the performance of simple and well-learned skills is enhanced when others are present as spectators, performers, or competitors, but social influence impairs the performance of complex or less well-learned skills.

Social influence also occurs through various teaching and coaching strategies. Modeling or demonstration is one of the most common and powerful teaching tactics in sport. Research indicates that actions do speak louder and have greater impact than words, but we have much more to learn about how observers acquire and perform modeled behaviors. Smoll and Smith's systematic research on coaching behaviors reveals that coaching style, or the overall pattern of coaching behaviors, is a social influence factor that has considerable impact on children's attitudes and reactions to youth sport. In general, social influence is a pervasive and powerful phenomenon in sport and exercise. Social interaction, from the mere presence of spectators to complex teaching styles, exerts powerful influences on sport participants. We have far to go, however, toward understanding how these various social influences operate in sport and exercise.

# CHAPTER 12

# *Aggression in Sport*

Aggressive behavior is quite visible in sport. To observe aggressive sport behavior, we could attend a basketball game and watch players "fight" for rebounds, or we could watch runners throw elbows and jostle for position in a 1,500-meter race. At the more extreme end of the spectrum, we could read the reports on the rampage of English soccer fans in Brussels prior to the start of a European Cup match between British and Italian teams that left 38 people dead and more than 400 injured (Lacayo, 1985). Closer to home, we might note that the night of "celebration" in Detroit following the Tigers' 1984 World Series victory left one person dead, 80 injured, and 41 arrested and caused more than $100,000 in property damage (Leo, 1984b). Of course, not all aggressive behavior in sport is violent and destructive. In fact, many forms of aggressive behavior are accepted and even promoted; often aggression is "part of the game."

Our use of the term *aggression* to refer to such a wide range of sport behaviors can cause confusion. We use the term aggression to label violent outbursts in sport, but we also talk about the "aggressive" player who dives for the ball or takes chances in a close contest. Our understanding of aggression is further clouded by value judgments and emotional connotations. We teach and encourage certain aggressive behaviors and praise individuals who use "good" aggressive tactics, but we consider other, "bad" aggressive acts shocking and repulsive. Most aggressive behaviors in sport are neither clearly desirable nor clearly undesirable. Instead, most aggressive acts are seen as distasteful by some people and justifiable by others. Thus you will find it easier to define and explain aggression in sport if you do not think of aggression as totally positive or negative, desirable or undesirable, but simply as behavior that we want to understand.

## Defining Aggression

Before we discuss theories and explanations of aggression, we need to clarify terms. Certainly, we could all agree that some behaviors constitute aggression. For example, when basketball player Kermit Washington punched opposing player Rudy Tomjanovich hard enough to require extensive surgery and effectively end Tomjanovich's professional career, that was aggression. Take a minute and try to write down a definition that will clearly delineate behaviors that you consider aggression. Now, let's see how well your definition works in the following scenario: You are watching the play-off game between the Blue Bombers and the Red Barons, two local youth ice hockey teams.

1. Mark, one of the Bombers' top players, slams Jeff, a Baron forward, into the boards to keep him away from the puck (a perfectly legal move).

2. Jeff retaliates by swinging his stick and smashing Mark in the ribs (*not* a perfectly legal move).

3. When the same thing occurs later in the game, Jeff again tries to retaliate by swinging his stick at Mark, but Mark skates away and Jeff misses.

4. Tim, Mark's younger brother and the least skilled player of the Bombers, finally gets into the game for his required ice time in the final minute. Tim is defending the goal as Baron forward Marcia skates toward it to take a shot that could tie the game. Tim tries to take the puck away from Marcia, catches his stick on her skate, and accidentally trips her.

5. Missing her chance to make the tying goal and become the first girl to score a hat trick in a play-off game, Marcia jumps up and yells at Tim that he's a wimp who "should stick to figure skating and eating quiche."

6. Gary, Marcia's father and the Barons' assistant coach, seeing his team's championship hopes come to an end as the time runs out, grabs the nearest hockey stick and smashes it over the bench.

How many of those incidents do you define as aggression? Does your definition include only those incidents that you want to include and exclude the others? Do you define legal tactics as aggression? What about accidental injuries? What if someone tries to hit you but misses? Can aggression be verbal? Is kicking a bench or throwing a golf club aggression? Everyone may not agree on all those issues. However, most people agree that aggression involves the *intent* to injure. Most people would say that when Jeff swings his stick at Mark and misses, that is aggression, but Tim's accidental tripping of Marcia is not aggression. Most of the many authors who have written about aggression incorporate this notion of *intention to harm* into their definitions.

In *Human Aggression*, Baron (1977) offered the following representative definition:

Aggression is any form of behavior directed toward the goal of harming or injuring another living being who is motivated to avoid such treatment. (p. 7)

Baron's definition raises several key points. First, aggression is *behavior*. Aggression is not an attitude, emotion, or motive. *Thinking* negative thoughts or *wanting* to hurt someone is not aggression; anger is not aggression. Anger and other thoughts and motives might play a role in the occurrence of aggressive behavior, but they are neither necessary nor defining characteristics of aggression.

Second, aggression is *directed* or *intentional* behavior. Accidental harm is not aggression, but acts that are intended to injure others are aggression, whether or not they are successful.

The third dimension of aggression is that it involves *harm or injury*. Aggression is not limited to physical assaults but may include verbal acts intended to embarrass another person or acts that deprive someone of something, such as destroying a teammate's equipment.

The fourth criterion is that aggression involves *living beings*. According to Baron, kicking your dog is aggression, but kicking a bench is not.

Finally, Baron limits aggression to incidents in which the victim is motivated to avoid such treatment. Actually this is not much of a limitation because most people obviously want to avoid harm, and most definitions do not add such a qualification. The criterion of an avoidance-motivated victim eliminates sadomasochistic and suicidal acts from Baron's definition of aggression, including some apparently sadomasochistic sport behaviors.

Baron's definition delineates aggression as we commonly understand it, but many individuals see the need for further clarification. By definition, a defensive back who makes a hard tackle to stop a runner and a football player who gives an opponent an extra punch under the pile are both committing aggression, but most of us look at those two behaviors quite differently. The aggression literature differentiates *instrumental aggression*, which is aggressive behavior committed to achieve a nonaggressive goal, from *hostile aggression*, which usually involves anger and has harm or injury as its primary goal. Much aggression in sport is instrumental as participants use aggressive behaviors to get the ball, score points, or stop opponents. Hostile aggression also occurs in sport, and often the dividing line between hostile and instrumental aggression is quite fuzzy.

Husman and Silva (1984) point out that we should also distinguish aggression from *assertive behavior*. Diving into the stands to retrieve a basketball, looking for the "kill" shot in volleyball, and rushing the net in tennis are not aggression, despite what we often say. Such behaviors do not involve intended harm. Instead, they are purposeful, goal-directed, assertive behaviors. Performers who strive for competitive success or make forceful, decisive plays are not necessarily aggressive, and in this chapter we will restrict the term *aggression* to behaviors intended to harm or injure others.

# Theories of Aggression

Having defined aggression as behavior intended to harm or injure others, we now turn our attention to explanations of that behavior. Unlike many sport psychology topics, the aggression literature is rich in theory. Because of the prevalence of aggressive behavior and its social implications, people want to know why aggression occurs, which individual characteristics predispose a person to aggression, which environmental and social factors elicit aggressive behaviors, and whether aggression can be directed or controlled. Many authors have studied and written about aggression. Their explanations and approaches to understanding aggression fall into three major categories: instinct theories, drive theories, and social learning theories.

## Instinct Theories

Instinct theories, as the name implies, propose that aggressiveness is an innate characteristic of all individuals. According to instinct theory, we are born with an aggressive instinct that makes aggressive behavior inevitable. Instinct theories fall into two main categories: psychoanalytic and ethological approaches.

Psychoanalytic approaches, of course, are associated with Freudian concepts. Freud held that human beings have two basic instincts, including *eros*, the energizing life force, and *thanatos*, the death instinct or destructive force. Aggression occurs when the death instinct is turned outward, away from the individual and toward others.

The other major instinct theory of aggression, the ethological approach, is most widely known through the work of Konrad Lorenz (1966). Lorenz and other ethologists assert that the aggressive instinct is an innate fighting instinct that developed through evolution. Much of the ethological literature draws comparisons between the aggressive behaviors of humans and those of other species. Ardrey (1966), for example, discusses the instinctive tendency of animals to defend their territory with aggressive behaviors and notes that humans do the same thing. For example, do you feel like throwing out another student who occupies "your" seat in a class? Do you consider it an invasion if another person bypasses all the empty tables in the library to sit right next to you?

Lorenz proposes that the fighting instinct spontaneously generates aggressive energy at a constant rate and that aggressive energy continues to build up until it is released through an aggressive act. The more energy builds up, the more easily aggressive behavior is triggered. Aggressive energy builds up like steam in a boiler. If not released before reaching the boiling point, it may erupt in a violent, destructive outburst.

According to Lorenz, because aggressive energy always accumulates, the best way to prevent destructive violence is to ensure that aggressive energy is released in less destructive ways. Ethologists strongly advocate competitive sport as one of the best ways for people to "let off steam." Lorenz asserted that the greatest value of sport is that it provides an outlet for aggressive energy, and Storr (1968) presented the following view:

> It is obvious that the encouragement of competition in all possible fields is likely to diminish the kind of hostility which leads to war rather than to increase it. . . . Rivalry between nations in sport can do nothing but good. (p. 132)

Many coaches and teachers seem to adhere to an instinct theory of aggression when they make similar statements to sport participants and the public to promote their competitive programs.

Although instinct theories might provide a nice justification for some competitive sport programs, most researchers actively investigating aggression accept neither the psychoanalytic nor the ethological explanations of aggressive behavior. Instinct theories predict that all individuals and cultures have the same innate urges, generate similar levels of aggressive energy, and should exhibit similar levels of aggressive behavior. Cross-cultural comparisons suggest that this is not the case. Instinct theories also imply that the cultures or societies that have the most nondestructive outlets for aggression, or the most aggressive games, will be the least warlike. Again, anthropological evidence suggests otherwise. Are the athletes who participate in the most aggressive, competitive sports and who thus have the most opportunity to release aggressive energy the calmest and least aggressive people off the field? Perhaps some are, but this generalization would probably not hold across many comparisons. Most psychologists do not accept the generalizations that arise from instinct theories. Instead, most believe that reasoning plays a critical role in human behavior. Thus instinct theories have limited influence in current aggression research.

## Drive Theories

Drive theory, the second major theoretical perspective on aggression, has more credibility among psychologists. The most notable drive approach is the frustration-aggression hypothesis proposed by Dollard, Doob, Miller, Mowrer, and Sears (1939). The two key proposals of Dollard et al.'s hypothesis are that (a) frustration always leads to some form of aggression and (b) aggression always stems from frustration. Actually, frustration does not cause aggression directly. Instead, frustration, which is any blocking of a goal-oriented behavior, induces an instigation toward aggression known as *aggressive drive*. That aggressive drive in turn facilitates aggressive behavior.

The proposition that frustration leads to aggression makes sense and fits with many of our observations of aggression in sport. When former Ohio State football coach Woody Hayes slugged the Clemson player who had just intercepted a pass and eliminated any chance of an Ohio State victory, didn't frustration seem like the obvious cause of his aggressive behavior?

On the other hand, I can recall incidents in which individuals who were clearly frustrated by their lack of success did not commit any aggressive acts but took nonaggressive action or simply gave up in despair. Furthermore, many aggressive sport behaviors occur with no evidence of preceding frustration. Thus the frustration-aggression relationship may not be as inevitable as the hypothesis states. Miller, Dollard, and others did modify the original frustration-aggression hypothesis, but most current aggression researchers do not accept the mediating role of aggressive drive as inevitable.

Although the original frustration-aggression hypothesis is not widely advocated today, one of the most prominent authorities in this area, Leonard Berkowitz (1962, 1965, 1969, 1974), adopts some of Dollard et al.'s ideas in his revision of the frustration-aggression hypothesis. In many ways Berkowitz's views are closer to social learning theory than to drive theory, but he does propose that learning and innate sources of aggression coexist. According to Berkowitz, frustration plays a role by arousing anger and creating a "readiness" for aggressive behavior. Frustration is not a sufficient cause for aggression, however, and readiness for aggression is not a drive that must be released. Instead, learning and situational cues are critical in determining whether or not aggressive behavior actually occurs.

Berkowitz is one of the most productive researchers in the aggression area. In a typical experiment, a subject was angered or not angered and was then given the opportunity to aggress against a victim, usually by administering shocks. Within that general framework, Berkowitz examined several cues and situational factors. In general, anger arousal appeared to influence aggressive behavior as subjects who were angered usually gave more shocks than other subjects gave. However, situational cues often exerted an even greater influence on aggressive behavior. Watching an aggressive film, the presence of aggressive weapons, and characteristics of the victim that were associated with aggression—such as being a boxer rather than a speech major and having the same name as an aggressive character in a film—all increased aggressive behavior.

## Social Learning Theory

Proponents of the social learning perspective, most notably Albert Bandura (1973), assert that aggression is a learned social behavior and as such is acquired, elicited, and maintained in the same manner as other behaviors. According to Bandura, we learn or acquire aggressive behaviors in two ways: through direct reinforcement and through observational learning. Clearly, many aggressive behaviors are encouraged and reinforced in sport. For example, fans cheer when you slam an opponent into the boards in ice hockey, and giving an opponent a hard elbow under the boards may keep that opponent "off your back" for the rest of a basketball game. Similarly, when you "take out" the shortstop on your slide into second base, you interfere with the throw and allow your softball teammate to reach first base safely. All of these incidents reinforce aggressive behavior.

Sometimes the reinforcement is more subtle. Perhaps the youth soccer coach and league rules severely punish aggressive acts, but when Alan gets home his parents tell him he did a great job intimidating the opposing star forward with his tough, aggressive play. Perhaps another coach formally abides by the rules against aggressive play but cheers when a team member pushes an opponent to get to the ball.

Bandura's (Bandura, 1965; Bandura, Ross, & Ross, 1963a, 1963b) "Bobo doll" studies on the modeling of aggressive behavior are widely known. In a typical study children watched a model playing with various toys. In one condition the model threw and punched the Bobo doll while making statements such as "Sock him in the nose," "Hit him down," etc., whereas another model did not demonstrate aggressive behaviors. Invariably, observing an aggressive model increased the children's aggressive behavior, whether the model was live or on film. Seeing an aggressive model praised or rewarded especially elicited aggressive behavior, whereas children who saw a model punished for aggressive behavior did not display as much aggressive behavior. When those same children were offered rewards for imitating the aggressive model, however, they displayed just as much aggressive behavior as the children who had seen the aggressive model rewarded. The vicarious rewards and punishments to the model influenced the children's actual display of aggressive behaviors, but apparently all of the children learned or acquired the aggressive behaviors equally well.

Unlike instinct and drive theories, social learning theory does not propose any constant drive toward aggression. According to social learning theory, aggression is learned through reinforcement and modeling, and individuals aggress only under conditions that elicit or facilitate aggressive behaviors. Social learning theory is the most optimistic approach to aggression and violence. If people can learn aggressive responses to certain situations and cues, then they can also learn nonaggressive responses to those same situations.

Whereas instinct and drive theories see aggression as inevitable, social learning theory purports that aggression is learned and can be directed or controlled.

# Aggression and Sport

Sport psychology research into the relationship between aggression and sport has taken three main routes. Some researchers have approached aggression in sport as a catharsis that allows for the release of aggressive impulses and reduces aggressive behavior in nonsport settings. Other investigators have examined the antecedents and consequences of aggression in sport, and still others have focused on the effects of aggressive behavior on sport performance. The following review highlights the major findings of these three approaches.

## Sport as a Catharsis for Aggression

The most thoroughly discussed aggression issue in sport psychology is whether sport, especially highly competitive, contact sport, can act as a catharsis to reduce aggressive behavior in nonsport settings. The social implications of the relationship between sport and aggression are potentially wide ranging and profound. Will bigger and better Olympic games reduce the likelihood of war? Will our streets be safer if we start a community rugby program? Proponents of sport programs often claim that sport can reduce antisocial, destructive behaviors in the larger society, and many individual participants adhere to similar beliefs. For example, former professional football player and current coach Mike Ditka once stated,

> There's no question about it. I feel a lot of football players build up a lot of anxieties in the off-season because they have no outlets for them. . . . I'm an overactive person anyway and if I don't get rid of this energy, it just builds up in me and then I blow it off in some other way which is not really the proper way. (Fisher, 1976, pp. 251-252)

Many sport participants and promoters maintain that sport acts as a catharsis for aggressive behavior. The theoretical and empirical evidence, however, does not support such claims. As noted earlier, instinct theories support and advocate sport as a catharsis. The original frustration-aggression hypothesis in drive theory also implies that sport acts as a catharsis by releasing the aggressive drive. Those theories are not major forces in today's aggression literature, however, and neither social learning theory nor the revised frustration-aggression hypothesis provide any support for the catharsis phenomenon. In fact, both Bandura and Berkowitz argue that learning and reinforcement of aggressive behavior, which often occur in sport, should *increase* rather than decrease the probability of later aggressive behavior.

The question of whether engaging in aggressive behavior reduces the tendency to engage in subsequent aggressive behavior may be debated, but evidence clearly indicates that merely *observing* aggressive behavior has no cathartic effect. As Berkowitz (1970) emphatically concludes,

> A decade of laboratory research has virtually demolished the contention that people will lessen their aggressive tendencies by watching other persons beat each other up. (p. 2)

Just as laboratory research refutes the cathartic value of observing aggression, field studies demonstrate that watching aggressive sport actually *increases* rather than decreases hostility. In a unique field study, Goldstein and Arms (1971) questioned spectators at an Army-Navy football game and at an Army-Temple gymnastics meet. Spectators at the football game experienced increased feelings of hostility after the game, whereas spectators at the gymnastics meet showed no such rise in hostility. In a more extensive and controlled replication, Arms, Russell, and Sandilands (1979) reported that individuals who watched aggressive sport contests (wrestling and ice hockey) experienced increased feelings of hostility, but individuals who watched a swimming meet did not. Based on the aggression research of Berkowitz and others and some key sport studies, we can conclude that observing aggressive sports has no cathartic benefits. If anything, watching aggressive sports increases the probability of aggressive behavior in the observer.

Even though observing aggressive sport has no cathartic value, actually participating in vigorous, aggressive activity often seems better than doing nothing when we are angry. Perhaps performing an aggressive act, even a relatively noninjurious one, lowers arousal and reduces the probability of further aggressive actions, at least in some situations.

A few studies (Doob, 1970; Doob & Wood, 1972; Konechi, 1975) indicate that aggressing directly against the person who annoyed you may reduce aggressive behavior. For example, if you give an extra elbow to an opposing player who has been on your back during most of a game, that act may reduce your anger and make you less likely to commit other aggressive acts. Other studies, however (Berkowitz, 1966; Geen, Stonner, & Shope, 1975), contradict those findings and indicate that even if you do not hit anyone else during that particular game, the success and reinforcement you experience through elbowing your opponent may increase the chances that you will commit similar aggressive acts in future games.

The few existing studies on catharsis and physical activity indicate that vigorous activity does *not* act as a catharsis. Following the Berkowitz paradigm, Ryan (1970) compared the aggressive behaviors of individuals in a control condition to those of individuals who (a) engaged in vigorous physical activity (pounding a mallet), (b) won in competition, or (c) lost in competition. Ryan found no support for the catharsis hypothesis; the pounding activity did not reduce aggressive behavior. Ryan also found that individuals who won in competition were less aggressive than those who lost.

In another test of physical exercise as a catharsis, Zillman, Katcher, and Milavsky (1972) compared the aggressive behaviors of individuals who had been provoked and then rode a bicycle ergometer to those who were provoked and performed a nonarousing task. The results not only failed to support catharsis, but individuals who exercised behaved *more* aggressively than those who performed the nonarousing activity. These findings suggest that the arousal created by exercise could actually *facilitate* aggressive behavior.

A subsequent experiment (Zillman, Johnson, & Day, 1974) revealed that exercise-induced arousal did not increase aggressive behavior if the individuals knew that their increased arousal was due to exercise. When individuals sat quietly after the exercise before having an opportunity to aggress, however, they were more aggressive. Zillman et al. reasoned that when heightened arousal clearly stems from exercise, competition, noise, or other sources unrelated to aggression, individuals do not become more aggressive. But when the source of arousal is not easily identified—as when time has elapsed after exercise—the arousal may be labeled as anger or irritation and may increase aggressive behavior. Considering all the research on catharsis, Baron (1977) concluded that aggressive acts sometimes reduce arousal but that the evidence does not indicate that such aggressive acts reduce the probability of later aggression even if arousal is reduced.

## Antecedents of Aggression in Sport

Despite the prevalence of aggressive behavior in sport and the numerous related issues and implications, very few investigators have attempted to determine its antecedents and consequences. The theoretical work of Berkowitz and Bandura offers some suggestions, but only a few researchers have explored those suggestions. High arousal levels are obviously common in sport, and many incidents in sport provoke or anger participants. Those conditions do not necessarily elicit aggression, however. As Berkowitz and Bandura propose, whether or not individuals actually behave aggressively depends on the situational cues and the responses that have been learned and reinforced.

Of course, many aggressive responses are encouraged, reinforced, and expected in sport. Silva (1979b) compared basketball players' guilt reactions to aggressive behavior in sport and to aggressive behavior in a competitive nonsport setting. As Silva suspected, the players expressed less guilt for aggressive behavior in sport, implying that aggressive behavior is more acceptable in sport than in nonsport settings.

Michael Smith is one of the few people who has written extensively about the causes of aggression in sport and, in particular, the causes of violence in youth ice hockey. Smith (1978, 1979) discounts the instinct and drive theory arguments that speed, contact, intensity, frustration, or a need for catharsis account for the violence in hockey. With specific reference to amateur youth hockey, Smith takes a social learning perspective and emphatically states that violence is caused by the influence of the professional game. First, the hockey system encourages aggressive behavior as a way for players to advance to higher levels. Smith notes that the majority of young hockey players agree with the statement, "If you want personal recognition in hockey, it helps to play rough." The hockey system not only encourages aggression, but significant others (parents, coaches, teammates) accept and praise aggressive acts. Additionally, the communications media reward such behavior by focusing on violent incidents. Thus young hockey players learn aggressive behaviors through reinforcement and modeling, just as Bandura would predict.

Smith's work suggests that situational reinforcements and modeling play key roles in sport aggression. Smith's data are limited, however, and few controlled studies have examined any situational factors or individual characteristics that might influence aggression in sport behavior. For example, some of the psychology literature suggests that gender differences exist in aggressive behavior, but gender differences in sport aggression have not been examined. Some reviewers (Deaux, 1976; Maccoby & Jacklin, 1974) conclude that males exhibit more aggressive behavior than females exhibit, but others (Baron, 1977; Frodi, Macauley, & Thome, 1977) disagree. These authors suggest that gender differences in aggression are more complex and may be decreasing with changes in society. The changing roles of women in sport and the increasing presence of females in highly competitive, aggressive sports may be changing gender differences in aggressive sport behavior quite dramatically. Silva (1983) observed that males tended to see aggression in sport as more legitimate than did females, but few others have investigated gender differences in perceptions, behaviors, and reactions to aggression in sport. Enterprising investigators could find countless issues to examine in relation to gender and individual differences and how they interact with situational factors to influence aggressive behavior in sport.

## Aggression and Sport Performance

Few researchers have examined factors that influence aggressive behavior in sport. Likewise, investigators have seldom examined the consequences of sport aggression. We currently know very little about how aggression affects performance and other sport behaviors either immediately or over time, how aggression influences our thoughts and feelings about the sport experience, or how sport participants react to their own aggressive behaviors and the aggressive behaviors of others. Perhaps the first issue to consider is how aggression affects sport performance.

A few investigators have considered the relationship between aggressive behavior and sport performance, but the limited data provide little insight into the underlying processes. Some individuals insist that aggression aids sport performance. We often encourage athletes to play tough, hit hard, or intimidate opponents. As mentioned in chapter 3, aggressiveness is one of the key personality characteristics of successful athletes on the *Athletic Motivation Inventory* (Tutko, Ogilvie, & Lyon, 1969). The empirical evidence, however, is not so convincing.

McCarthy and Kelly (1978a, 1978b) did find a positive correlation between aggressive behavior (penalty minutes) and assists and goals scored in ice hockey. Wankel (1973), however, found no difference in the aggressive penalties of winning and losing teams in university hockey. Widmeyer and Birch (1979) reported that elite, all-star university hockey players were *either* extremely aggressive or extremely nonaggressive, whereas those who were not all-stars were moderately aggressive. Thus even the data from the limited setting of ice hockey are equivocal. Furthermore, even if penalty minutes did relate positively to success, we could not conclude that aggression causes success; other factors might affect both penalties and success.

Few studies on aggression involve sports other than hockey, but Sachs (1978), in one of the few studies on women, reported that softball success was not related to either reactive (hostile) or instrumental aggression. In the only controlled investigation that I know of, Silva (1979a) used confederates to provoke hostile aggression in individuals playing competitive pegboard and three-person basketball. Players provoked into hostile aggression exhibited less concentration and poorer performance than individuals in a nonprovoked condition for both the pegboard and basketball tasks. Silva concluded that hostile aggression may increase arousal, which interferes with concentration and consequently impairs performance.

The existing research, limited as it is, provides no evidence that aggressive behavior improves sport performance. On the contrary, it appears that hostile aggression quite likely creates anger and arousal, interferes with concentration, and has no apparent benefits. Some aggressive acts may, of course, have instrumental value in sport. The value of such aggressive behaviors probably varies with the situation and individuals involved. Research findings also suggest that the consequences of both hostile and instrumental aggression may extend beyond immediate performance effects. Sport psychologists have far to go before the factors that influence aggressive behavior and its consequences can be discussed with any certainty.

# Prosocial Behavior in Sport

We have discussed aggressive behavior, which involves the intent to injure others, at length. I would like to devote equal time to the other side of social behavior, prosocial or helping behavior in sport. Unfortunately, neither theoretical work nor empirical data permit such an extended discourse. In fact, research and writing on prosocial, helping behavior in sport are virtually nonexistent. Sport psychologists have neither documented the existence of helping behaviors in sport nor investigated the factors that elicit and maintain prosocial behaviors and the consequences of such actions for sport participants.

Individuals in sport often discuss "sportsmanship," "sportspersonship," or simply "sporting behavior." Discussions of *sporting behavior*, which might be defined as ethical or moral behavior in sport, typically extend beyond psychological observations into more abstract value judgments or statements of opinion. Sport programs and activities reflect our moral values, and careful consideration of those values is appropriate and useful. Sport psychologists could contribute to the discussion with theoretical statements and evidence about the antecedents and consequences of various prosocial behaviors in sport. To date, however, such topics have not been explored by sport psychology researchers.

Kroll (1975) presented a paper on the psychology of sportsmanship and proposed that ethical behaviors develop in sport situations when the individual must choose between an ethically correct strategy and a success strategy. Many sport critics decry the emphasis on competition and winning in sport and insist that we can best encourage ethical behavior by eliminating that competitive emphasis. Kroll countered that view by arguing that ethical choices are important only if success is also important. In other words, if a sport participant has nothing to lose by acting in an ethical or prosocial way, then ethical or prosocial actions in a sport situation become less significant. Consider, for example, the following scenarios: (a) A basketball player refrains from intentionally fouling an opponent and allows the opponent to make an uncontested breakaway lay-up when the team has a 20-point lead, and (b) A basketball player refrains from making the intentional foul when the score is tied in the last minute. Which scenario do you consider the more strikingly ethical behavior? Avoiding a foul or injury when the score does not matter does not strike us as especially ethical.

Most of the dramatic incidents of sporting behavior that you can recall probably involved sacrificing success. Kroll suggests that those situations in which the individual must choose between an ethical or "sporting" action and a success action are the situations that develop our moral or sporting standards and values. If we want to encourage the development of ethical behaviors, we should encourage sport participants to make ethical choices in situations that force a choice between success and some moral criterion. All ethical and sporting decisions do not require sacrificing success, but we should not ignore ethical issues as we pursue success. In fact, we should make choices based on relevant ethical criteria.

Although sport psychologists have seldom investigated ethical decisions and prosocial behaviors or the factors that influence them, Bredemeier and Shields (Bredemeier, 1984; Shields & Bredemeier, 1984) have initiated a systematic investigation of the development of moral behavior in sport. Most of the earlier writing implied either that sport was the ideal arena to develop ethical values or that sport destroyed moral judgment. Bredemeier and Shields take a structural developmental approach and assert that sport can affect moral development either positively or negatively. They report that college basketball players use less mature forms of moral reasoning than college nonathletes and suggest that the tendency to objectify opponents, project responsibility for moral decisions onto coaches and officials, and take an unbalanced interest in one's own gain may all discourage moral growth. On the other hand, they report that sport enhanced the moral reasoning of children in a summer camp in both a social learning situation in which moral behavior was reinforced and modeled and in a structural developmental group that included peer-oriented moral dialogues. Thus, depending upon the situation, participation in sport can either positively or negatively influence moral development.

## Summary

Many people have written about and discussed aggression in sport, but few have conducted systematic research on aggression in sport and exercise settings. The strongest theoretical work suggests that aggression is learned through the modeling and reinforcement of aggressive behaviors. Research does *not* support the popular notion that sport acts as a catharsis to release aggressive urges. Instead, the modeling and reinforcement of aggression in sport probably increases the probability of aggressive behaviors in both sport and nonsport settings. Like aggression, the topic of prosocial or sporting behavior abounds with issues and questions but offers few answers and conclusions. Sport psychologists could build upon the work of Berkowitz and Bandura or explore other possibilities within the unique context of sport to clarify the role of aggressive and prosocial behaviors and the characteristics and factors that interact with and influence such behaviors in sport.

# PART V

# *The Dynamics of Sport Groups*

In part V we will conclude our progression through the sport psychology literature by reviewing the research on the dynamics of sport groups. Group performance, a critical concern for many sport participants, is the focus of chapter 13. Our review of the research will reveal that the relationship of individual abilities to group performance is far from simple. Complex coordination and motivation processes affect group performance, and research indicates that recognition of individual efforts is critical in group activities.

In chapter 14 we will review the sport psychology literature on interpersonal relationships in groups, concentrating on the topics of cohesiveness and leadership. We often claim that cohesive teams win more games, but the research does not confirm that popular belief. As you will discover, many factors must be considered to clarify the relationship between cohesiveness and performance for sport teams. Leadership is another topic that is often discussed by sport participants, and sport psychologists are just beginning to investigate the specific factors and relationships in sport leadership. In fact, sport psychologists are just beginning to unravel many of the complex leadership and group dynamics issues that concern sport participants. Those efforts are discussed in chapter 14.

# CHAPTER 13

# *Individual and Group Performance in Sport*

Most sport activities involve groups or teams. Even so-called individual sports are conducted as team competitions. We also play informal volleyball matches with friends, join racquetball clubs, participate in exercise groups, and learn sport skills in physical education classes. Clearly, the psychological processes and dynamics of sport groups are crucial issues in sport psychology. Despite the predominance of group activities in sport, however, sport psychologists are not avid pursuers of group dynamics research.

The reluctance of sport psychologists and others to tackle sport group research may be attributed, at least in part, to the overwhelming complexity of group dynamics. Sport teams, like other groups, involve several individuals with varying relationships to each other interacting through various processes over changing times and environmental conditions. Groups, by definition, involve interaction, and the dynamic nature of group processes makes it difficult to identify researchable questions, let alone to reach conclusions. Even if we limit our attention to team performance, which is a primary concern of sport participants and one of the most identifiable and easily measured aspects of group dynamics, we need to consider the interactions of many factors and relationships within a group dynamics framework.

First, we should consider what we mean by a *group*. Certainly a professional basketball team or a youth soccer team is a group. A swimming class at the community center and the noon exercise club at a local business are also groups. But what about several individuals who are jogging on a track at the same time or the crowd at a football game? Most authors who have written about groups (e.g., McGrath, 1984; Shaw, 1976) agree that a collection of individuals is not necessarily a group. *Interaction* is the key defining characteristic of a group. Group members must be aware of each other, relate to each other in some way, and have the ability to interact with each other through group processes.

McGrath (1984) states, "Groups are those social aggregates that involve mutual awareness and potential interaction" (p. 7). Several joggers who happen to be running on the same track are not concerned with each other, do not interact, and are therefore not a group. McGrath also excludes crowds and organizations that are too large for mutual awareness and interaction, although those larger aggregates might include many groups. Groups must contain at least two persons but be small enough to provide for interaction, mutual awareness, some interdependence, and continuity over time. McGrath acknowledges that the dividing line between groups and nongroups is vague and notes that even groups that we all recognize and define as groups vary tremendously. Most sport teams, exercise groups, and skill classes clearly fall within McGrath's definition, however, and application of a group dynamics framework may clarify some sport group processes.

## McGrath's Conceptual Framework for the Study of Groups

McGrath (1984) recently advanced a conceptual framework that specifies factors and relationships in the group dynamics process. In its entirety, McGrath's model is complex and presents few clear, simple relationships. McGrath's model is not designed, however, to provide simple answers but rather to serve as a guide to investigating and understanding the interactive relationships and processes within group dynamics.

Group interaction, the defining characteristic of a group, is the central element of the model. The rest of the model specifies factors and relationships that both influence and are influenced by the interactive processes. Individual characteristics influence group structures and patterns, environmental properties affect the group task and situation, and those factors collectively influence the behavioral setting under which group interaction takes place. Group interaction is influenced by all those components as well as by forces internal to the interaction process itself. Furthermore, the interaction process may in turn lead to changes in the group's members, the environment, and the relationships present in the group. Given the complexities of the model, it is not surprising that researchers have not delineated the factors that affect sport group dynamics. This text will not unravel all the mysteries of sport groups, but in the remainder of this chapter we will examine some insights into group performance that are provided by the extant literature.

## Group Performance in Sport

Group performance is one of the most pressing practical issues in sport. Coaches and others who work with sport groups devote prodigious effort to maximizing team performance. Perhaps the maxim most accepted by both sport researchers and participants is that the best individuals make the best team. In general this rule is undoubtedly true; obviously, five intercollegiate basketball players will consistently defeat five intramural players. However, the relationship between individual abilities and group performance is not perfect. Most of us can recall incidents in which teams with all the talent to win the championship did not or times when teams without individual stars performed exceptionally well as teams. Simply summing the abilities of individual group members does not accurately describe the group performance. Thus we must consider the group process as well as individual abilities to understand group performance.

## Steiner's Model of Group Performance

Steiner (1972) has proposed a theoretical model that may clarify the individual/group performance relationship in sport. The essence of Steiner's model is expressed by the following equation:

Actual productivity = Potential productivity − Losses due to faulty process

Potential productivity is the group's best possible performance given its resources and the task demands. The group's resources comprise all relevant knowledge and skills of individual members, including the overall level and distribution of such talents.

Individual ability, demonstrated by individual performance, is probably the most important resource for sport groups. According to Steiner's model, greater resources increase potential productivity, and, as in the general maxim, the best individuals make the best team. Steiner's model, however, goes beyond the general maxim.

To contribute to potential performance, resources must be relevant to the task. Thus height is a relevant resource for a volleyball team but not for a track relay team. Task demands, or the rules and requirements imposed by the task, determine which resources are relevant to performance. When a group effectively uses its available resources to meet task demands, its actual productivity or performance approaches its potential.

In Steiner's model, a group's actual performance falls short of its potential performance because of faulty *process*. Process includes all individual and interactive actions by which a group transforms its resources into a collective product or performance, or what we often refer to as the process of "putting it all together." Process losses may be subdivided into the two general categories of coordination losses and motivation losses. Coordination losses occur when poor timing or ineffective strategies detract from the group's potential, such as when a basketball team fails to get the ball to the top scorer or when volleyball setters and spikers are unable to execute the timing on a short set. Motivational losses occur when group members slack off or give less than their best efforts.

These process losses, which involve both group actions and interactions of group members, are critical considerations when working with sport groups. Coaches have some influence on group resources when they recruit individual talent or provide instructions to improve individual abilities, but otherwise resources and task demands are relatively stable. The main role of a teacher or coach working with a sport team is to reduce process losses by developing and practicing organizational strategies that reduce coordination losses and maintain optimal motivation levels.

Process losses and the strategies needed to reduce such losses vary with the sport task. Activities that require considerable interaction or cooperation, such as basketball, are more susceptible to coordination losses than activities that demand less interaction, such as softball or swimming. Consequently, the basketball coach spends considerable time, thought, and effort developing strategies and drills to achieve correct timing and team movement patterns. The softball coach spends some time working on interactive skills, such as double plays, but also devotes considerable time to developing individual batting and fielding skills. The swimming coach may try to develop efficient transitions among relay team members but otherwise spends little time on interactive skills.

## Research on Individual and Group Motor Performance

The most cited works on individual and group motor performance are those of Comrey (1953) and Wiest, Porter, and Ghiselli (1961). Both Comrey, using a pegboard task, and Wiest et al., using puzzles, had subjects perform a series of individual trials followed by a series of group trials. In all cases the individual scores of both partners were positively related to group performance, and combining the two individual scores in a multiple correlation yielded a moderate positive relationship with group performance.

In a study directly involving sport teams, Jones (1974) compared team performance (rankings or final win/loss records) to individual statistics (i.e., singles rankings in tennis; points for and against in football; runs batted in and earned run averages in baseball; and points, assists, and rebounds in basketball) for professional teams. Jones concluded that group effectiveness was positively related to individual effectiveness in all cases. The relationship was weakest for basketball, the sport with the greatest interaction, which suggests that interaction requirements may reduce the individual ability/group performance relationship.

Those studies suggest a positive individual/group performance relationship, but the data are correlational and do not indicate whether we can predict team performance. In a more controlled study, I (Gill, 1979) matched partners in two-person teams to see how well individual scores predicted group performance. In each of two experiments, individual performance scores on a motor maze task were used to form two-person groups representing a range of average ability levels and discrepancies between partners for a group performance session. Multiple regression analyses revealed a moderate positive correlation between group performance and the combination of average ability and ability discrepancy in both experiments. Average ability was the primary predictor, but ability discrepancy (a large difference between partners) had a negative effect on cooperative performance.

In the second experiment, a control group performed as individuals in both task sessions to check the reliability of individual performance. Individual performance was not especially reliable from session to session and almost completely unreliable from trial to trial. Sport performance, which is subject to numerous influences that were controlled in the laboratory, is probably even less reliable or consistent. A baseball batter, for example, often goes 3-for-4 in one game and 1-for-4 in the next game. Thus individual abilities relate to group motor performance, but in light of the variability of both individual and group performance, more than a moderate positive prediction of team performance is not realistic.

## The Ringelmann Effect

Most of the research on sport groups has assessed individual performance and group performance without considering the intervening group process. One line of research that has developed into a systematic investigation of group process stems from an obscure, unpublished study of individual and group performance on a rope-pulling task. Nearly 100 years ago a French agricultural engineer named Ringelmann observed individuals and groups of two, three, and eight persons pulling on a rope (cited in Ingham, Levinger, Graves, & Peckham, 1974; Kravtiz & Martin, 1986). Groups in Ringelmann's study pulled with more force than individuals but not with as much force as would be predicted by adding individual scores. Eight-person groups did not pull eight times as hard as individuals but only four times as hard. The average individual force exerted by members of two-person groups was 93% of the average individual force in solo performance, and this percentage decreased to 85% for three-person groups and 49% for eight-person groups. This phenomenon in which average individual performance decreases with increases in group size is known as the *Ringelmann effect*.

The Ringelmann effect was mentioned frequently in discussions of group performance but was not actually demonstrated until Ingham, Levinger, Graves, and Peckham (1974) resurrected the original Ringelmann paradigm with updated controls and modifications. Ingham et al.'s first step was to replicate the Ringelmann effect with individuals and groups of two, three, four, five, and six persons. Experiment 1 of Ingham et al.'s study partially replicated the Ringelmann effect; the average performance of individuals in two-person groups was 91% of the average individual solo performance, and average performance dropped to 82% in three-person groups. Groups of four, five, and six persons, however, did not exhibit further decreases as the average performance in six-person groups was 78% of the average individual solo performance. (See Figure 13.1 for a comparison of the Ingham et al. and Ringelmann findings.)

Ingham et al. not only demonstrated the Ringelmann effect but extended their investigation to determine whether the performance decreases were due to coordination losses or motivation losses. Possible motivation losses were examined by eliminating the coordination requirements of the group task. In Experiment 2 only one real subject pulled on the rope, but by using blindfolds and trained confederates who pretended to pull, subjects were led to believe that they were performing in groups of from one to six members. The results were virtually identical to results in Experiment 1. Average performance dropped to 85% in three-person groups, and no further drops were observed. Ingham et al. concluded that the decreases in average performance were due to motivational losses within groups.

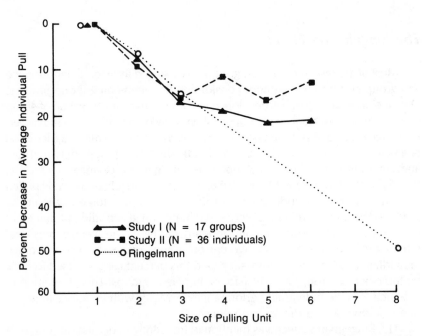

**Figure 13.1**  Individual rope-pulling scores as a function of group size. *Note.* From "The Ringlemann Effect: Studies of Group Size and Group Performance" by A. Ingham, G. Levinger, J. Graves, and V. Peckham, 1974, *Journal of Personality and Social Psychology, 10*, p. 377. Copyright 1974 by the American Psychological Association. Reprinted with permission.

**Social Loafing in Groups.** More recently, Latane and his colleagues undertook a systematic investigation of group performance and process, and, in light of Ingham et al.'s findings, dubbed the motivational losses noted in groups "social loafing." The first study of the series (Latane, Williams, & Harkins, 1979) included two experiments using clapping and shouting as group tasks. Experiment 1 confirmed the Ringelmann effect as the average sound produced per person decreased from the solo performance to 71% in two-person groups, 51% in four-person groups, and 40% in six-person groups.

Experiment 2 included pseudo groups as well as actual groups. In the pseudo groups, instructions and constant background noise played through earphones led subjects to believe that they were clapping or shouting in groups when in fact they were performing alone. Actual groups in Experiment 2 performed much like the groups in Experiment 1 as the average sound produced by members of two- and six-person groups was 66% and 36% of the average sound in solo performances. Pseudo groups also exhibited social loafing with the average sound dropping to 82% in two-person groups and 74% in six-person groups. Because coordination losses (e.g., interfering sound waves) were eliminated in the pseudo groups, Latane et al. concluded that this performance drop was due to motivation losses or social loafing. The greater performance drop for actual groups represented a combination of coordination and motivation losses. Unlike Ingham et al., Latane et al. thus observed both coordination losses and motivation losses in their groups' task performances.

After confirming the motivation losses, Latane and his colleagues pursued the issue by probing the causes and explanations of social loafing. Williams, Harkins, and Latane (1981) proposed that *identifiability* of individual performance is critical. When individual efforts are "lost in the crowd," performance decreases. In two experiments, Williams et al. demonstrated that when group members believed that their individual outputs were identifiable (i.e., known to others), social loafing was eliminated.

Introducing the identifiability factor reconciles the apparently conflicting coaction effects in social facilitation literature and the social loafing phenomenon in group performance literature. In typical coaction situations, evaluation potential *increases* with an increase in the number of coactors. In typical social loafing situations, evaluation potential *decreases* as group size increases. When identifiability remains high in group performance situations, evaluation potential does not decrease, and Williams et al.'s findings indicate that performance does not decrease.

**Social Incentives in Groups.** If simply monitoring individual performance can eliminate social loafing, perhaps other factors can provide a social incentive and actually *increase* individual efforts in groups. Sport teams are natural examples of groups that seem to provide social incentives in the form of social support and peer pressure from teammates. After noting that many people believe athletes perform better when in a relay or group than when alone, Latane, Harkins, and Williams (1980) decided to examine social loafing and identifiability in a sport setting.

Latane and his colleagues first checked individual and relay times at the 1977 Big Ten intercollegiate swim meet. A comparison of the times of swimmers who swam both individual and relay events with the same stroke and distance revealed no social loafing; instead, times for relay events were faster than individual times. Because the faster start in relay events could account for the difference, they designed a controlled experiment to test their observations.

A competition was set up with 16 members of an intercollegiate swim team who swam in two 100-meter individual freestyle events and in one lap of each of two 400-meter freestyle relays. Because relay starts are typically faster than flat starts, the starts were standardized by having all swimmers use the faster anticipated starts. Along with the individual and relay conditions, identifiability was manipulated by announcing or not announcing individuals' lap times.

An identifiability by individual-relay interaction was found for performance times. Under low identifiability, when individual times were not announced, individual times were faster (61.34 seconds) than relay times (61.66), implying social loafing. Under high identifiability, however, individual times were slower (60.95) than relay times (60.18). Not only was social loafing eliminated with high identifiability, but the group situation seemed to provide a social incentive. Although the time differences due to identifiability were small (1.48 seconds for relay times and .39 seconds for individual times), such small differences often determine places in a competitive event.

## Implications for Sport Teams

Perhaps the most basic finding of the group performance research is support for our common belief in the general individual ability/group performance relationship. The best individuals make the best team. No evidence suggests any reason for selecting any but the most skilled or capable individual performers. Selecting the best individuals, however, is not easy. Individual performance is not necessarily the most appropriate measure. A group task, especially a task requiring high interaction, may require skills not evident in individual performance. For example, a track relay involves the skills of passing and receiving the baton as well as individual speed. Sports requiring greater interaction impose many skill requirements not present in individual performance, such as timing passes, double plays, and playing zone defenses.

Identifying persons who possess individual interactive skills as well as individual performance skills could greatly reduce coordination losses in sport groups. In lieu of selecting the best individuals, or when selecting the best individuals is not possible, coaches and instructors might direct their efforts toward developing team members' interactive skills and reducing coordination losses. Indeed, a large portion of most coaches' efforts is directed at reducing coordination losses. Drills in interactive skills, set plays, and formations all reduce uncertainty and variability in the group process and probably reduce losses due to ineffective coordination of effort. At this point, neither social psychologists nor sport psychologists can offer much additional advice to coaches and instructors on reducing those losses.

# Group Motivation

Psychologists have a great deal to say about motivation, although most of the motivational work deals with individuals rather than groups. The motivational concepts discussed in part III apply to individuals in groups. Group interaction also introduces group motivation issues, specifically the desire for *group success* and concern for *group goals* as well as individual goals.

## The Desire for Group Success

Zander (1971, 1975) is one of the few social psychologists to address the issue of group motivation and to apply his work to sport teams. Using constructs analogous to those in the Atkinson model of achievement motivation, Zander proposes the *desire for group success* $(D_{gs})$ as a key element in group motivation. Unlike the analogous *motive to approach success* $(M_s)$ in Atkinson's model, the $D_{gs}$ is situation-specific. Like $M_s$, however, $D_{gs}$ spurs group members to set and strive for challenging goals. As with individuals, challenging but realistic goals with approximately a 50% chance of success elicit optimal achievement behavior from groups.

Emerson's (1966) unique participant observation study of a Mt. Everest climbing team revealed that team members directed their communication toward maintaining uncertainty (a 50% chance of success) to keep themselves operating at maximum effort. When the environment was encouraging and things were going well, climbers talked about things to be wary of and potential problems. In contrast, bad weather and difficulties brought out more optimistic talk. Similarly, many coaches alter pregame talks depending on the opponent. When faced with a far superior opponent, coaches typically downplay that superiority and emphasize their own team's strengths. In contrast, when faced with a much weaker opponent, coaches often stress taking the opponent seriously and playing with full effort.

With specific reference to sport, Zander advocates developing $D_{gs}$ through a pride-in-team approach. One could interpret Zander as emphasizing group goals and de-emphasizing individual goals (there is no "I" in team), but this is not necessarily true. Zander stresses the importance of ensuring that each member's individual contribution is valued and recognized.

## Individual Recognition in Groups

The research of Ingham, Latane, and their colleagues clearly points out the inadvisability of submerging individuals within the team. Group goals, like individual goals, must be specific and behavior-oriented to influence performance effectively. Ultimately, however, the specific behaviors contributing to group goals are individual behaviors. Those desired behaviors may involve interactions with teammates in tasks or processes that are not as evident as individual and group performance outcomes (e.g., points, win/loss). Indeed, key interactive behaviors are often overlooked when we focus on performance outcomes in sport. The task for anyone working with sport groups is to identify individual behaviors that contribute to group performance and to apply strategies that encourage those behaviors.

Performance feedback is a relatively simple but effective tactic for enhancing individual and group performance. Research (Zajonc, 1962; Zander & Wolfe, 1964) indicates that feedback to group members that includes individual scores as well as group scores elicits better performance than feedback of group scores only. Along with providing information feedback, we should encourage and reinforce positive individual behaviors. As research on individual motivation and rewards indicates, however, overemphasis on extrinsic rewards can reduce intrinsic motivation (see chapter 10). Thus verbal encouragement and specific, informative evaluations of positive behaviors will probably have fewer negative consequences than adding extensive extrinsic reward systems.

Effective coaches identify and recognize individual contributions to team performance. Latane et al. (1980) cited the example of football linemen at Ohio State University whose individual contributions could easily go unrecognized by focusing exclusively on the group outcome. Latane et al. noted that both Woody Hayes and Earle Bruce used several techniques to increase the identifiability and recognition of the individual efforts of linemen, including filming and specifically grading each player on each play, "lineman of the week" honors, and decals to signify individual effort.

While at the University of Iowa, basketball coach Lute Olson developed a "total performance chart" to rate each player's performance in each game. Total performance was calculated by including assists, steals, blocked shots, and forced turnovers as well as points and rebounds and then subtracting errors such as missed shots, fouls, and turnovers. Many of the components are not included in typical game reports, but Olson considered those behaviors essential for optimal group performance. Many other coaches apply similar techniques to recognize individual performances, and those who do not would be well advised to do so.

# *Summary*

Group performance, and particularly the relationship of individual abilities to group performance, is an important concern for sport teams. Although research confirms a positive relationship between individual abilities and group performance, suggesting that the best individuals make the best team, that relationship is far from perfect. Many aspects of group interaction, including coordination of individual efforts and motivational processes, affect group performance. Considerable research indicates that social loafing occurs when group outcomes are emphasized and individual efforts go unrecognized and unrewarded. Perhaps the most promising finding in the group performance literature is that social incentives may not only reduce social loafing but may enhance individual efforts.

At present, the research presents more questions than answers about the incentive properties of groups, but the preliminary findings are encouraging. Identifiability of individual contributions, increased evaluation potential, feedback, behavioral and cognitive motivational techniques, and any number of personal and interpersonal psychological factors not yet examined may enhance individual performance in teams. The investigation of precise influences and interactive effects of those and other variables within sport teams warrant extensive future research. In the meantime, the following suggestions are offered to those who work with sport groups:

- Identify the individual behaviors that contribute to desired group performance, and be especially alert to interactive behaviors that are often overlooked.

- Ensure that those individual behaviors are recognized and encouraged.

# CHAPTER 14

# *Interpersonal Relationships in Sport Groups*

Sport group dynamics involve much more than group performance and team success or failure. The psychological implications of the social relationships and interpersonal processes within sport groups are equally compelling topics. Even coaches of highly competitive, task-oriented teams often devote time and effort to improving group communication or cohesiveness, and participants in recreational sport activities are often more concerned with interpersonal relationships than with performance outcomes.

Sport psychologists might pose many questions about interpersonal relationships within sport groups. We might consider how group goals and norms are developed and maintained or examine the implications of varying interaction processes for the group and its members. Do new recruits decide how much to hustle in practice by observing veterans? Do certain players have more influence than others on group goals and standards? If so, why? How does the turnover of team members each season affect group structure, goals, relationships, and performance? Do starters and reserves relate differently to each other or to the coach? What types of communication and influence patterns develop in informal, recreational sport groups, and how do those patterns affect the participants?

We could pose countless questions about sport group dynamics, but we will find few answers. Issues related to interpersonal relationships within sport groups have received scant attention from sport psychologists and sport sociologists. The general social psychology literature on group dynamics does not provide much assistance because that literature usually involves decision making, problem solving, or verbal behavior rather than physical activity, and the formal organizational models studied are quite removed from the unique structure and relationships of sport teams and groups. Most of the existing research on sport group relationships focuses on two general areas: leadership and cohesiveness. Even that work, however, is limited in scope. The sport leadership research has centered primarily on the leadership role of the coach, and the sport cohesiveness literature has focused on the relationship between cohesiveness and team performance. In the remainder of this chapter we will consider these two topics in more detail.

# Leadership in Sport

Leadership is a prominent interpersonal issue in any group. In sport we typically think of the team coach, class instructor, or exercise director as the leader. However, leadership is not simply a characteristic of single persons but rather a complex social relationship that may be defined as "the behavioral process of influencing individuals and groups toward set goals" (Barrow, 1977, p. 232). Thus defined, leadership is not limited to coaches, instructors, or team captains, and even sport groups without formal leaders include individuals who clearly influence the group. Furthermore, leadership is a complex relationship that cannot be understood without considering not only the leader but also the situation and the persons who are being influenced (followers).

Early research on leadership ignored the followers and the situational context in attempts to describe the personality characteristics of leaders. Much of that work attempted to identify common characteristics of selected great leaders and hence is often called the *Great Man Theory of Leadership* (the theory was a theory about great *men*, literally). Like the early personality research that focused on traits and ignored situational factors and interactions, the early work on leadership traits yielded few conclusive findings. The leadership research gradually shifted from a focus on traits to an interactive model that considered the relative effectiveness of various leadership styles and behaviors in varying group situations.

## Fiedler's Contingency Model of Leadership

Fiedler's (1967) contingency model of leadership effectiveness is the predominant theoretical approach to the interaction of leader characteristics and situational factors. Within Fiedler's model leaders are classified as *task-oriented* and primarily focused on performance or as *person-oriented* and primarily concerned with interpersonal relationships. The effectiveness of a task-oriented or person-oriented leader depends on the favorableness of the situation. Situation favorableness is the product of three factors: leader/member relations, task structure, and the leader's position power or authority. The situation is most favorable with warm, positive leader/member relations; a clearly and highly defined task structure; and strong leader position power. Conversely, the situation is least favorable with poor leader/member relations, an unstructured task, and weak leader position power. Other combinations lead to varying degrees of situation favorableness falling between the two extremes.

According to Fiedler, task-oriented leaders are more effective in both the most favorable and least favorable situations, whereas person-oriented leaders are more effective in moderately favorable situations. Fiedler's model is widely discussed in sport psychology, and a few investigators have tried to test the model (e.g., Bird, 1977). To date, however, the findings are inconclusive. Although Fiedler's model is appealing, the variables are difficult to assess, sport situations may not represent all combinations of the model's variables, and some authors question the appropriateness of the model for specific and unique sport groups.

## Chelladurai's Multidimensional Model of Leadership

Chelladurai and his colleagues are engaged in one of the few current attempts to explore leadership in sport behavior. Chelladurai's (Chelladurai, 1984b; Chelladurai & Carron, 1978) model, pictured in Figure 14.1, considers the influence of situational, leader, and member characteristics on leader behaviors and the subsequent influence of leader behaviors on group performance and satisfaction. The model's major proposition is that the degree of congruence among the three components of leadership behavior is positively related to performance and satisfaction. In other words, the more the leader's actual behaviors match the preferences of the group members and the situation requirements, the better the group's performance and the greater the group members' satisfaction will be.

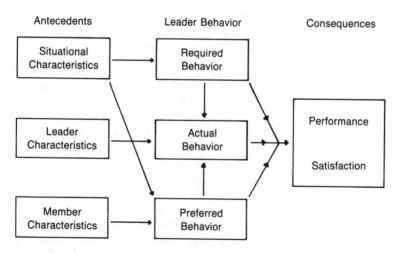

**Figure 14.1** Chelladurai's multidimensional model of leadership. *Note.* From "Leadership in Sports" by P. Chelladurai, 1984, in J.M. Silva and R.S. Weinberg (Eds.), *Psychological Foundations of Sport* (p. 338), Champaign, IL: Human Kinetics. Copyright 1984 by John M. Silva and Robert S. Weinberg. Reprinted by permission.

As an initial step, Chelladurai and Saleh (1980) developed the *Leadership Scale for Sports* (LSS). Psychometric testing revealed good internal consistency and test-retest reliability. Factor analysis yielded five factors or dimensions of leader behaviors in sport: training and instruction, democratic, autocratic, social support, and rewarding behaviors. A brief description of each LSS dimension is presented in Table 14.1.

Research on the multidimensional model is just beginning. Chelladurai and Saleh (1978) examined gender differences in preferred leader behaviors and noted that males preferred more autocratic and social support behaviors than did females. However, other studies of gender and personality differences in preferred leadership styles have yielded inconsistent findings. Chelladurai and Carron (1983) failed to find the expected relationships between athletic experience and preferred leader behaviors.

In a test of the congruence prediction, Chelladurai (1984a) reported that the discrepancy between preferred and actual leader behavior was related to satisfaction. Athletes in wrestling, basketball, and track and field preferred an emphasis on training and instruction, and the more the coach matched those preferences and actually emphasized training and instruction, the greater was athletes' satisfaction. Basketball players were more satisfied when positive

**Table 14.1** Dimensions of the Leadership Scale for Sports (LSS)

| Dimension | Description |
| --- | --- |
| Training and instruction behavior | Coaching behavior aimed at improving athletes' performance by emphasizing and facilitating hard and strenuous training; instructing them in the skills, techniques, and tactics of the sport; clarifying the relationship among the members; and by structuring and coordinating the members' activities. |
| Democratic behavior | Coaching behavior which allows greater participation by the athletes in decisions pertaining to group goals, practice methods, and game tactics and strategies. |
| Autocratic behavior | Coaching behavior which involves independent decision making and stresses personal authority. |
| Social support behavior | Coaching behavior characterized by a concern for the welfare of individual athletes, positive group atmosphere, and warm interpersonal relations with members. |
| Rewarding (positive feedback) behavior | Coaching behavior which reinforces an athlete by recognizing and rewarding good performance. |

*Note.* From "Leadership in sports" by P. Chelladurai, 1984, in J.M. Silva and R.S. Weinberg (Eds.), *Psychological foundations of sport* (p. 332), Champaign, IL: Human Kinetics. Copyright 1984 by John M. Silva and Robert S. Weinberg. Reprinted by permission.

feedback or rewards met or exceeded their preferences, but similar trends were not found for athletes in wrestling and track. Those findings may reflect Smoll and Smith's observation (discussed in chapter 11) that youth sport coaches who provided more instruction and encouragement were better liked and had players who were more satisfied with the sport experience. Further investigations of specific coach and instructor behaviors, as well as participant preferences and reactions in different sport activities, may help to clarify the influence of varying leader behaviors on different sport groups and members.

## Group Structure and Leadership

Chelladurai's research is currently the most prominent sport-specific work on leadership psychology. Several years ago, however, Grusky (1963) examined some unique aspects of leadership in sport by applying a model of group structure and organizational leadership to professional baseball. Grusky proposed that players in more central playing positions were more likely to be recruited as managers than players in more peripheral positions. Specifically, Grusky theorized that players in more central positions would perform more dependent, coordinative tasks and interact more with players in other positions. Grusky expected that players who were high interactors would develop leadership skills and be selected as managers more often than low interactors. The high interactors in baseball, as you can probably guess, are the infielders and catchers. The pitchers and outfielders are low interactors. Grusky's examination of baseball records confirmed his theory; catchers and infielders did indeed become managers more often than did pitchers and outfielders.

Subsequent studies supported Grusky's contention that high interactors are more likely to become leaders than low interactors (see Loy, Curtis, & Sage, 1979, for a review of that literature). Studies with high school baseball teams (Loy & Sage, 1970) and women's intercollegiate softball teams (Gill & Perry, 1979) confirmed that infielders and catchers were selected as captains more often or rated higher on leadership than pitchers and outfielders, but others (Chelladurai & Carron, 1977; Tropp & Landers, 1979) proposed alternatives or modifications to Grusky's model. Tropp and Landers examined playing position and leadership in field hockey and specifically measured interaction by recording the number of passes players received. They observed that goalies rated high on leadership despite being low interactors in peripheral positions. This study suggests that performing independent, critical tasks may be more important to leadership than spatial location and interaction in a highly dynamic sport such as field hockey.

Grusky's model and the subsequent related research provided some insight into the relationships among player positions, interactions, and leadership in sport. However, that research has not extended far beyond his original propositions. Interactionist approaches that consider both individual characteristics and situational factors offer the best prospects for understanding leadership in sport. Chelladurai's model is a promising step, but research on that or other interactionist approaches remains sparse. Although sport psychologists have conducted few studies on leadership, they have devoted more research to cohesiveness, and we will consider that work in the next section.

## Cohesiveness in Sport

Anyone who has been involved in any team sport knows the value of cohesiveness. Coaches try to develop cohesiveness in their teams because they believe cohesive teams win more games. Surely you have heard spectators and sports announcers as well as coaches and players praise the unity, teamwork, and cohesiveness of successful teams, especially when the teams win without individual superstars. Conversely, lack of cohesion or team dissension is often cited when a team of talented individuals fails to meet expectations. Given the popularity of cohesiveness in sports talk, it is not surprising that cohesiveness is a popular research topic. Many sport psychologists have examined the relationship between cohesiveness and team performance, and according to the results we can answer the question "Do cohesive teams win more games?" with "Yes," "No," and "Maybe."

Some evidence does indicate a positive relationship between team cohesiveness and team success. One of the most extensive and representative investigations in the sport cohesiveness literature, involving over 1,200 male intramural basketball players on 144 teams, provides strong evidence that team cohesiveness and success are positively related. In the first study of the overall investigation, Martens and Peterson (1971) examined the influence of preseason cohesiveness on team success and reported that highly cohesive teams won more games than teams with low cohesiveness. In the second study, Peterson and Martens (1972) looked at the influence of team success on postseason cohesiveness and observed that successful teams were more cohesive than less successful teams. Other studies have confirmed the positive relationship between cohesiveness and success for basketball teams (Arnold & Straub, 1972; Klein & Christiansen, 1969; Nixon, 1977; Widmeyer & Martens, 1978), football teams (Stogdill, 1963), baseball teams (Landers & Crum, 1971), ice hockey teams (Ball & Carron, 1976; Carron & Ball, 1977), rifle teams (Myers, 1962), and volleyball teams (Bird, 1977).

Those findings might provide convincing support for our popular notions about cohesiveness, but several other studies have yielded contradictory findings. Melnick and Chemers (1974), using the same questionnaire and similar procedures as Martens and Peterson, found no relationship between preseason cohesiveness and team success in intramural basketball. Other authors actually report negative relationships in which high cohesiveness appeared to impair performance for basketball (Fiedler, 1954), bowling (Landers & Lueschen, 1974), rifle (McGrath, 1962), and rowing (Lenk, 1969) teams.

Obviously, further research does not always clarify or help us to understand a phenomenon, especially if the research is haphazard with no systematic progression that builds upon and extends previous work. As Carron (1982) notes, to date the overall strategy of sport cohesiveness research can be described as a generally erratic, "shotgun" approach. No overall conceptual model has emerged to integrate the findings in any meaningful way, and, as with the sport personality research discussed in chapter 3, the findings are as diverse as the studies themselves. Although the sport cohesiveness literature is somewhat less diverse and more "cohesive" than the sport personality research, the absence of an integrating framework and clear, standard definitions and measures continues to be a major problem.

## Carron's Conceptual System for Cohesiveness in Sport Teams

Carron (1982) went beyond criticism of earlier research and advanced a conceptual model specifying antecedents and consequences of cohesiveness in sport teams. Before exploring related variables, however, we should clarify the term *cohesiveness*. We all understand the idea of cohesiveness and have our own intuitive definitions, but a precise, unambiguous definition that will clearly delineate cohesiveness for researchers is elusive. Most authors routinely cite Festinger, Schachter, and Back's (1963) classic definition of cohesiveness as "the total field of forces which act on members to remain in the group" (p. 164). Obviously, a "total field of forces" is a far-reaching, nebulous concept. Most cohesiveness investigators suggest attraction-to-group as a key aspect of cohesiveness, and Carron (1982) defines cohesion as "a dynamic process which is reflected in the tendency for a group to stick together and remain united in the pursuit of its goals and objectives" (p. 124). Carron's definition is more precise and appropriate for sport teams than Festinger et al.'s more general statement, but investigators still have considerable leeway in approach and interpretation.

Carron's conceptual system helps to clarify the role of cohesiveness in sport teams and provides a framework for research. As pictured in Figure 14.2, Carron's model identifies four antecedents or contributors to sport cohesiveness, including environmental, personal, leadership, and team factors. Environmental factors, which are the most general and remote, include contractual and organizational regulations such as NCAA recruiting rules or local rules that specify playing time in a children's baseball program. Personal factors are the individual characteristics of team members, and leadership factors refer to coaching behaviors. Environmental, personal, and leadership factors all contribute to the most specific antecedent, team factors. Team factors include characteristics and relationships of the group itself, such as group task characteristics, norms, and stability.

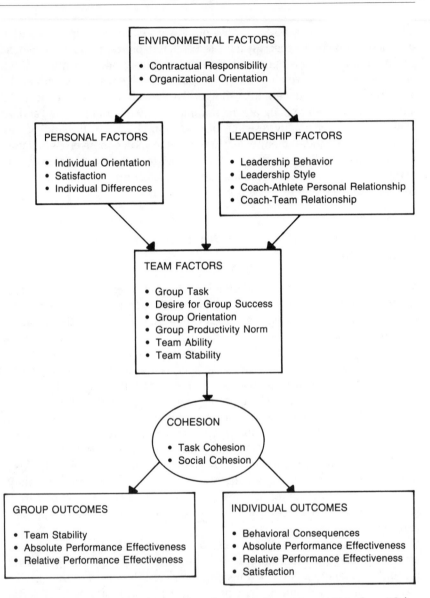

**Figure 14.2** Carron's conceptual system for cohesiveness in sport teams. *Note.* From "Cohesiveness in Sport Groups: Interpretations and Considerations" by A.V. Carron, 1982, *Journal of Sport Psychology,* **4**, p. 131. Copyright 1984 by Human Kinetics Publishers, Inc. Reprinted by permission.

All of these factors contribute to cohesiveness, which Carron describes as a dynamic process rather than a static characteristic. Carron further advocates differentiating at least two dimensions of cohesion, including (a) *task cohesion,* which relates to commitment to team goals and performance objectives, and

(b) *social cohesion*, which refers to more interpersonal concerns such as friendship, affiliation, and social-emotional support.

Cohesiveness has consequences or outcomes for both the team as a whole and for individual team members. However, sport cohesiveness research focuses almost exclusively on absolute team performance, usually in terms of a team's win/loss record. Researchers could just as easily consider other variables such as individual satisfaction and team stability or measure performance in terms of individual or team goals and standards other than the win/loss statistic.

## Cohesiveness and Performance in Sport

Carron's conceptual system raises numerous research possibilities, but so far sport cohesiveness research has focused almost exclusively on the cohesiveness/performance relationship. Conflicting findings on cohesiveness and performance were cited earlier in this section. Now we will consider factors that help clarify those findings. These factors are discussed in more detail elsewhere (Gill, 1978a).

The first step in sorting out the literature is to consider the definition and measurement of cohesiveness in the research. Most of the sport cohesiveness studies used the same measure, the *Sport Cohesiveness Questionnaire* (Martens, Landers, & Loy, 1972), thus providing a basis for comparing findings. The Martens et al. questionnaire includes two categories of items: (a) direct ratings of closeness or attraction to the group and (b) interpersonal attraction or friendship ratings. The direct items and friendship ratings are not highly related to each other, and they often relate differently to team performance. When the research findings are sorted out by type of measure, some consistency emerges. Most of the positive relationships involve direct cohesiveness ratings, and most of the negative relationships are found with interpersonal attraction measures. All of the major studies reporting negative relationships used an interpersonal attraction measure (Fiedler, 1954; Landers & Lueschen, 1974; Lenk, 1969; McGrath, 1962). In several studies with mixed results, positive relationships were found when direct measures were used, but not when friendship ratings were used (Landers & Crum, 1971; Martens & Peterson, 1971; Widmeyer & Martens, 1978).

A second approach to clarifying the literature on cohesiveness and performance is to consider key mediating variables, particularly the team factors from Carron's conceptual system. Of the team factors listed, the one receiving the most attention and the one that seems to have the most impact on the sport cohesiveness/performance relationship is the nature of the group task. Positive cohesiveness/performance relationships are reported most often for team sports that require extensive interaction and cooperation among players, such as basketball and volleyball. With sports that require independent performances and little interaction, such as bowling and rifle teams, cohesiveness may relate negatively to performance.

Although some negative relationships have been observed, cohesiveness should not necessarily impair performance, even in primarily individual or independent sports. Zander (1971) asserts that cohesiveness increases motivation and commitment to team goals, and hence cohesiveness should enhance performance. As discussed in chapter 13, however, if emphasizing team goals detracts from the recognition and encouragement of individual contributions and goals, performance may suffer. Also, high social cohesion or interpersonal attraction could detract from performance if team members sacrifice performance goals and task interaction strategies to maintain friendship patterns. Social support and encouragement from teammates certainly have potential positive effects on performance, however, if individuals are committed to performance and task goals.

Research with nonsport groups suggests that the commitment to performance goals and to other group norms affects the cohesiveness/performance relationship. A classic experiment by Schachter, Ellerton, McBride, and Gregory (1951) and several subsequent studies revealed that highly cohesive groups outperform less cohesive groups only if the group norms call for better performance. Most sport teams are highly task-oriented with performance success as their primary goal so that group norms present few performance problems. However, the degree of commitment to performance success likely varies from high-level, competitive teams to informal, recreational sport groups. Also, even highly competitive teams may hold a norm that encourages members to take it easy in practice or to avoid showing up teammates. Such norms could detract from performance success.

Even considering the cohesiveness measures and the group task, the cohesiveness/performance literature is not entirely consistent. One final consideration that helps sort out the findings is the direction of causality in the cohesiveness/performance relationship. Our discussions of sport cohesiveness usually imply that cohesiveness leads to success, but the evidence makes a stronger case that success leads to greater cohesiveness. Causality is difficult to establish because most data are correlational. In general, however, studies looking at the relationship of team success to postseason cohesiveness (e.g., Landers & Crum, 1971; Myers, 1962; Peterson & Martens, 1972) yield stronger, more consistent findings than studies examining preseason cohesiveness and later team success (e.g., Martens & Peterson, 1971; McGrath, 1962; Widmeyer & Martens, 1978).

In a more direct test of causality, Bakeman and Helmreich (1975) used a cross-lagged panel design to examine the cohesiveness and performance of aquanaut teams over time. Bakeman and Helmreich concluded that cohesiveness was not an important determinant of performance but that good performance may have been a cause of cohesiveness. Carron and Ball (1977) applied the same design in a study of ice hockey teams and similarly observed stronger relationships from performance success to cohesiveness than vice versa.

Two recent studies applied path analyses and partial correlations as well as cross-lagged panel analyses to determine causality in the cohesiveness/ performance relationship. Landers, Wilkinson, Hatfield, and Barber (1982) found evidence for both the influence of cohesiveness on performance and the influence of performance on cohesiveness with cross-lagged techniques, but most relationships disappeared with path analyses. Williams and Hacker (1982) reported that the cross-lagged technique supported both directions of the cohesiveness/performance causality, but path analyses suggested that the causal flow was stronger from performance to cohesiveness.

Obviously, the sport cohesiveness research contains many methodological flaws, and some of its data are suspect. Nevertheless, we can tentatively suggest that cohesiveness, defined and measured as attraction-to-group, is positively related to success in interactive sport teams. However, cohesiveness is not necessarily a cause, or even a partial cause, of success. Cohesiveness may influence performance, but the evidence indicates that success enhances cohesiveness and provides only weak indications that cohesiveness affects performance.

## Current Trends in Sport Cohesiveness Research

Although we can draw tentative conclusions about the relationship of cohesiveness to team performance, we can make few statements about how cohesiveness is developed and maintained in sport teams or about the relationship of cohesiveness to nonperformance variables. Questionable methodology and the lack of an integrating framework are still problems, but the future may be brighter. Carron's conceptual system offers some guidance, and two recently developed sport cohesiveness measures may advance the research process.

Until recently the Martens et al. questionnaire was standard in sport cohesiveness research despite the fact that it was never validated or tested psychometrically. Two recently developed measures, the *Multidimensional Sport Cohesion Instrument* (Yukelson, Weinberg, & Jackson, 1984) and the *Group Environment Questionnaire* (Carron, Widmeyer, & Brawley, 1985) both assess cohesiveness as a multidimensional construct in sport-specific terms and show promise as useful, psychometrically sound measures. Yukelson et al.'s inventory incorporates both task and social forces, and initial testing reveals good internal consistency. Factor analyses yielded four factors or dimensions within the inventory, including (a) attraction to the group (e.g., pride in group membership, feelings of acceptance), (b) unity of purpose (e.g., clarity of team goals, commitment to team operations), (c) quality of teamwork (e.g., teamwork, role compatibility), and (d) valued roles (e.g., sense of belongingness, role valued by teammates).

Carron et al. also separated task cohesion from social cohesion by starting from a conceptual model of cohesion composed of group integration, which reflects the degree of unification of the group field, and individual attraction to the group, which reflects the interaction of motives working on the individual to stay in the group. Those two dimensions were further subdivided into task and social components. Initial testing reveals good reliability, internal consistency, and content validity, whereas factor analyses confirm the differentiation into the four subscales of (a) group integration–task, (b) group integration–social, (c) attraction to group–task, and (d) attraction to group–social. Although both measures are new and have not yet been extensively tested, initial research suggests that they should be reliable, valid tools to aid sport cohesiveness researchers.

Armed with improved measures developed within a conceptual framework, sport psychologists may begin to explore antecedents and consequences of sport cohesiveness. Carron clearly depicts cohesiveness as a dynamic process, and several authors (e.g., Peterson & Martens, 1972; Williams & Hacker, 1982) propose circular, dynamic relationships between cohesiveness and other variables. To date, however, we have little information on how cohesiveness develops and changes in varying sport situations. Karen Ruder and I (Ruder & Gill, 1982) looked at the immediate effects of winning and losing a single contest on perceptions of cohesiveness and found that winning teams increased in cohesiveness whereas losing teams decreased. It appears likely that accumulated wins and losses over time gradually modify cohesiveness in sport teams. Many other factors and events could influence the immediate perceptions and long-term development of cohesiveness. Investigators might consider the effects on cohesiveness of personnel changes (e.g., injuries to key players), coaching strategy changes, rule changes, role changes (e.g., shifting players between starter and reserve status), the integration of women and girls into previously all-male teams, or countless other factors.

## Summary

A great deal remains to be learned about cohesiveness and group dynamics in sport teams. Even the cohesiveness/performance relationship, which has been examined in many studies, needs further research and clarification. We have even further to go to understand the interactive influences of participant characteristics, team relationships, and group processes on both individual members and the group as a whole. Sport psychologists have discussed leadership for some time but are only now beginning to consider sport-specific aspects of leadership. Many other group dynamics issues of concern to sport participants have yet to be addressed, such as the development of group goals, interpersonal communication and interaction patterns within groups and subgroups, the starter/reserve relationship, and the turnover of group members. As we have proposed for other areas, an interactionist approach that considers both individual characteristics and relevant situational factors offers the most promise for meaningful progress in sport cohesiveness research. With group dynamics issues, we must consider not only the complex, interactive influences on individual behavior but also how individual behaviors combine in varying group relationships and processes. The study of group dynamics in sport highlights a recurring principle that we have stated in other chapters: Human behavior in sport and exercise is complex, and understanding that behavior requires consideration of many complex factors, relationships, and interactions.

# *Epilogue*

We will now conclude our review and discussion of sport psychology. If you have read the text and perhaps discussed the material in a class or with colleagues, you should have a good grasp of the theories and research on human behavior in sport and exercise. After a brief overview of sport psychology, we began with a discussion of individual differences and personality characteristics and their effects upon sport and exercise behavior. We then examined the role of arousal, anxiety management, and motivational approaches in sport and exercise. In the latter parts of the text we focused on the social dimensions of sport behavior, specifically the influence of other people on performance and the complex social interactions that occur in sport groups.

We have covered a great deal of information. If you return to the questions posed at the beginning of chapter 1, you probably will discover that you can now answer them easily. Your answers should reflect the depth of your understanding of sport psychology theory and research. You may wonder why you were unable to offer the same insightful explanations when you first tried to answer those questions.

Answering those same questions again is not the best test of your sport psychology knowledge. I hope that you can use the information presented in this text to help answer questions about human behavior as they arise in your future sport and exercise activities. Perhaps you will use anxiety management skills to prepare for a competitive contest. Perhaps you will consider the research on rewards and intrinsic motivation when you plan a corporate fitness program. Perhaps you will think twice about the behaviors you are modeling and reinforcing when you coach a youth soccer team. Perhaps some of you will use the information in this text as a starting point for asking more questions, conducting your own research, and expanding our sport psychology knowledge base. It is clear that we need more research to clarify issues and extend our understanding into new areas.

Much has been learned about human behavior in sport and exercise from the time that sport psychology first emerged as an identifiable discipline in the late 1960s. We have applied theories and research models from psychology, and we have begun to examine the unique aspects of sport and exercise behavior with sport-specific measurement techniques and approaches. The current research and applied work differ greatly from early sport psychology efforts. This text reflects our current sport psychology knowledge. A sport psychology text written 20 years from now may differ radically in topics and approaches.

In writing this text I have shared my knowledge and views of sport psychology with you, the readers. I now invite you to do the same. Specifically, I invite you to offer your comments, insights, and suggestions about sport psychology issues and concerns. Sport psychology continues to expand in new and exciting directions. I hope you will participate as we advance our understanding of human behavior in sport and exercise.

# APPENDIX A

# *Sport Competition Anxiety Test for Adults*

Directions: Below are some statements about how persons feel when they compete in sports and games. Read each statement and decide if you HARDLY EVER, or SOMETIMES, or OFTEN feel this way when you compete in sports and games. If your choice is HARDLY EVER, blacken the square labeled A; if your choice is SOMETIMES, blacken the square labeled B; and if your choice is OFTEN, blacken the square labeled C. There are no right or wrong answers. Do not spend too much time on any one question. Remember to choose the word that describes how you *usually* feel when competing in *sports and games*.

|  | Hardly Ever | Sometimes | Often |
|---|---|---|---|
| 1. Competing against others is socially enjoyable. | A ☐ | B ☐ | C ☐ |
| 2. Before I compete I feel uneasy. | A ☐ | B ☐ | C ☐ |
| 3. Before I compete I worry about not performing well. | A ☐ | B ☐ | C ☐ |
| 4. I am a good sportsman when I compete. | A ☐ | B ☐ | C ☐ |
| 5. When I compete I worry about making mistakes. | A ☐ | B ☐ | C ☐ |
| 6. Before I compete I am calm. | A ☐ | B ☐ | C ☐ |
| 7. Setting a goal is important when competing. | A ☐ | B ☐ | C ☐ |
| 8. Before I compete I get a queasy feeling in my stomach. | A ☐ | B ☐ | C ☐ |
| 9. Just before competing I notice my heart beats faster than usual. | A ☐ | B ☐ | C ☐ |
| 10. I like to compete in games that demand considerable physical energy. | A ☐ | B ☐ | C ☐ |
| 11. Before I compete I feel relaxed. | A ☐ | B ☐ | C ☐ |
| 12. Before I compete I am nervous. | A ☐ | B ☐ | C ☐ |
| 13. Team sports are more exciting than individual sports. | A ☐ | B ☐ | C ☐ |
| 14. I get nervous wanting to start the game. | A ☐ | B ☐ | C ☐ |
| 15. Before I compete I usually get uptight. | A ☐ | B ☐ | C ☐ |

## Instructions for Scoring SCAT for Adults

For each item three responses are possible: (a) Hardly ever, (b) Sometimes, and (c) Often. The 10 test items are 2, 3, 5, 6, 8, 9, 11, 12, 14, and 15. The spurious items (1, 4, 7, 10, and 13) are *not* scored. Items 2, 3, 5, 8, 9, 12, 14, and 15 are worded so that they are scored according to the following key:

$$1 = \text{Hardly ever}$$
$$2 = \text{Sometimes}$$
$$3 = \text{Often}$$

Items 6 and 11 are scored according to the following key:

$$1 = \text{Often}$$
$$2 = \text{Sometimes}$$
$$3 = \text{Hardly ever}$$

The range of scores on SCAT is from 10 (low competitive A-trait) to 30 (high competitive A-trait).

If a person deletes 1 of the 10 test items, a prorated full-scale score can be obtained by computing the mean score for the 9 items answered, multiplying this value by 10, and rounding the product to the next whole number. When two or more items are omitted, the respondent's questionnaire should be invalidated.

Selected raw scores and corresponding percentile norms for college-age adults are included in the following section. A more detailed discussion of SCAT scores and additional norms are included in Martens' (1977) SCAT monograph.

## SCAT-A Norms for Normal College-Age Adults

| Raw Score | Male Percentile | Female Percentile |
|---|---|---|
| 30 | 99 | 99 |
| 28 | 97 | 88 |
| 26 | 89 | 75 |
| 24 | 82 | 59 |
| 22 | 74 | 47 |
| 20 | 61 | 35 |
| 18 | 40 | 22 |
| 16 | 24 | 10 |
| 14 | 14 | 6 |
| 12 | 7 | 3 |
| 10 | 1 | 1 |

*Note.* Instructions and norms modified from *Sport Competition Anxiety Test* (pp. 91 & 99). By R. Martens, 1977, Champaign, IL: Human Kinetics. Copyright 1977 by Rainer Martens. Reprinted by permission.

# *Progressive Relaxation Exercise*

This exercise is adapted from the progressive relaxation procedures described by Bernstein and Borkovec (1973).

*Introduction.* As the name implies, progressive relaxation involves the progressive tensing and relaxing of various muscle groups. Although the exercise is a relaxation technique, we start with tension because most individuals find it easier to go from a tensed state to a relaxed state than to simply relax muscles. Progressing from a tensed state to relaxation also helps to develop the ability to recognize and differentiate the feelings of tension and relaxation in the muscles. The first session of progressive relaxation training might take 30 to 45 minutes. As training continues, however, the sessions become shorter; muscle groups can be combined and the tension phase can be omitted. The goal of progressive relaxation training is self-control. With practice an individual can learn to recognize subtle levels of muscle tension and immediately relax those muscles.

*General Instructions.* As we proceed through this exercise, various muscle groups will be tensed for a short time and then relaxed on the following cues: *NOW* for tension and the word *RELAX* for relaxation. On the word *NOW*, you should tense the muscles and hold the tension until the word *RELAX*, and then you should let all the tension go at once, not gradually.

As we go through tension and relaxation, I will ask you to pay attention to the feelings of tension and relaxation. This is in part a concentration exercise; try to focus attention on the feelings in your muscles. Today try to remain awake and pay attention to the feelings in your muscles. Later you can also use this exercise as a sleep aid.

Once a muscle group has been relaxed, try not to move it except to be comfortable; try to tense only the particular muscle group that we are working on.

Do not talk during the exercise; ignore distracting sounds and activities; and keep your attention on the feelings in your muscles.

We will go through each of 16 muscle groups twice. Each time I will remind you about the tension methods, give you the signal to tense (the word

*NOW*), then the signal to *RELAX*. We will go through the tension and relaxation a second time, and then we will go on to the next muscle group.

The 16 muscle groups that we will go through and the general instruction for tensing those muscles include the following:

1. Dominant (right) hand and lower arm: Make a fist.
2. Dominant biceps and upper arm: push elbow down and pull back, without moving the lower arm.
3. Nondominant (left) hand and lower arm: Same as 1.
4. Nondominant biceps and upper arm: Same as 2.
5. Forehead (upper face): Lift eyebrows as high as possible and wrinkle forehead.
6. Central face: Squint and wrinkle nose.
7. Lower face and jaw: Clench teeth and pull back corners of mouth.
8. Neck: Pull chin forward and neck back.
9. Chest, back, and shoulders: Pull shoulder blades together and take a deep breath; continue to take a deep breath while tensing and release with slow, easy breathing as you are relaxing.
10. Stomach/abdomen: Make stomach hard.
11. Dominant (right) upper leg: Counterpose top and bottom thigh muscles.
12. Dominant calf and lower leg: Pull toes toward head.
13. Dominant foot: Curl toes and foot inward (do not hold too long to avoid foot cramps).
14. Nondominant upper leg: Same as 11.
15. Nondominant calf and lower leg: Same as 12.
16. Nondominant foot: Same as 13.

For a shorter session, the muscle groups may be combined as follows:

1. Dominant hand and arm (hand, lower arm, upper arm).
2. Nondominant hand and arm.
3. Face (upper, central, and lower face muscles).
4. Neck.
5. Trunk area (chest, back, shoulders, stomach, abdomen).
6. Dominant leg and foot (upper leg, lower leg, foot).
7. Nondominant leg and foot.

*Specific Instructions.* Make yourself comfortable; remove any constraining items that might get in your way such as watches, glasses, or shoes. Close your eyes and take three deep, relaxed breaths. Breathe in slowly and completely, and breathe out slowly and relaxed.

Focus your attention on the muscles of your dominant (right) lower arm and hand. When I give the signal, make a fist and tense the muscles of your dominant lower arm and hand. Ready . . . *NOW.*

*Tension talk.* "Feel the tension. . . . Focus on the tension. . . . Feel the muscles pull. . . . Notice the tightness. . . . Hold the tension. . . . Put tension in the muscle. . . . Hold it. . . ." (5-7 seconds) and—*RELAX.*

*Relaxation talk.* "Let all the tension go. . . . Let the muscles get more and more relaxed. . . . Let go. . . . Notice how you feel as relaxation takes place. . . . Notice the feelings of relaxation. . . . Relax deeper and deeper. . . . Just let the muscles go. . . . more and more completely. . . . Notice the pleasant feelings of relaxation. . . . Continue letting the muscles relax. . . . Keep relaxing. . . . Let yourself relax. . . . Feel the relaxation through the muscles. . . . Continue letting go. . . . Let the muscles keep relaxing. . . . Nothing to do but let the muscles relax. . . . Feel the relaxation come into the muscles. . . . Pay attention to the feelings of relaxation as the muscles relax more and more . . . more and more completely . . . deeply relaxed. . . . Let the muscles loosen up and smooth out. . . . Relax. . . . Notice how you feel as the muscles relax. . . . Let the tension go away. . . . Feel calm, peaceful relaxation. . . . Let the tension go as you breathe slow and easy. . . . Feel calm, rested. . . . With each breath the muscles relax more and more. . . . Notice the difference between tension and relaxation. . . . See if the muscles of the arm feel as relaxed as those of the hand. . . . Just let the muscles continue to relax. . . . Relax. . . . Relax. . . ." (30-40 seconds).

We're going to repeat the tension/relaxation sequence again for the dominant hand and lower arm. All right, I'd like you to again make a fist and tense the muscles of the dominant hand and lower arm. Ready, *NOW.* (Repeat tension phase 5-7 seconds.) And *RELAX.* (Repeat relaxation phase 45-60 seconds.)

All right. Now I'd like you to shift your attention to the muscles of the upper arm and biceps of your dominant arm. Ignore the lower arm and focus only on the upper arm throughout the exercise. (Continue to go through each of the 16 muscle groups twice following the same tension and relaxation phases as for the dominant hand and lower arm.)

*General Relaxation Talk.* "Notice the relaxation in all the muscles. . . . Complete and deep relaxation. . . . Check the muscles in your dominant hand; let those muscles keep relaxing. . . . Check your other muscles. . . . If you notice tension, just let the muscle keep relaxing. . . . Let the tension go. . . . Let the face muscles relax. . . . Let your shoulders relax. . . . Breathe slowly and easily. . . . With each breath, the muscles relax more and more. . . . Enjoy the feelings of relaxation. . . ." (45-60 seconds).

*End of Exercise.* "In a moment I will count backwards from four to one. On the count of four, you should move your legs and feet; on three, move your arms and hands; on two, move your head and neck; and on one you can open your eyes and get up slowly. All right. *Four:* Move your legs and feet; stretch out. *Three:* Move your hands and arms. *Two:* Move your head and neck. *One:* Open your eyes, get up, and move around when you're ready. You may feel a little dizzy, so move slowly as you become more alert."

# References

Abramson, L.Y., Seligman, M.E.P., & Teasdale, J.D. (1978). Learned helplessness in humans: Critique and reformulation. *Journal of Abnormal Psychology, 87*, 49-74.

Albrecht, R.R., & Feltz, D.L. (1985, May). *Relationships among a sport-specific measure of attentional style, anxiety, and performance of collegiate baseball and softball batters.* Paper presented at the North American Society for the Psychology of Sport and Physical Activity Conference, Gulfpark, MS.

Alderman, R.B. (1970). A sociopsychological assessment of attitude toward physical activity in champion athletes. *Research Quarterly, 41*, 1-9.

Allard, F., Graham, S., & Paarsalu, M.T. (1980). Perception in sport: Basketball. *Journal of Sport Psychology, 2*, 14-21.

Allard, F., & Starkes, J.L. (1980). Perception in sport: Volleyball. *Journal of Sport Psychology, 2*, 22-33.

Allison, M.G., & Ayllon, T. (1980). Behavioral coaching in the development of skills in football, gymnastics, and tennis. *Journal of Applied Behavior Analysis, 13*, 297-314.

Allport, F.H. (1924). *Social psychology.* Boston: Houghton Mifflin.

Allport, G.W. (1935). Attitudes. In C. Murchison (Ed.), *Handbook of social psychology* (pp. 798-844). Worcester, MA: Clark University Press.

Al-Talib, N.M. (1970). Effects of consonant and dissonant role playing with high or low justification on attitude change toward physical education courses. *Research Quarterly, 41*, 467-471.

Ardrey, R. (1966). *The territorial imperative.* New York: Atheneum.

Arms, R.L., Russell, G.W., & Sandilands, M.L. (1979). Effects of viewing aggressive sports on the hostility of spectators. *Social Psychology Quarterly, 42*, 275-279.

Arnold, G.E., & Straub, W.F. (1972). Personality and group cohesiveness as determinants of success among interscholastic basketball teams. *Proceedings: Fourth Canadian Symposium on Psychomotor Learning and Sport Psychology.* Ottawa: Health and Welfare Canada.

Atkinson, J.W. (1964). *An introduction to motivation.* Princeton, NJ: Van Nostrand.

Atkinson, J.W. (1974). The mainsprings of achievement-oriented activity. In J.W. Atkinson & J.O. Raynor (Eds.), *Motivation and achievement* (pp. 13-41). New York: Halstead.

Babad, E., Inbar, J., & Rosenthal, R. (1982). Pygmalion, galatea and the golem: Investigations of biased and unbiased teachers. *Journal of Educational Psychology, 74*, 459-474.

Bakan, D. (1966). *The duality of human existence.* Chicago: Rand McNally.

Bakeman, R., & Helmreich, R. (1975). Cohesiveness and performance: Co-variation and causality in an undersea environment. *Journal of Experimental Social Psychology, 11*, 478-489.

Ball, J.R., & Carron, A.V. (1976). The influence of team cohesion and partici-pation motivation upon performance success in intercollegiate ice hockey. *Canadian Journal of Applied Sport Sciences, 1*, 271-275.

Bandura, A. (1965). Influence of models' reinforcement contingencies on the acquisition of imitative responses. *Journal of Personality and Social Psychology, 1*, 589-595.

Bandura, A. (1973). *Aggression: A social learning analysis.* Englewood Cliffs, NJ: Prentice-Hall.

Bandura, A. (1977a). *Social learning theory.* Englewood Cliffs, NJ: Prentice-Hall.

Bandura, A. (1977b). Self-efficacy: Toward a unifying theory of behavioral change. *Psychological Review, 84*, 191-215.

Bandura, A. (1982). Self-efficacy mechanism in human agency. *American Psychologist, 37*, 122-147.

Bandura, A., & Jeffery, R.W. (1973). Role of symbolic coding and rehearsal processes in observational learning. *Journal of Personality and Social Psychology, 26*, 122-130.

Bandura, A., Ross, D., & Ross, S.A. (1963a). Imitation of film-mediated aggres-sive models. *Journal of Abnormal and Social Psychology, 66*, 3-11.

Bandura, A., Ross, D., & Ross, S.A. (1963b). Vicarious reinforcement and imi-tative learning. *Journal of Abnormal and Social Psychology, 67*, 601-607.

Bandura, A., & Schunk, D. (1981). Cultivating competence, self-efficacy, and intrinsic interest through proximal self-motivation. *Journal of Personality and Social Psychology, 41*, 586-598.

Baron, R.A. (1977). *Human aggression.* New York: Plenum.

Baron, R., Moore, D., & Sanders, G.S. (1978). Distraction as a source of drive in social facilitation research. *Journal of Personality and Social Psychology, 36*, 816-824.

Barrow, J.C. (1977). The variables of leadership: A review and conceptual framework. *Academy of Management Review, 74,* 231-251.

Baumeister, R.F. (1984). Choking under pressure: Self-consciousness and paradoxical effects of incentives on skillful performance. *Journal of Personality and Social Psychology, 46,* 610-620.

Baumeister, R.F., & Steinhilber, A. (1984). Paradoxical effects of supportive audiences on performance under pressure: The home field disadvantage in sport championships. *Journal of Personality and Social Psychology, 47,* 85-93.

Bem, S.L. (1974). The measurement of psychological androgyny. *Journal of Consulting and Clinical Psychology, 42,* 155-162.

Bem, S.L. (1978a). Beyond androgyny: Some presumptuous prescriptions for a liberated sexual identity. In J. Sherman & F. Denmark (Eds.), *Psychology of women: Future directions for research* (pp. 1-23). New York: Psychological Dimensions.

Bem, S.L. (1978b). *The short Bem Sex-Role Inventory.* Palo Alto, CA: Consulting Psychologists Press.

Benson, H. (1976). *The relaxation response.* New York: William Morrow.

Berkowitz, L. (1962). *Aggression: A social psychological analysis.* New York: McGraw-Hill.

Berkowitz, L. (1965). The concept of aggressive drive: Some additional considerations. In L. Berkowitz (Ed.), *Advances in experimental social psychology* (Vol. 2, pp. 301-329). New York: Academic Press.

Berkowitz, L. (1966). On not being able to aggress. *British Journal of Social and Clinical Psychology, 5,* 130-139.

Berkowitz, L. (1969). *Roots of aggression.* New York: Atherton Press.

Berkowitz, L. (1970). Experimental investigations of hostility catharsis. *Journal of Consulting and Clinical Psychology, 35,* 1-7.

Berkowitz, L. (1974). Some determinants of impulsive aggression: The role of mediated associations with reinforcements for aggression. *Psychological Review, 81,* 165-176.

Bernstein, D.A., & Borkovec, T.D. (1973). *Progressive relaxation: A manual for the helping professions.* Champaign, IL: Research Press.

Berridge, H. (1935). An experiment in the psychology of competition. *Research Quarterly, 6,* 37-42.

Betts, G.H. (1909). *The distribution and functions of mental imagery.* New York: Teachers College, Columbia University.

Bird, A.M. (1977). Development of a model for predicting team performance. *Research Quarterly, 48,* 24-32.

Bird, A.M., & Brame, J.M. (1978). Self versus team attributions: A test of the "I'm OK, but the team's so-so" phenomenon. *Research Quarterly,* **49,** 260-268.

Bradley, B. (1976). *Life on the run.* New York: Quadrangle, New York Times Book Co.

Brawley, L.R. (1984). Attributions as social cognitions: Contemporary perspectives in sport. In W.F. Straub & J.M. Williams (Eds.), *Cognitive sport psychology* (pp. 212-230). Lansing, NY: Sport Science Associates.

Brawley, L.R., Landers, D.M., Miller, L., & Kearns, K.M. (1979). Sex bias in evaluating motor performance. *Journal of Sport Psychology,* **1,** 15-24.

Brawley, L.R., Powers, R.C., & Phillips, K.A. (1980). Sex bias in evaluating motor performance: General or task-specific performance expectancy? *Journal of Sport Psychology,* **2,** 279-287.

Brawley, L.R., & Roberts, G.C. (1984). Attributions in sport: Research foundations, characteristics, and limitations. In J.M. Silva & R.S. Weinberg (Eds.), *Psychological foundations of sport* (pp. 197-213). Champaign, IL: Human Kinetics.

Bredemeier, B.J. (1984). Sport, gender, and moral growth. In J.M. Silva & R.S. Weinberg (Eds.), *Psychological foundations of sport* (pp. 400-413). Champaign, IL: Human Kinetics.

Brophy, J.E. (1982). *Research on the self-fulfilling prophecy and teacher expectations.* Educational Resources Information Center, National Institute of Education, U.S. Department of Education, Washington, D.C.

Brophy, J.E., & Good, T.L. (1970). Teachers' communication of differential expectations for children's classroom performance: Some behavioral data. *Journal of Educational Psychology,* **61,** 365-374.

Bryan, J.H. (1969, December). How adults teach hypocrisy. *Psychology Today,* **3,** 50-52, 65.

Bryan, J.H., & Walbek, N.H. (1970). Preaching and practicing generosity: Some determinants of sharing in children. *Child Development,* **41,** 329-354.

Buffone, G.W. (1984). Exercise as a therapeutic adjunct. In J.M. Silva & R.S. Weinberg (Eds.), *Psychological foundations of sport* (pp. 445-451). Champaign, IL: Human Kinetics.

Bukowski, W.M., & Moore, D. (1980). Winners' and losers' attributions for success and failure in a series of athletic events. *Journal of Sport Psychology,* **2,** 195-210.

Burwitz, L., & Newell, K.M. (1972). The effects of the mere presence of co-actors on learning a motor skill. *Journal of Motor Behavior,* **4,** 99-102.

Callahan, T. (1984a, July 30). No limit to what he can do. *Time,* pp. 52-59.

Callahan, T. (1984b, July 30). Star-spangled home team. *Time,* pp. 60-63.

Carron, A.V. (1982). Cohesiveness in sport groups: Interpretations and considerations. *Journal of Sport Psychology,* **4,** 123-138.

Carron, A.V., & Ball, J.R. (1977). Cause-effect characteristics of cohesiveness and participation motivation in intercollegiate hockey. *International Review of Sport Sociology,* **12,** 49-60.

Carron, A.V., Widmeyer, M.N., & Brawley, L.R. (1985). The development of an instrument to assess cohesion in sport teams: The Group Environment Questionnaire. *Journal of Sport Psychology,* **7,** 244-266.

Chase, W.G., & Simon, H.A. (1973). Perception in chess. *Cognitive Psychology,* **4,** 55-81.

Chelladurai, P. (1984a). Discrepancy between preferences and perceptions of leadership behavior and satisfaction of athletes in varying sports. *Journal of Sport Psychology,* **6,** 27-41.

Chelladurai, P. (1984b). Leadership in sports. In J.M. Silva & R.S. Weinberg (Eds.), *Psychological foundations of sport* (pp. 329-339). Champaign, IL: Human Kinetics.

Chelladurai, P., & Carron, A.V. (1977). A reanalysis of formal structure in sport. *Canadian Journal of Applied Sport Sciences,* **2,** 9-14.

Chelladurai, P., & Carron, A.V. (1978). *Leadership* (Monograph). Ottawa: Canadian Association for Health, Physical Education, and Recreation.

Chelladurai, P., & Carron, A.V. (1983). Athletic maturity and preferred leadership. *Journal of Sport Psychology,* **5,** 371-380.

Chelladurai, P., & Saleh, S.D. (1978). Preferred leadership in sports. *Canadian Journal of Applied Sport Sciences,* **3,** 85-92.

Chelladurai, P., & Saleh, S.D. (1980). Dimensions of leader behavior in sports: Development of a leadership scale. *Journal of Sport Psychology,* **2,** 34-45.

Church, R.M. (1962). The effects of competition on reaction time and palmar skin conductance. *Journal of Abnormal and Social Psychology,* **65,** 32-40.

Church, R.M. (1968). Applications of behavior theory to social psychology: Imitation and competition. In E.C. Simmel, R.A. Hoppe, & G.A. Milton (Eds.), *Social facilitation and imitative behavior* (pp. 135-168). Boston: Allyn & Bacon.

Colker, R., & Widom, C.S. (1980). Correlates of female athletic participation: Masculinity, femininity, self-esteem, and attitudes toward women. *Sex Roles,* **6,** 47-58.

Comrey, A.L. (1953). Group performance in a manual dexterity task. *Journal of Applied Psychology,* **37,** 207-210.

Condry, J., & Dyer, S. (1976). Fear of success: Attribution of cause to the victim. *Journal of Social Issues, 32*, 63-83.

Connor, J.M., Schackman, M.E., & Serbin, L.A. (1978). Sex-related differences in response to practice on a visual-spatial test and generalization to a related test. *Child Development, 49*, 24-29.

Constantinople, A. (1973). Masculinity-femininity: An exception to a famous dictum? *Psychological Bulletin, 80*, 389-407.

Corbin, C.B. (1972). Mental practice. In W.P. Morgan (Ed.), *Ergogenic aids and muscular performance* (pp. 93-118). New York: Academic Press.

Corbin, C.B. (1980). *A textbook of motor development*. Dubuque, IA: William C. Brown.

Corbin, C.B., & Nix, C. (1979). Sex-typing of physical activities and success predictions of children before and after cross-sex competition. *Journal of Sport Psychology, 1*, 43-52.

Corbin, C.B., Stewart, M.J., & Blair, W.O. (1981). Self-confidence and motor performance of preadolescent boys and girls studied in different feedback situations. *Journal of Sport Psychology, 3*, 30-34.

Cottrell, N.B. (1968). Performance in the presence of other human beings: Mere presence, audience, and affiliation effects. In E.C. Simmel, R.A. Hoppe, & G.A. Milton (Eds.), *Social facilitation and imitative behavior* (pp. 91-110). Boston: Allyn & Bacon.

Crandall, V.C. (1969). Sex differences in expectancy of intellectual and academic reinforcement. In C.P. Smith (Ed.), *Achievement-related motives in children* (pp. 11-45). New York: Russell Sage Foundation.

Cratty, B.J. (1983). *Psychology in contemporary sport* (2nd ed.). Englewood Cliffs, NJ: Prentice-Hall.

Csikszentmihalyi, M. (1975). *Beyond boredom and anxiety*. San Francisco: Jossey-Bass.

Dashiell, J.F. (1935). Experimental studies of the influence of social situations on the behavior of individual human adults. In C. Murchison (Ed.), *A handbook of social psychology* (pp. 1097-1158). Worcester, MA: Clark University Press.

Deaux, K. (1976). *The behavior of men and women*. Monterey, CA: Brooks/Cole.

Deaux, K. (1984). From individual differences to social categories: Analysis of a decade's research on gender. *American Psychologist, 39*, 105-116.

Deaux, K. (1985). Sex and gender. *Annual Review of Psychology, 36*, 49-81.

Deaux, K., & Lewis, L.L. (1984). The structure of gender stereotypes: Interrelationships among components and gender label. *Journal of Personality and Social Psychology, 46*, 991-1004.

Deci, E.L. (1971). Effects of externally mediated rewards on intrinsic motivation. *Journal of Personality and Social Psychology,* **18**, 105-115.

Deci, E.L. (1975). *Intrinsic motivation.* New York: Plenum.

Deci, E.L., Betley, G., Kahle, J., Abrams, L., & Porac, J. (1981). When trying to win: Competition and intrinsic motivation. *Personality and Social Psychology Bulletin,* **7**, 79-83.

Del Rey, P., & Sheppard, S. (1981). Relationship of psychological androgyny in female athletes to self-esteem. *International Journal of Sport Psychology,* **12**, 165-175.

Dickinson, J. (1977). *A behavioral analysis of sport.* Princeton, NJ: Princeton Books.

Diener, C.I., & Dweck, C.S. (1978). An analysis of learned helplessness: Continuous changes in performance, strategy, and achievement cognitions following failure. *Journal of Personality and Social Psychology,* **36**, 451-462.

Diener, C.I., & Dweck, C.S. (1980). An analysis of learned helplessness: II. The processing of success. *Journal of Personality and Social Psychology,* **39**, 940-952.

Dishman, R.K. (1982). Contemporary sport psychology. In R.L. Terjung (Ed.), *Exercise and Sport Sciences Reviews* (Vol. 10, pp. 120-159). Philadelphia: Franklin Institute Press.

Dishman, R.K. (1984). Motivation and exercise adherence. In J.M. Silva & R.S. Weinberg (Eds.), *Psychological foundations of sport* (pp. 420-434). Champaign, IL: Human Kinetics.

Dishman, R.K., & Ickes, W. (1981). Self-motivation and adherence to therapeutic exercise. *Journal of Behavioral Medicine,* **4**, 421-438.

Dishman, R.K., Ickes, W., & Morgan, W.P. (1980). Self-motivation and adherence to habitual physical activity. *Journal of Applied Social Psychology,* **10**, 115-132.

Dollard, J., Doob, J., Miller, N., Mowrer, O., & Sears, R. (1939). *Frustration and aggression.* New Haven, CT: Yale University Press.

Donahue, J.A., Gillis, J.H., & King, K. (1980). Behavior modification in sport and physical education. *Journal of Sport Psychology,* **2**, 311-328.

Doob, A.N. (1970). Catharsis and aggression: The effect of hurting one's enemy. *Journal of Experimental Research in Personality,* **4**, 291-296.

Doob, A.N., & Wood, L. (1972). Catharsis and aggression: The effects of annoyance and retaliation on aggressive behavior. *Journal of Personality and Social Psychology,* **22**, 156-162.

Duda, J. (1983, May). *A multidimensional approach to the study of sex and cultural differences in motivation.* Paper presented at the North American

Society for the Psychology of Sport and Physical Activity Conference, East Lansing, MI.

Dweck, C.S. (1975). The role of expectations and attributions in the alleviation of learned helplessness. *Journal of Personality and Social Psychology*, **31**, 674-685.

Dweck, C.S. (1978). Achievement. In M.E. Lamb (Ed.), *Social and personality development* (pp. 114-130). New York: Holt, Rinehart & Winston.

Dweck, C.S. (1980). Learned helplessness in sport. In C.M. Nadeau, W.R. Halliwell, K.M. Newell, & G.C. Roberts (Eds.), *Psychology of motor behavior and sport—1979* (pp. 1-11). Champaign, IL: Human Kinetics.

Dweck, C.S., & Goetz, T.E. (1978). Attributions and learned helplessness. In J.H. Harvey, W.J. Ickes, & R.F. Kidd (Eds.), *New directions in attribution research* (Vol. 2, pp. 158-181). Hillsdale, NJ: Erlbaum.

Dweck, C.S., & Reppucci, N.D. (1973). Learned helplessness and reinforcement responsibility in children. *Journal of Personality and Social Psychology*, **25**, 109-116.

Easterbrook, J.A. (1959). The effect of emotion on cue utilization and the organization of behavior. *Psychological Review*, **66**, 183-201.

Eccles (Parsons), J. (1983). Expectations, values, and academic behaviors. In J.T. Spence (Ed.), *Achievement and achievement motives* (pp. 75-145). San Francisco: W.H. Freeman.

Eccles (Parsons), J., Adler, T., & Meece, J.L. (1984). Sex differences in achievement: A test of alternate theories. *Journal of Personality and Social Psychology*, **46**, 26-43.

Emerson, R. (1966). Mount Everest: A case study of communication feedback and sustained goal striving. *Sociometry*, **29**, 213-277.

Epstein, M.L. (1980). The relationship of mental imagery and mental rehearsal to performance of a motor task. *Journal of Sport Psychology*, **2**, 211-220.

Espenschade, A.S., & Eckert, H.M. (1980). *Motor development*. Columbus, OH: Charles E. Merrill.

Feltz, D.L. (1982). Path analysis of the causal elements in Bandura's theory of self-efficacy and an anxiety-based model of avoidance behavior. *Journal of Personality and Social Psychology*, **42**, 764-781.

Feltz, D.L. (1984). Self-efficacy as a cognitive mediator of athletic performance. In W.F. Straub & J.M. Williams (Eds.), *Cognitive sport psychology* (pp. 191-198). Lansing, NY: Sport Science Associates.

Feltz, D.L., & Landers, D.M. (1977). Informational-motivational components of a model's demonstration. *Research Quarterly*, **48**, 525-533.

Feltz, D.L., & Landers, D.M. (1983). The effects of mental practice on motor skill learning and performance: A meta-analysis. *Journal of Sport Psychology, 5,* 25-57.

Feltz, D.L., Landers, D.M., & Raeder, U. (1979). Enhancing self-efficacy in high-avoidance motor tasks: A comparison of modeling techniques. *Journal of Sport Psychology, 1,* 112-122.

Feltz, D.L., & Mugno, D.A. (1983). A replication of the path analysis of the causal elements in Bandura's theory of self-efficacy and the influence of autonomic perception. *Journal of Sport Psychology, 5,* 262-277.

Fenz, W. (1975). Coping mechanisms and performance under stress. In D.M. Landers (Ed.), *Psychology of sport and motor behavior II* (pp. 3-24). University Park, PA: Pennsylvania State University.

Fenz, W.D., & Jones, G.B. (1974). Cardiac conditioning in a reaction time task and heart rate control during real life stress. *Journal of Psychosomatic Research, 18,* 199-203.

Festinger, L.A. (1957). *A theory of cognitive dissonance.* New York: Harper & Row.

Festinger, L., Schachter, S., & Back, K. (1963). *Social pressures in informal groups.* New York: Harper & Row.

Fiedler, F.E. (1954). Assumed similarity measures as predictors of team effectiveness. *Journal of Abnormal and Social Psychology, 49,* 381-388.

Fiedler, F.E. (1967). *A theory of leadership effectiveness.* New York: McGraw-Hill.

Fishbein, M., & Ajzen, I. (1974). Attitudes toward objects as predictors of single and multiple behavioral criteria. *Psychological Review, 81,* 59-74.

Fishbein, M., & Ajzen, I. (1975). *Belief, attitude, intention, and behavior: An introduction to theory and research.* Reading, MA: Addison-Wesley.

Fisher, A.C. (1976). *Psychology of sport.* Palo Alto, CA: Mayfield.

Fisher, A.C., Ryan, E.D., & Martens, R. (1976). Current status and future directions of personality research related to motor behavior and sport: Three panelists' views. In A.C. Fisher (Ed.), *Psychology of sport* (pp. 400-431). Palo Alto, CA: Mayfield.

Folkins, C.H., & Sime, W.E. (1981). Physical fitness training and mental health. *American Psychologist, 36,* 373-389.

Frieze, I.H., Parsons, J.E., Johnson, P.B., Ruble, D.N., & Zellman, G.L. (1978). *Women and sex roles: A social psychological perspective.* New York: W.W. Norton.

Frodi, A., Macauley, J., & Thome, P.R. (1977). Are women always less aggressive than men? A review of the experimental literature. *Psychological Bulletin, 84*, 638-660.

Gaebelein, J., & Taylor, S. (1971). The effects of competition and attack on physical aggression. *Psychonomic Science, 24*, 65-67.

Galton, F. (1883). *Inquiries into human faculty and its development.* London: MacMillan.

Geen, R.G., & Gange, J.G. (1977). Drive theory of social facilitation: Twelve years of theory and research. *Psychological Bulletin, 84*, 1267-1288.

Geen, R.G., Stonner, D., & Shope, G.L. (1975). The facilitation of aggression by aggression: Evidence against the catharsis hypothesis. *Journal of Personality and Social Psychology, 31*, 721-726.

Gill, D.L. (1977). The influence of group success-failure and relative ability on intrapersonal variables. *Research Quarterly, 48*, 685-694.

Gill, D.L. (1978a). Cohesiveness and performance in sport groups. In R.S. Hutton (Ed.), *Exercise and sport sciences reviews* (Vol. 5, pp. 131-155). Santa Barbara, CA: Journal Publishing Affiliates.

Gill, D.L. (1978b). The influence of competition on individual and group motor performance. *Journal of Human Movement Studies, 4*, 36-43.

Gill, D.L. (1979). The prediction of group motor performance from individual member abilities. *Journal of Motor Behavior, 11*, 113-122.

Gill, D.L. (in press). Competitiveness among females and males in physical activity classes. *Sex Roles.*

Gill, D.L., Deeter, T.E., & Gruber, C. (1985, May). *Competitive orientations of males and females in competitive and noncompetitive physical activities.* Paper presented at the North American Society for the Psychology of Sport and Physical Activity Conference, Gulfpark, MS.

Gill, D.L., & Gross, J.B. (1979). The influence of group success-failure on selected intrapersonal variables. In G.C. Roberts & K.M. Newell (Eds.), *Psychology of motor behavior and sport—1978* (pp. 61-71). Champaign, IL: Human Kinetics.

Gill, D.L., Gross, J.B., Huddleston, S., & Shifflett, B. (1984). Sex differences in achievement cognitions and performance in competition. *Research Quarterly for Exercise and Sport, 55*, 340-346.

Gill, D.L., & Martens, R. (1975). The informational and motivational influence of social reinforcement on motor performance. *Journal of Motor Behavior, 7*, 171-182.

Gill, D.L., & Perry, J.L. (1979). A case study of leadership in women's intercollegiate softball. *International Review of Sport Sociology, 14*, 83-91.

Gill, D.L., Ruder, M.K., & Gross, J.B. (1982). Open-ended attributions in team competition. *Journal of Sport Psychology, 4*, 159-169.

Gill, D.L., & Strom, E.H. (1985). The effect of attentional focus on performance of an endurance task. *International Journal of Sport Psychology, 16*, 217-223.

Goldstein, J., & Arms, R. (1971). Effects of observing athletic contests on hostility. *Sociometry, 54*, 83-91.

Gordon, R. (1949). An investigation into some of the factors that favour the formation of stereotyped images. *British Journal of Psychology, 39*, 156-167.

Gould, D.R. (1978). *The influence of motor task types on model effectiveness.* Unpublished doctoral dissertation, University of Illinois at Urbana-Champaign.

Gould, D., & Weiss, M. (1981). The effects of model similarity and model talk on self-efficacy and muscular endurance. *Journal of Sport Psychology, 3*, 17-29.

Gould, D., Weiss, M., & Weinberg, R. (1981). Psychological characteristics of successful and nonsuccessful Big Ten wrestlers. *Journal of Sport Psychology, 3*, 69-81.

Greene, D., & Lepper, M.R. (1974). Effects of extrinsic rewards on children's subsequent intrinsic interest. *Child Development, 45*, 1141-1145.

Griffith, C.R. (1926). *Psychology of coaching.* New York: Scribners.

Griffith, C.R. (1928). *Psychology and athletics.* New York: Scribners.

Gross, J.B., & Gill, D.L. (1982). Competition and instructional set effects on the speed and accuracy of a throwing task. *Research Quarterly for Exercise and Sport, 53*, 125-132.

Grusky, O. (1963). The effects of formal structure on managerial recruitment: A study of baseball organization. *Sociometry, 26*, 345-353.

Halliwell, W.R. (1978). The effect of cognitive development on children's perceptions of intrinsically motivated behavior. In D.M. Landers & R.W. Christina (Eds.), *Psychology of motor behavior and sport—1977* (pp. 403-419). Champaign, IL: Human Kinetics.

Hanin, Y., & Martens, R. (1978, Winter). Sport psychology in the USSR. *NASPSPA Newsletter, 3*(2), 1-3.

Harney, D.M., & Parker, R. (1972). Effects of social reinforcement, subject sex, and experimenter sex on children's motor performance. *Research Quarterly, 43*, 187-196.

Harres, B. (1968). Attitudes of students toward women's athletic competition. *Research Quarterly, 39*, 278-284.

Harris, D.V., & Harris, B.L. (1984). *The athlete's guide to sports psychology: Mental skills for physical people.* New York: Leisure Press.

Harris, D.V., & Jennings, S.E. (1977). Self-perceptions of female distance runners. *Annals of the New York Academy of Sciences,* **301,** 808-815.

Hastorf, A.H., & Cantril, H. (1954). They saw a game: A case study. *Journal of Abnormal and Social Psychology,* **49,** 129-134.

Haywood, K. (1986). *Concepts in lifespan motor development.* Champaign, IL: Human Kinetics.

Healey, R.R., & Landers, D.M. (1973). Effect of need achievement and task difficulty on competitive and noncompetitive motor performance. *Journal of Motor Behavior,* **5,** 121-128.

Heider, F. (1958). *The psychology of interpersonal relations.* New York: Wiley.

Helmreich, R., & Spence, J.T. (1977). Sex roles and achievement. In R.W. Christina & D.M. Landers (Eds.), *Psychology of motor behavior and sport—1976* (Vol 2, pp. 33-46). Champaign, IL: Human Kinetics.

Helmreich, R.L., & Spence, J.T. (1978). The Work and Family Orientation Questionnaire: An objective instrument to assess components of achievement motivation and attitudes toward family and career. *Catalog of Selected Documents in Psychology,* **8,** 35.

Helmreich, R.L., Spence, J.T., & Holohan, C.K. (1979). Psychological androgyny and sex role flexibility: A test of two hypotheses. *Journal of Personality and Social Psychology,* **37,** 1631-1644.

Highlen, P.S., & Bennett, B.B. (1979). Psychological characteristics of successful and nonsuccessful elite wrestlers: An exploratory study. *Journal of Sport Psychology,* **1,** 123-137.

Horn, T.S. (1984a). Expectancy effects in the interscholastic setting: Methodological considerations. *Journal of Sport Psychology,* **6,** 60-76.

Horn, T.S. (1984b). The expectancy process: Causes and consequences. In W.F. Straub & J.M. Williams (Eds.), *Cognitive sport psychology* (pp. 199-211). Lansing, NY: Sport Science Associates.

Horner, M.S. (1968). *Sex differences in achievement motivation and performance in competitive and noncompetitive situations.* Unpublished doctoral dissertation, University of Michigan.

Horner, M.S. (1969, November). Fail: Bright women. *Psychology Today,* **3,** 36-38, 62.

Horner, M.S. (1972). Toward an understanding of achievement-related conflicts in women. *Journal of Social Issues,* **28,** 157-176.

Hovland, C.I., Janis, I.L., & Kelley, H.H. (1953). *Communication and persuasion.* New Haven, CT: Yale University Press.

Hughes, J.R. (1984). Psychological effects of habitual aerobic exercise: A critical review. *Preventive Medicine,* **13**, 66-78.

Hull, C.L. (1943). *Principles of behavior.* New York: Appleton-Century-Crofts.

Husman, B.F., & Silva, J.M. (1984). Aggression in sport: Definitional and theoretical considerations. In J.M. Silva & R.S. Weinberg (Eds.), *Psychological foundations of sport* (pp. 246-260). Champaign, IL: Human Kinetics.

Hyde, J.S. (1981). How large are cognitive gender differences? A meta-analysis using $\omega^2$ and d. *American Psychologist,* **36**, 892-901.

Ingham, A.G., Levinger, G., Graves, J., & Peckham, V. (1974). The Ringelmann effect: Studies of group size and group performance. *Journal of Experimental Social Psychology,* **10**, 371-384.

Iso-Ahola, S. (1977). Effects of team outcome on children's self-perception: Little League baseball. *Scandinavian Journal of Psychology,* **18**, 38-42.

Jacobson, E. (1938). *Progressive relaxation.* Chicago: University of Chicago Press.

James, W. (1890). *The principles of psychology* (Vol. I). New York: Henry Holt.

Jones, M.B. (1974). Regressing group on individual effectiveness. *Organizational Behavior and Human Performance,* **11**, 426-451.

Kauss, D.R. (1980). *Peak performance.* Englewood Cliffs, NJ: Prentice-Hall.

Keele, S.W. (1973). *Attention and human performance.* Pacific Palisades, CA: Goodyear.

Kenyon, G.S. (1968a). A conceptual model for characterizing physical activity. *Research Quarterly,* **39**, 96-105.

Kenyon, G.S. (1968b). Six scales for assessing attitudes toward physical activity. *Research Quarterly,* **39**, 566-574.

Keough, J. (1962). Analysis of general attitudes toward physical education. *Research Quarterly,* **33**, 239-244.

King, B.J., with Chapin, K. (1974). *Billie Jean.* New York: Harper & Row.

Klein, M., & Christiansen, G. (1969). Group composition, group structure and group effectiveness of basketball teams. In J.W. Loy & G.S. Kenyon (Eds.), *Sport, culture and society* (pp. 397-408). New York: Macmillan.

Komaki, J., & Barnett, F. (1977). A behavioral approach to coaching football: Improving the play execution of the offensive backfield on a youth football team. *Journal of Applied Behavior Analysis,* **10**, 657-664.

Konecni, V.J. (1975). Annoyance, type and duration of postannoyance activity, and aggression: The "cathartic" effect. *Journal of Experimental Psychology: General,* **104**, 76-102.

Kosslyn, S.M. (1983). *Ghosts in the mind's machine: Creating and using images in the brain.* New York: W.W. Norton.

Kravitz, D.A., & Martin, B. (1986). Ringelmann rediscovered: The original article. *Journal of Personality and Social Psychology, 50*, 936-941.

Kroll, W. (1975, March). *Psychology of sportsmanship.* Paper presented at the AAHPER Convention, Atlantic City, NJ.

Kroll, W., & Lewis, G. (1970). America's first sport psychologist. *Quest, 13*, 1-4.

Lacayo, R. (1985, June 10). Blood in the stands. *Time,* pp. 38-41.

Lan, L.Y., & Gill, D.L. (1984). The relationships among self-efficacy, stress responses and a cognitive feedback manipulation. *Journal of Sport Psychology, 6*, 227-238.

Landers, D.M. (1978). Motivation and performance: The role of arousal and attentional factors. In W.F. Straub (Ed.), *Sport psychology: An analysis of athlete behavior* (pp. 91-103). Ithaca, NY: Mouvement.

Landers, D.M. (1980). The arousal/performance relationship revisited. *Research Quarterly for Exercise and Sport, 51*, 77-90.

Landers, D.M. (1981). Arousal, attention and skilled performance: Further considerations. *Quest, 33*, 271-283.

Landers, D.M. (1985, May). *Beyond the TAIS: Alternative behavioral and psychophysiological measures for determining an internal vs. external focus of attention.* Paper presented at the North American Society for the Psychology of Sport and Physical Activity Conference, Gulfpark, MS.

Landers, D.M., Bauer, R.S., & Feltz, D.L. (1978). Social facilitation during the initial stage of motor learning: A re-examination of Martens' audience study. *Journal of Motor Behavior, 10*, 325-337.

Landers, D.M., & Courtet, P. (1979, May). *Peripheral narrowing among experienced and inexperienced rifle shooters under low and high stress conditions.* Paper presented at the North American Society for the Psychology of Sport and Physical Activity Conference, Trois Rivieres, Canada.

Landers, D.M., & Crum, T. (1971). The effects of team success and formal structure on interpersonal relationships and cohesiveness of baseball teams. *International Journal of Sport Psychology, 2*, 88-96.

Landers, D.M., & Landers, D.M. (1973). Teacher versus peer models: Effects of model's presence and performance level on motor behavior. *Journal of Motor Behavior, 5*, 129-139.

Landers, D.M., & Lueschen, G. (1974). Team performance outcome and the cohesiveness of competitive coacting groups. *International Review of Sport Sociology, 9*, 57-71.

Landers, D.M., & McCullagh, P.D. (1976). Social facilitation of motor performance. In J. Keough & R.S. Hutton (Eds.), *Exercise and sport sciences reviews* (Vol. 4, pp. 125-162). Santa Barbara, CA: Journal Publishing Affiliates.

Landers, D.M., Wilkinson, M.O., Hatfield, B.D., & Barber, H. (1982). Causality and the cohesion-performance relationship. *Journal of Sport Psychology*, **4**, 170-183.

Lane, J.F. (1980). Improving athletic performance through visuo-motor behavior rehearsal. In R.M. Suinn (Ed.), *Psychology in sports: Methods and applications* (pp. 316-320). Minneapolis: Burgess.

LaPiere, R.T. (1934). Attitudes vs. action. *Social Forces*, **13**, 230-237.

Latane, B., Harkins, S.G., & Williams, K.D. (1980). *Many hands make light the work: Social loafing as a social disease*. Unpublished manuscript, The Ohio State University, Columbus.

Latane, B., Williams, K.D., & Harkins, S.G. (1979). Many hands make light the work: The causes and consequences of social loafing. *Journal of Personality and Social Psychology*, **37**, 823-832.

Lau, R.R., & Russell, D. (1980). Attributions in the sport pages. *Journal of Personality and Social Psychology*, **39**, 29-38.

Lazarus, R.S., & Monat, A. (1979). *Personality* (3rd ed.). Englewood Cliffs, NJ: Prentice-Hall.

Lenk, H. (1969). Top performance despite internal conflict: An antithesis to a functionalistic proposition. In J.W. Loy & G.S. Kenyon (Eds.), *Sport, culture and society* (pp. 393-397). New York: Macmillan.

Lenney, E. (1977). Women's self-confidence in achievement situations. *Psychological Bulletin*, **84**, 1-13.

Leo, J. (1984a, July 30). Leading the invasion. *Time*, pp. 64-67.

Leo, J. (1984b, October 29). Take me out to the brawl game. *Time*, p. 87.

Lepper, M.R., & Greene, D. (1975). Turning play into work: Effects of adult surveillance and extrinsic rewards on children's intrinsic motivation. *Journal of Personality and Social Psychology*, **31**, 479-486.

Lepper, M.R., Greene, D., & Nisbett, R.E. (1973). Undermining children's intrinsic interest with extrinsic rewards: A test of the overjustification hypothesis. *Journal of Personality and Social Psychology*, **28**, 129-137.

Lewin, K. (1935). *A dynamic theory of personality*. New York: McGraw-Hill.

Liebert, R.M., & Morris, L.W. (1967). Cognitive and emotional components of test anxiety: A distinction and some initial data. *Psychological Reports*, **20**, 975-978.

Likert, R.A. (1932). A technique for the measurement of attitudes. *Archives of Psychology*, **140**, 1-55.

Locke, E.A., Saari, L.M., Shaw, K.N., & Latham, G.P. (1981). Goal setting and task performance: 1969-1980. *Psychological Bulletin*, **90**, 125-152.

Locksley, A., & Colten, M.E. (1979). Psychological androgyny: A case of mistaken identity? *Journal of Personality and Social Psychology, 37*, 1017-1031.

Lorenz, K. (1966). *On aggression.* New York: Harcourt, Brace & World.

Loy, J.W., Curtis, J.E., & Sage, J.N. (1979). Relative centrality of playing position and leadership recruitment in team sports. In R.S. Hutton (Ed.), *Exercise and sport sciences reviews* (Vol 6, pp. 257-284). Santa Barbara, CA: Journal Publishing Affiliates.

Loy, J.W., & Sage, J.N. (1970). The effects of formal structure on organizational leadership: An investigation of interscholastic baseball teams. In G.S. Kenyon & T.M. Grogg (Eds.), *Contemporary psychology of sport* (pp. 363-373). Chicago: Athletic Institute.

Maccoby, E., & Jacklin, C. (1974). *The psychology of sex differences.* Stanford, CA: Stanford University Press.

Magill, R.A. (1980). *Motor learning: Concepts and applications.* Dubuque, IA: William C. Brown.

Mahoney, M.J. (1979). Cognitive skills and athletic performance. In P.C. Kendall & S.D. Hollon (Eds.), *Cognitive-behavioral intervention: Theory, research, and procedures* (pp. 423-443). New York: Academic Press.

Mahoney, M.J., & Avener, M. (1977). Psychology of the elite athlete: An exploratory study. *Cognitive Therapy and Research, 1*, 135-141.

Mandler, G., & Sarason, S.B. (1952). A study of anxiety and learning. *Journal of Abnormal and Social Psychology, 47*, 166-173.

Marks, D.F. (1973). Visual imagery differences in the recall of patterns. *British Journal of Psychology, 64*, 17-24.

Marks, D.F. (1977). Imagery and consciousness: A theoretical review from an individual differences perspective. *Journal of Mental Imagery, 2*, 275-290.

Marteniuk, R.G. (1976). *Information processing in motor skills.* New York: Holt, Rinehart & Winston.

Martens, R. (1969). Effect of an audience on learning and performance of a complex motor skill. *Journal of Personality and Social Psychology, 12*, 252-260.

Martens, R. (1970). Social reinforcement effects on preschool children's motor performance. *Perceptual and Motor Skills, 81*, 787-792.

Martens, R. (1971). Internal-external control and social reinforcement effects on motor performance. *Research Quarterly, 42*, 107-113.

Martens, R. (1972). Social reinforcement effects on motor performance as a function of socio-economic status. *Perceptual and Motor Skills, 35*, 215-218.

Martens, R. (1975). *Social psychology and physical activity*. New York: Harper & Row.

Martens, R. (1976a). *Competitiveness and sport*. Paper presented at the International Congress of Physical Activity Sciences, Quebec City.

Martens, R. (1976b). Competition: In need of a theory. In D.M. Landers (Ed.), *Social problems in athletics*. Urbana, IL: University of Illinois Press.

Martens, R. (1977). *Sport Competition Anxiety Test*. Champaign, IL: Human Kinetics.

Martens, R. (1979). The significance of nonsignificant findings: A reply to Landers, Bauer, and Feltz. *Journal of Motor Behavior, 11*, 225-228.

Martens, R., Burton, D., Vealey, R.S., Bump, L.A., & Smith, D.E. (1983). *Competitive State Anxiety Inventory—2*. Unpublished manuscript, University of Illinois at Urbana-Champaign.

Martens, R., Burwitz, L., & Newell, K.M. (1972). Money and praise: Do they improve motor learning and performance? *Research Quarterly, 43*, 429-442.

Martens, R., Burwitz, L., & Zuckerman, J. (1976). Modeling effects on motor performance. *Research Quarterly, 47*, 277-291.

Martens, R., & Gill, D.L. (1976). State anxiety among successful and unsuccessful competitors who differ in competitive trait anxiety. *Research Quarterly, 47*, 698-708.

Martens, R., & Landers, D.M. (1969). Coaction effects on a muscular endurance task. *Research Quarterly, 40*, 733-737.

Martens, R., & Landers, D.M. (1970). Motor performance under stress: A test of the inverted-U hypothesis. *Journal of Personality and Social Psychology, 16*, 29-37.

Martens, R., & Landers, D.M. (1972). Evaluation potential as a determinant of coaction effects. *Journal of Experimental Social Psychology, 8*, 347-359.

Martens, R., Landers, D.M., & Loy, J.W. (1972). *Sport cohesiveness questionnaire*. Unpublished report, University of Illinois at Urbana-Champaign.

Martens, R., & Peterson, J.A. (1971). Group cohesiveness as a determinant of success and member satisfaction in team performance. *International Review of Sport Sociology, 6*, 49-61.

Martens, R., & White, V. (1975). Influence of win-loss ratio on performance, satisfaction and preference for opponents. *Journal of Experimental Social Psychology, 11*, 343-362.

Martinek, T.J. (1981). Pygmalion in the gym: A model for the communication of teacher expectations in physical education. *Research Quarterly for Exercise and Sport, 52*, 58-67.

Martinek, T.J., & Johnson, A.B. (1979). Teacher expectations: Effects on dyadic interactions and self-concept in elementary age children. *Research Quarterly, 50,* 60-70.

McAuley, E. (1985). Modeling and self-efficacy: A test of Bandura's model. *Journal of Sport Psychology, 7,* 283-295.

McCarthy, J.F., & Kelly, B.R. (1978a). Aggression, performance variables, and anger self-report in ice hockey players. *Journal of Psychology, 99,* 97-101.

McCarthy, J.F., & Kelly, B.R. (1978b). Aggressive behavior and its effect on performance over time in ice hockey athletes: An archival study. *International Journal of Sport Psychology, 9,* 90-96.

McClelland, D.C., Atkinson, J.W., Clark, R.A., & Lowell, E.C. (1953). *The achievement motive.* New York: Appleton-Century-Crofts.

McClements, J.D., & Botterill, C.B. (1979). Goal setting in shaping of future performances of athletes. In P. Klavora & J.V. Daniel (Eds.), *Coach, athlete, and the sport psychologist* (pp. 199-210). Toronto: University of Toronto.

McClements, J.D., & Botterill, C.B. (1980). Goal setting and performance. In R.M. Suinn (Ed.), *Psychology in sports: Methods and applications* (pp. 269-279). Minneapolis: Burgess.

McElroy, M.A., & Willis, J.D. (1979). Women and the achievement conflict in sport: A preliminary study. *Journal of Sport Psychology, 1,* 241-247.

McGrath, J.E. (1962). The influence of positive interpersonal relations on adjustment and effectiveness in rifle teams. *Journal of Abnormal and Social Psychology, 65,* 365-375.

McGrath, J.E. (1984). *Groups: Interaction and performance.* Englewood Cliffs, NJ: Prentice-Hall.

McKenzie, T., & Rushall, B. (1974). Effects of self-recording on attendance and performance in a competitive swimming training environment. *Journal of Applied Behavior Analysis, 7,* 199-206.

NcNally, J., & Orlick, T. (1975). Cooperative sport structures: A preliminary analysis. *Mouvement, 7,* 267-271.

Mehrabian, A. (1968). Male and female scales of tendency to achieve. *Educational and Psychological Measurement, 23,* 493-502.

Melnick, M.J., & Chemers, M.M. (1974). Effects of group structure on the success of basketball teams. *Research Quarterly, 45,* 1-8.

Meyers, A.W., Cooke, C.J., Cullen, J., & Liles, L. (1979). Psychological aspects of athletic competitors: A replication across sports. *Cognitive Therapy and Research, 3,* 361-366.

Mihevic, P.M. (1981). Anxiety, depression, and exercise. *Quest, 33,* 140-153.

Miller Brewing Company (1983). *The Miller Lite Report on American Attitudes Toward Sports*. Milwaukee, WI: Author.

Minas, S.C. (1980). Acquisition of a motor skill following guided mental and physical practice. *Journal of Human Movement Studies, 6*, 127-141.

Mischel, W. (1968). *Personality and adjustment*. New York: Wiley.

Mischel, W. (1973). Toward a cognitive social learning reconceptualization of personality. *Psychological Review, 80*, 252-283.

Morgan, W.P. (1978). Sport personology: The credulous-skeptical argument in perspective. In W.F. Straub (Ed.), *Sport psychology: An analysis of athlete behavior* (pp. 330-339). Ithaca, NY: Mouvement.

Morgan, W.P. (1980). The trait psychology controversy. *Research Quarterly for Exercise and Sport, 51*, 50-76.

Morgan, W.P. (1981a). Psychological benefits of physical activity. In F.J. Nagle & H.J. Montoye (Eds.), *Exercise in health and disease* (pp. 299-315). Springfield, IL: Thomas.

Morgan, W.P. (1981b). Psychophysiology of self-awareness during vigorous physical activity. *Research Quarterly for Exercise and Sport, 52*, 385-427.

Morgan, W.P. (1985). Affective beneficence of vigorous physical activity. *Medicine and Science in Sports and Exercise, 17*, 94-100.

Morgan, W.P., Horstman, D.H., Cymerman, A., & Stokes, J. (1983). Facilitation of physical performance by means of a cognitive strategy. *Cognitive Therapy and Research, 7*, 251-264.

Morgan, W.P., & Pollock, M.L. (1977). Psychologic characterization of the elite distance runner. *Annals of the New York Academy of Sciences, 301*, 382-403.

Morris, L., Davis, D., & Hutchings, C. (1981). Cognitive and emotional components of anxiety: Literature review and revised worry-emotionality scale. *Journal of Educational Psychology, 73*, 541-555.

Moyer, K.E. (1973, July). The physiology of violence. *Psychology Today, 7*, 35-38.

Murray, H.A. (1938). *Explorations in personality*. New York: Oxford University Press.

Myers, A.E. (1962). Team competition, success, and adjustment of group members. *Journal of Abnormal and Social Psychology, 65*, 325-332.

Myers, A.M., & Lips, H.M. (1978). Participation in competitive amateur sports as a function of psychological androgyny. *Sex Roles, 4*, 571-578.

Neale, J.M., & Liebert, R.M. (1973). *Science and behavior: An introduction to methods and research*. Englewood Cliffs, NJ: Prentice-Hall.

Nelson, L.L., & Kagan, S. (1972, September). Competition: The star-spangled scramble. *Psychology Today, 5,* 53-56; 90-91.

Ness, R.G., & Patton, R.W. (1979). The effects of beliefs on maximum weight-lifting performance. *Cognitive Therapy and Research, 3,* 205-211.

Nideffer, R.M. (1976a). *The inner athlete.* New York: Crowell.

Nideffer, R.M. (1976b). Test of attentional and interpersonal style. *Journal of Personality and Social Psychology, 34,* 394-404.

Nisbett, R.E., & Gordon, A. (1967). Self-esteem and susceptibility to social influence. *Journal of Personality and Social Psychology, 5,* 268-276.

Nixon, H.L. (1977). "Cohesiveness" and team success: A theoretical reformulation. *Review of Sport and Leisure, 2,* 36-57.

Norman, D.A. (1976). *Memory and attention: An introduction to human information processing* (2nd ed.). New York: Wiley.

Obermeier, G.E., Landers, D.M., & Ester, M.A. (1977). Social facilitation of speed events: The coaction effect in racing dogs and trackmen. In R.W. Christina & D.M. Landers (Eds.), *Psychology of motor behavior and sport—1976* (Vol. 2, pp. 9-23). Champaign, IL: Human Kinetics.

O'Block, F.R., & Evans, F.H. (1984). Goal setting as a motivational technique. In J.M. Silva & R.S. Weinberg (Eds.), *Psychological foundations of sport* (pp. 188-196). Champaign, IL: Human Kinetics.

Ogilvie, B.C. (1968). Psychological consistencies within the personality of high-level competitors. *Journal of the American Medical Association, 205,* 156-162.

Orlick, T. (1978). *Winning through cooperation.* Washington, DC: Hawkins.

Orlick, T.D., & Mosher, R. (1978). Extrinsic rewards and participant motivation in a sport-related task. *International Journal of Sport Psychology, 9,* 27-39.

Osgood, C.E., Suci, G.J., & Tannenbaum, P.H. (1957). *The measurement of meaning.* Urbana, IL: University of Illinois Press.

Ostrow, A.C. (1976). Goal-setting behavior and need achievement in relation to competitive motor activity. *Research Quarterly, 47,* 174-183.

Ostrow, A.C. (1981). Age grading: Implications for physical activity participation among older adults. *Quest, 33,* 112-123.

Ostrow, A.C., Jones, D.C., & Spiker, D.A. (1981). Age role expectations and sex role expectations for selected sport activities. *Research Quarterly for Exercise and Sport, 52,* 216-227.

Oxendine, J.B. (1970). Emotional arousal and motor performance. *Quest, 13,* 23-32.

Paivio, A. (1971). *Imagery and verbal processes*. New York: Holt, Rinehart & Winston.

Paulus, P.B., & Cornelius, W.L. (1974). An analysis of gymnastic performance under conditions of practice and spectator observation. *Research Quarterly, 45*, 56-63.

Paulus, P.B., Judd, B.B., & Bernstein, I.H. (1977). Social facilitation in sports. In R.W. Christina & D.M. Landers (Eds.), *Psychology of motor behavior and sport—1976* (Vol. 2, pp. 2-8). Champaign, IL: Human Kinetics.

Pedhazur, E.J., & Tetenbaum, T.J. (1979). BSRI: A theoretical and methodological critique. *Journal of Personality and Social Psychology, 37*, 996-1016.

Pennebaker, J.W., & Lightner, J.M. (1980). Competition of internal and external information in an exercise setting. *Journal of Personality and Social Psychology, 39*, 165-174.

Peterson, J.A., & Martens, R. (1972). Success and residential affiliation as determinants of team cohesiveness. *Research Quarterly, 43*, 62-76.

Petty, R.E., & Cacioppo, J.T. (1981). *Attitudes and persuasion: Classic and contemporary approaches*. Dubuque, IA: William C. Brown.

Rejeski, W.J., & Brawley, L.R. (1983). Attribution theory in sport: Current status and new perspectives. *Journal of Sport Psychology, 5*, 77-99.

Rejeski, W.J., Darracott, C., & Hutslar, S. (1979). Pygmalion in youth sports: A field study. *Journal of Sport Psychology, 1*, 311-319.

Richardson, A. (1967a). Mental practice: A review and discussion. Part I. *Research Quarterly, 38*, 95-107.

Richardson, A. (1967b). Mental practice: A review and discussion. Part II. *Research Quarterly, 38*, 263-273.

Richardson, A. (1977). Verbalizer-visualizer: A cognitive style dimension. *Journal of Mental Imagery, 1*, 109-126.

Riddle, P.K. (1980). Attitudes, beliefs, behavioral intentions, and behavior of women and men toward regular jogging. *Research Quarterly for Exercise and Sport, 51*, 663-674.

Roberts, G.C. (1972). Effect of achievement motivation and social environment on performance of a motor task. *Journal of Motor Behavior, 4*, 37-46.

Roberts, G.C. (1974). Effect of achievement motivation and social environment on risk taking. *Research Quarterly, 45*, 42-55.

Roberts, G.C. (1978). Children's assignment of responsibility for winning and losing. In F.L. Smoll & R.E. Smith (Eds.), *Psychological perspectives in youth sports* (pp. 145-171). Washington, DC: Hemisphere.

Roberts, G.C., & Martens, R. (1970). Social reinforcement and complex motor performance. *Research Quarterly, 41*, 175-181.

Roberts, G.C., & Pascuzzi, D. (1979). Causal attributions in sport: Some theoretical implications. *Journal of Sport Psychology, 1,* 203-211.

Rosenthal, R. (1974). *On the social psychology of the self-fulfilling prophecy: Further evidence for Pygmalion effects and their mediating mechanisms.* New York: MSS Modular Publishing.

Rosenthal, R. (1976). Experimenter effects in behavior research (2nd ed.). New York: Irvington.

Rosenthal, R., & Jacobson, L. (1968). *Pygmalion in the classroom: Teacher expectations and pupils' intellectual development.* New York: Holt, Rinehart & Winston.

Rotter, J.B. (1966). Generalized expectancies for internal versus external control of reinforcement. *Psychological Monographs, 80* (1, Whole No. 609).

Ruder, M.K., & Gill, D.L. (1982). Immediate effects of win-loss on perceptions of cohesion in intramural volleyball teams. *Journal of Sport Psychology, 4,* 227-234.

Rush, D.B., & Ayllon, T. (1984). Peer behavioral coaching: Soccer. *Journal of Sport Psychology, 6,* 325-334.

Rushall, B.S., & Siedentop, D. (1972). *The development and control of behavior in sport and physical education.* Philadelphia: Lea & Febiger.

Rushall, B.S., & Smith, K.C. (1979). The modification of the quality and quantity of behavior categories in a swimming coach. *Journal of Sport Psychology, 1,* 138-150.

Ryan, E.D. (1968). Reaction to "Sport and personality dynamics." In the *Proceedings of the National College Physical Education Association for Men* (pp. 70-75).

Ryan, E.D. (1970). The cathartic effect of vigorous motor activity on aggressive behavior. *Research Quarterly, 41,* 542-551.

Ryan, E.D. (1977). Attribution, intrinsic motivation, and athletics. In L.I. Gedvilas & M.E. Kneer (Eds.), *Proceedings of the NAPECW/NCPEAM National Conference, 1977* (pp. 346-353). Chicago: Office of Publications Services, University of Illinois at Chicago Circle.

Ryan, E.D. (1980). Attribution, intrinsic motivation, and athletics: A replication and extension. In C.H. Nadeau, W.R. Halliwell, K.M. Newell, & G.C. Roberts (Eds.), *Psychology of motor behavior and sport—1979* (pp. 19-26). Champaign, IL: Human Kinetics.

Ryan, E.D., & Lakie, W.L. (1965). Competitive and noncompetitive performance in relation to achievement motive and manifest anxiety. *Journal of Personality and Social Psychology, 1,* 342-345.

Ryan, R.M., Vallerand, R.J., & Deci, E.L. (1984). Intrinsic motivation in sport: A cognitive evaluation theory interpretation. In W.F. Straub & J.M. Williams (Eds.), *Cognitive sport psychology* (pp. 231-242). Lansing, NY: Sport Science Associates.

Sachs, M.L. (1978). An analysis of aggression in female softball players. *Review of Sport and Leisure, 3*, 85-97.

Sachs, M.L. (1984). Psychological well-being and vigorous physical activity. In J.M. Silva & R.S. Weinberg (Eds.), *Psychological foundations of sport* (pp. 435-444). Champaign, IL: Human Kinetics.

Scanlan, T.K. (1977). The effects of success-failure on the perception of threat in a competitive situation. *Research Quarterly, 48*, 144-153.

Scanlan, T.K. (1978). Antecedents of competitiveness. In R.A. Magill, M.J. Ash, & F.L. Smoll (Eds.), *Children in sport: A contemporary anthology* (pp. 53-75). Champaign, IL: Human Kinetics.

Scanlan, T.K., & Passer, M.W. (1978). Factors related to competitive stress among youth sport participants. *Medicine and Science in Sports, 10*, 103-108.

Scanlan, T.K., & Passer, M.W. (1979). Sources of competitive stress in young female athletes. *Journal of Sport Psychology, 1*, 151-159.

Scanlan, T.K., & Passer, M.W. (1980). Self-serving biases in the competitive sport setting: An attributional dilemma. *Journal of Sport Psychology, 2*, 124-136.

Schachter, S., Ellerton, N., McBride, D., & Gregory, D. (1951). An experimental study of cohesiveness and productivity. *Human Relations, 4*, 229-238.

Scheer, J.K., & Ansorge, C.J. (1975). Effects of naturally induced judges' expectations on the ratings of physical performances. *Research Quarterly, 46*, 463-470.

Scheer, J.K., & Ansorge, C.J. (1979). Influence due to expectations of judges: A function of internal-external locus of control. *Journal of Sport Psychology, 1*, 53-58.

Schmidt, R.A. (1982). *Motor control and learning: A behavioral emphasis.* Champaign, IL: Human Kinetics.

Schunk, D.H. (1983). Developing children's self-efficacy and skills: The roles of social comparative information and goal setting. *Contemporary Educational Psychology, 8*, 76-86.

Schutz, R.W., Smoll, F.L., & Wood, T.M. (1981). Physical activity and sport: Attitudes and perceptions of young Canadian athletes. *Canadian Journal of Applied Sport Sciences, 6*, 32-39.

Schwartz, B., & Barsky, S.F. (1977). The home advantage. *Social Forces, 55,* 641-661.

Schwartz, G.E., Davidson, R.J., & Goleman, D.J. (1978). Patterning of cognitive and somatic processes in the self-regulation of anxiety: Effects of meditation versus exercise. *Psychosomatic Medicine, 40,* 321-328.

Scott, J. (1971, December). Sports. *Ramparts, 67.*

Scott, P.M. (1953). Attitudes toward athletic competition in elementary schools. *Research Quarterly, 24,* 352-361.

Selby, R., & Lewko, J. (1976). Children's attitudes toward females' participation in sports. *Research Quarterly, 47,* 453-463.

Selye, H. (1956). *The stress of life.* New York: McGraw-Hill.

Shaw, M.E. (1976). *Group dynamics: The psychology of small group behavior* (2nd ed.). New York: McGraw-Hill.

Sheehan, P.W. (1967). A shortened form of Betts' questionnaire upon mental imagery. *Journal of Clinical Psychology, 23,* 386-389.

Sheehan, P.W., Ashton, R., & White, K. (1983). Assessment of mental imagery. In A.A. Sheikh (Ed.), *Imagery: Current theory, research, and application* (pp. 189-221). New York: Wiley.

Sheldon, W.H., & Stevens, S.S. (1942). *The varieties of temperament: A psychology of constitutional differences.* New York: Harper & Row.

Shields, D.L., & Bredemeier, B.J. (1984). Sport and moral growth: A structural developmental perspective. In W.F. Straub & J.M. Williams (Eds.), *Cognitive sport psychology* (pp. 89-101). Lansing, NY: Sport Science Associates.

Siedentop, D. (1978). The management of practice behavior. In W.F. Straub (Ed.), *Sport psychology: An analysis of athlete behavior* (pp. 49-55). Ithaca, NY: Mouvement.

Silva, J.M. (1979a). Behavioral and situational factors affecting concentration and skill performance. *Journal of Sport Psychology, 1,* 221-227.

Silva, J.M. (1979b). Changes in the affective state of guilt as a function of exhibiting proactive assertion or hostile aggression. In G.C. Roberts & K.M. Newell (Eds.), *Psychology of motor behavior and sport—1978* (pp. 98-108). Champaign, IL: Human Kinetics.

Silva, J.M. (1983). The perceived legitimacy of rule violating behavior in sport. *Journal of Sport Psychology, 5,* 438-448.

Simon, J.A., & Smoll, F.L. (1974). An instrument for assessing children's attitudes toward physical activity. *Research Quarterly, 45,* 407-415.

Skinner, B.F. (1968). *The technology of teaching.* New York: Appleton-Century-Crofts.

Smith, M.D. (1978). Hockey violence: Interring some myths. In W.F. Straub (Ed.), *Sport psychology: An analysis of athlete behavior* (pp. 187-192). Ithaca, NY: Mouvement.

Smith, M.D. (1979). Social determinants of violence in ice hockey: A review. *Canadian Journal of Applied Sport Sciences, 4,* 76-82.

Smith, R.E. (1980). A cognitive-affective approach to stress management training for athletes. In C.H. Nadeau, W.R. Halliwell, K.M. Newell, & G.C. Roberts (Eds.), *Psychology of motor behavior and sport—1979* (pp. 54-72). Champaign, IL: Human Kinetics.

Smith, R.E., Smoll, F.L., & Curtis, B. (1978). Coaching behaviors in Little League baseball. In F.L. Smoll & R.E. Smith (Eds.), *Psychological perspectives in youth sports* (pp. 173-201). Washington, DC: Hemisphere.

Smith, R.E., Smoll, F.L., & Curtis, B. (1979). Coach effectiveness training: A cognitive-behavioral approach to enhancing relationship skills in youth sport coaches. *Journal of Sport Psychology, 1,* 59-75.

Smith, R.E., Smoll, F.L., & Hunt, E. (1977). A system for the behavioral assessment of athletic coaches. *Research Quarterly, 48,* 401-407.

Smoll, F.L., & Schutz, R.W. (1980). Children's attitudes toward physical activity: A longitudinal analysis. *Journal of Sport Psychology, 2,* 137-147.

Smoll, F.L., Schutz, R.W., & Keeney, J.K. (1976). Relationships among children's attitudes, involvement, and proficiency in physical activities. *Research Quarterly, 47,* 797-803.

Smoll, F.L., & Smith, R.E. (1984). Leadership research in youth sports. In J.M. Silva & R.S. Weinberg (Eds.), *Psychological foundations of sport* (pp. 371-386). Champaign, IL: Human Kinetics.

Sonstroem, R.J. (1978). Physical estimation and attraction scales: Rationale and research. *Medicine and Science in Sports, 10,* 97-102.

Sonstroem, R.J., & Bernardo, P.B. (1982). Intraindividual pregame state anxiety and basketball performance: a re-examination of the inverted-U curve. *Journal of Sport Psychology, 4,* 235-245.

Sonstroem, R.J., & Kampper, R.P. (1980). Prediction of athletic participation in middle-school males. *Research Quarterly for Exercise and Sport, 51,* 685-694.

Spence, J.T., & Helmreich, R.L. (1972). The Attitudes Toward Women Scale: An objective instrument to measure attitudes toward the rights and roles of women in contemporary society. *JSAS Catalog of Selected Documents in Psychology, 2,* 66.

Spence, J.T., & Helmreich, R.L. (1978). *Masculinity and femininity.* Austin, TX: University of Texas Press.

Spence, J.T., & Helmreich, R.L. (1980). Masculine instrumentality and feminine expressiveness: Their relationships with sex role attitudes and behaviors. *Psychology of Women Quarterly, 5*, 147-163.

Spence, J.T., & Helmreich, R.L. (1983). Achievement-related motives and behaviors. In J.T. Spence (Ed.), *Achievement and achievement motives: Psychological and sociological approaches* (pp. 7-74). San Francisco: W.H. Freeman.

Spence, J.T., Helmreich, R.L., & Stapp, J. (1974). The Personality Attributes Questionnaire: A measure of sex role stereotypes and masculinity-femininity. *JSAS Catalog of Selected Documents in Psychology, 4*, 127.

Spence, K.W. (1956). *Behavior theory and conditioning.* New Haven, CT: Yale University Press.

Spielberger, C.D. (1966). *Anxiety and behavior.* New York: Academic Press.

Spielberger, C.D., Gorsuch, R.L., & Lushene, R.E. (1970). *Manual for the State-Trait Anxiety Inventory.* Palo Alto, CA: Consulting Psychologists Press.

Starkes, J.L., & Allard, F. (1983). Perception in volleyball: The effects of competitive stress. *Journal of Sport Psychology, 5*, 189-196.

Start, K., & Richardson, A. (1964). Imagery and mental practice. *British Journal of Educational Psychology, 34*, 280-284.

Steiner, I.D. (1972). *Group process and productivity.* New York: Academic Press.

Stevenson, H.W. (1965). Social reinforcement of children's behavior. In L.P. Lipsitt & C.C. Spiker (Eds.), *Advances in child development and behavior* (Vol. 2, pp. 97-126). New York: Academic Press.

Stogdill, R.M. (1963). *Team achievement under high motivation.* Columbus, OH: Bureau of Business Research, Ohio State University.

Storr, A. (1968). *Human aggression.* New York: Atheneum.

Straub, W.F., & Felock, T. (1974). Attitudes toward physical activity of delinquent and nondelinquent junior high school age girls. *Research Quarterly, 45*, 21-27.

Suinn, R.M. (1976, July). Body thinking: Psychology for Olympic champs. *Psychology Today, 10*, 38-43.

Suinn, R.M. (1983). Imagery and sports. In A.A. Sheikh (Ed.), *Imagery: Current theory, research, and application* (pp. 507-534). New York: Wiley.

Taylor, J.T. (1953). A personality scale of manifest anxiety. *Journal of Abnormal and Social Psychology, 48*, 285-290.

Tharp, R.G., & Gallimore, R. (1976, Janurary). What a coach can teach a teacher. *Psychology Today, 9*, 74-78.

Thayer, R.E. (1967). Measurement of activation through self-report. *Psychological Reports,* **20**, 663-678.

Thomas, J.R., & Tennant, L.K. (1978). Effects of rewards on children's motivation for an athletic task. In F.L. Smoll & R.E. Smith (Eds.), *Psychological perspectives in youth sports* (pp. 123-144). Washington, DC: Hemisphere.

Thompson, C.E., & Wankel, L.M. (1980). The effects of perceived activity choice upon frequency of exercise behavior. *Journal of Applied Social Psychology,* **10**, 436-444.

Thurstone, L.L. (1928). Attitudes can be measured. *American Journal of Sociology,* **33**, 529-554.

Thurstone, L.L. (1938). Primary mental abilities. *Psychometrika Monographs,* No. 1.

Titley, R.W. (1976, September). The loneliness of the long-distance kicker. *The Athletic Journal,* 74-80.

Tresemer, D.W. (1977). *Fear of success.* New York: Plenum.

Triandis, H.C. (1971). *Attitude and attitude change.* New York: Wiley.

Triplett, N. (1898). The dynamogenic factors in pacemaking and competition. *American Journal of Psychology,* **9**, 507-553.

Tropp, L.J., & Landers, D.M. (1979). Team interaction and the emergence of leadership and interpersonal attraction in field hockey. *Journal of Sport Psychology,* **1**, 228-240.

Tutko, T.A., Lyon, L.P., & Ogilvie, B.C. (1969). *Athletic Motivation Inventory.* San Jose, CA: Institute for the Study of Athletic Motivation.

Vallerand, R.J. (1983). Effect of differential amounts of positive verbal feedback on the intrinsic motivation of male hockey players. *Journal of Sport Psychology,* **5**, 100-107.

Vallerand, R.J., & Reid, G. (1984). On the causal effects of perceived competence on intrinsic motivation: A test of cognitive evaluation theory. *Journal of Sport Psychology,* **6**, 94-102.

Vanek, M. (1985, Summer). A message from the President of ISSP: Prof. Dr. Miroslav Vanek. *ISSP Newsletter,* **1**(1), 1-2.

Van Schoyk, S.R., & Grasha, A.F. (1981). Attentional style variations and athletic ability: The advantages of a sports-specific test. *Journal of Sport Psychology,* **3**, 149-165.

Varca, P.E. (1980). An analysis of home and away game performance of male college basketball teams. *Journal of Sport Psychology,* **2**, 245-257.

Varca, P.E., Shaffer, G.S., & Saunders, V. (1984). A longitudinal investigation of sport participation and life satisfaction. *Journal of Sport Psychology,* **6**, 440-447.

Veroff, J. (1969). Social comparison and the development of achievement motivation. In C.P. Smith (Ed.), *Achievement-related motives in children* (pp. 46-101). New York: Russell Sage Foundation.

Vetere, V.A. (1977). *An attributional field study of male and female college varsity basketball players*. Unpublished master's thesis, University of Waterloo, Waterloo, Ontario.

Wankel, L.M. (1972). Competition in motor performance: An experimental analysis of motivational components. *Journal of Experimental Social Psychology, 8*, 427-437.

Wankel, L.M. (1973). An examination of illegal aggression in intercollegiate hockey. *Proceedings of the Fourth Canadian Psychomotor Learning and Sport Psychology Symposium*. Waterloo, Ontario: University of Waterloo.

Wankel, L.M. (1975). The effects of social reinforcement and audience presence upon the motor performance of boys with different levels of initial ability. *Journal of Motor Behavior, 7*, 207-216.

Wankel, L. (1984). Audience effects in sport. In J.M. Silva & R.S. Weinberg (Eds.), *Psychological foundations of sport* (pp. 293-314). Champaign, IL: Human Kinetics.

Weinberg, R.S. (1977). Anxiety and motor behavior: A new direction. In R.W. Christina & D.M. Landers (Eds.), *Psychology of motor behavior and sport—1976* (Vol. 2, pp. 132-139). Champaign, IL: Human Kinetics.

Weinberg, R.S. (1979). Intrinsic motivation in a competitive setting. *Medicine and Science in Sport, 11*, 146-149.

Weinberg, R.S. (1984). The relationship between extrinsic rewards and intrinsic motivation. In J.M. Silva & R.S. Weinberg (Eds.), *Psychological foundations of sport* (pp. 177-187). Champaign, IL: Human Kinetics.

Weinberg, R.S., Gould, D., & Jackson, A. (1979). Expectations and performance: An empirical test of Bandura's self-efficacy theory. *Journal of Sport Psychology, 1*, 320-331.

Weinberg, R.S., & Jackson, A. (1979). Competition and extrinsic rewards: Effect on intrinsic motivation and attribution. *Research Quarterly, 50*, 494-502.

Weinberg, R.S., & Ragan, J. (1979). Effects of competition, success/failure, and sex on intrinsic motivation. *Research Quarterly, 50*, 503-510.

Weinberg, R.S., Smith, J., Jackson, A., & Gould, D. (1984). Effect of association, dissociation, and positive self-talk strategies on endurance performance. *Canadian Journal of Applied Sport Sciences, 9*, 25-30.

Weiner, B. (1974). *Achievement motivation and attribution theory*. Morristown, NJ: General Learning Press.

Weiner, B. (1979). A theory of motivation for some classroom experiences. *Journal of Educational Psychology, 71*, 3-25.

Weiner, B., Frieze, I., Kukla, A., Reed, L., Rest, S., & Rosenbaum, R.M. (1972). Perceiving the causes of success and failure. In E.E. Jones, D.E. Kanouse, H.H. Kelley, R.E. Nisbett, S. Valins, & B. Weiner (Eds.), *Attribution: Perceiving the causes of behavior* (pp. 95-120). Morristown, NJ: General Learning Press.

Weiss, M.R. (1983). Modeling and motor performance: A developmental perspective. *Research Quarterly for Exercise and Sport, 54*, 190-197.

White, K.D., Ashton, R., & Lewis, S. (1979). Learning a complex skill: Effects of mental practice, physical practice and imagery ability. *International Journal of Sport Psychology, 10*, 71-78.

White, R.W. (1959). Motivation reconsidered: The concept of competence. *Psychological Review, 66*, 297-333.

Whittemore, J.C. (1924). Influence of competition on performance: An experimental study. *Journal of Abnormal and Social Psychology, 19*, 236-253.

Wickstrom, R.L. (1983). *Fundamental motor patterns* (3rd ed.). Philadelphia: Lea & Febiger.

Widmeyer, W.N., & Birch, J.S. (1979). The relationship between aggression and performance outcome in ice hockey. *Canadian Journal of Applied Sport Sciences, 4*, 91-94.

Widmeyer, W.N., & Martens, R. (1978). When cohesion predicts performance outcome in sport. *Research Quarterly, 49*, 372-380.

Wiest, W.M., Porter, L.W., & Ghiselli, E.E. (1961). Relationships between individual proficiency and team performance and efficiency. *Journal of Applied Psychology, 45*, 435-440.

Williams, J.M., & Hacker, C.M. (1982). Causal relationships among cohesion, satisfaction and performance in women's intercollegiate field hockey teams. *Journal of Sport Psychology, 4*, 324-337.

Williams, K., Harkins, S., & Latane, B. (1981). Identifiability and social loafing: Two cheering experiments. *Journal of Personality and Social Psychology, 40*, 303-311.

Wilmore, J.H. (1968). Influence of motivation on physical work capacity and performance. *Journal of Applied Physiology, 24*, 459-463.

Yerkes, R.M., & Dodson, J.D. (1908). The relation of strength of stimulus to rapidity of habit formation. *Journal of Comparative and Neurological Psychology, 18*, 459-482.

Yukelson, D., Weinberg, R., & Jackson, A. (1984). A multidimensional sport cohesion instrument for intercollegiate basketball teams. *Journal of Sport Psychology, 6*, 103-117.

Zajonc, R.B. (1962). The effects of feedback and probability of group success on individual and group performance. *Human Relations, 15*, 149-161.

Zajonc, R.B. (1965). Social facilitation. *Science, 149*, 269-274.

Zander, A. (1971). *Motives and goals in groups.* New York: Academic Press.

Zander, A. (1975). Motivation and performance of sports groups. In D.M. Landers (Ed.), *Psychology of sport and motor behavior II.* University Park, PA: Pennsylvania State University Press.

Zander, A., & Wolfe, D. (1964). Administrative rewards and coordination among committee members. *Administrative Science Quarterly, 9*, 50-69.

Zavoral, N. (1984, October 22). "Little-bitty" things mean a big win for Hawks. *Iowa City Press-Citizen*, p. 1.

Ziegler, S.G. (1978). An overview of anxiety management strategies in sport. In W.F. Straub (Ed.), *Sport psychology: An analysis of athlete behavior* (pp. 257-264). Ithaca, NY: Mouvement.

Zillmann, D., Johnson, R.C., & Day, K.D. (1974). Attribution of apparent arousal and proficiency of recovery from sympathetic activation affecting activation transfer to aggressive behavior. *Journal of Experimental Social Psychology, 10*, 503-515.

Zillman, D., Katcher, A.H., & Milavsky, B. (1972). Excitation transfer from physical exercise to subsequent aggressive behavior. *Journal of Experimental Social Psychology, 8*, 247-259.

# Author Index

# Subject Index